TO PAINT A WAR

TO PAINT A WAR

The lives of the Australian artists who
painted the Great War, 1914–1918

RICHARD TRAVERS

Thames & Hudson

First published in Australia 2017
by Thames & Hudson Australia Pty Ltd
11 Central Boulevard Portside Business Park
Port Melbourne Victoria 3207
ABN: 72 004 751 964

National Library of Australia Cataloguing-in-Publication entry
Creator: Travers, Richard, author.
Title: To paint a war: the lives of the Australian artists who painted the Great War, 1914–18/RichardTravers.
ISBN: 9780500500903 (paperback)
Subjects: War artists – Australia.
Painters – Australia.
World War, 1914–18 – Art and the war.
War in art.
Art, Australian – 20th century.
Dewey Number: 759.06

Cover, internal designer and typesetter Helen Semmler
Editor Jean Kingett
Publishing consultant Richard Smart
Printed in China through Red Planet Management
Front cover image Hilda Rix Nicholas, *A Man*, AWM
Title page image George Coates, *Australian Official War Artists 1916–1918*, AWM

For Heather

ACKNOWLEDGEMENTS

Making a book is a joyful task, not entirely done in solitude. This book would not have seen the light of day but for the persistence and encouragement of Richard Smart. In a wonderful career as a publisher, Richard has produced a body of work for which all Australians should be grateful. It is an honour to work with him.

The artists have contributed so much to the beauty of this book, but I am sure they would join with me in paying tribute to Helen Semmler for its design and presentation. From the outset, Helen sensed just how the book should look and feel. Her work has been inspired.

I thank Walter Di Qual, who painted three beautiful maps that are themselves fine works of art; Jean Kingett, who, as editor, provided rigour, discipline, patience and a sense of humour; and Jenny Zimmer at Thames & Hudson, who has been a constant supporter.

For permission to reproduce work still under copyright, I thank Ann Mills (Grace Cossington Smith), Simon Hearder (Dora Meeson), Bronwyn Wright (Hilda Rix Nicholas), Anthony White (Cyril Leyshon-White) and Barbara Mobbs (Norman Lindsay).

The collections of our great galleries and museums are a wonderful resource. Their individual contributions are acknowledged in the List of Images. I thank them all.

Richard Travers
November 2016

CONTENTS

Acknowledgements...................................... vi

Introduction.. 1

Principal Artists... 3

1   Being Australian...................................... 6

2   Painting Australia.................................... 9

3   From Heidelberg to London – or Paris.................... 25

4   Sydney Follows Melbourne................................ 32

5   Life in London.. 37

6   War.. 60

7   Gallipoli... 71

8   The 3rd London General Hospital........................ 80

9   The Western Front, 1916................................ 95

10 The Western Front, 1917............................... 113

11 The Middle East....................................... 132

12 Face Wounds... 142

13 Away from the Front................................... 149

14 The Western Front, 1918............................... 154

15 Peace, Memory and Commemoration....................... 174

    Epilogue.. 207

    Artists Who Served with the AIF....................... 210

    Notes... 211

    List of Images.. 225

    Bibliography.. 232

    Index... 235

INTRODUCTION

War art is as old as warfare. It is found in the pyramids of Egypt, on classical Greek vases, on the triumphal arches and columns of ancient Rome, on Chinese stone reliefs and in the tapestry at Bayeux in France. For the most part, it is the victors who produce war art – losers are less inclined to commemorate their defeats. War art is biased, almost by definition.

Among painters of the Napoleonic wars, for example, Ingres painted Bonaparte as the conquering hero (*Napoleon I on his Imperial Throne*). Goya painted a French firing squad executing Spanish patriots (*Third of May, 1808*). Lejeune painted glorious pictures of the advance to Moscow (*The Battle of Borodino*). Vereshchagin painted quite different pictures of the retreat (*On the Road – Retreat and Escape December, 1812*). After Waterloo, Pieneman painted Wellington as the conquering hero, with Napoleon nowhere to be seen (*The Duke of Wellington and Officers and Soldiers of the Allied Army at the End of the Battle of Waterloo*).

The paintings say as much about their artists as they do about their subjects. Ingres idolised Napoleon – his fortunes ebbed and flowed with those of the Napoleon family. Goya was court painter to the Spanish Crown. Lejeune was one of Napoleon's generals. Vereshchagin – a Russian working at the end of the nineteenth century – painted Napoleon's 1812 retreat in 1893, after publication of Tolstoy's *War and Peace*. Pieneman was Dutch. His painting of Wellington featured the Dutch Crown Prince, later King William II, gallantly wounded in the foreground, making the painting suitable to hang in Amsterdam's Rijksmuseum.

In the years leading up to the Great War, Australia exported many of her best artists to Europe. When war broke out, they had to decide how they might contribute to the war effort. Told that painting was too frivolous a pastime for total war, the artists were channelled into a variety of unpleasant and demanding wartime occupations. That changed in 1916. As the war dragged into its third year, the artists were called back to their easels to make a painterly record of the war. Over the next two years, they drew and sketched as eyewitnesses of the unfolding tragedy. Their work continued after the Armistice, as they made paintings that became part of the memory and commemoration of the war.

To Paint a War is the story of the Australians who painted the Great War. It asks: what do their paintings say about the war, about the artists, and about Australia?

PRINCIPAL ARTISTS

*T*o *Paint a War* is the story of the generation of Australian artists who painted between 1900 and 1920.

Tom Roberts was the undisputed leader of the generation. His friend and biographer, Robert Croll, called him the 'Father of Australian Landscape Painting'.[1] James MacDonald, who was, in succession, the director of the National Art Gallery of New South Wales, and the director of the National Gallery of Victoria, and an acerbic critic of modern art, credited Roberts with recognising that 'the likeness of this new country [Australia] could best be arrived at by impressionistic means'.[2]

A messianic figure, Roberts converted fellow artists Charles Conder and Arthur Streeton to his way of painting. With the addition of Frederick McCubbin, the four – the backbone of what was to become known as the 'Heidelberg School' – were the inspiration for the younger artists who followed them.

Eleven years younger than Roberts, Arthur Streeton was the disciple who outshone his mentor. At any rate, MacDonald believed so. He called Streeton 'the best landscapist Australia has produced'.[3] Together, Roberts and Streeton made a formidable partnership. There was little to choose between them as painters of Australian subjects, but both would struggle for recognition and acclaim when painting in England. Away from the easel, Streeton challenged Roberts, whilst Roberts provided a worldly perspective that tempered Streeton's impetuosity. The result was that the two men could achieve more working in tandem than each could separately.

George Coates was the leader of a group of young Melbourne artists who sought to emulate the feats of Roberts and Streeton. The group,

Tom Roberts
Self Portrait AGNSW

Tom Roberts
Smike Streeton age 24 AGNSW

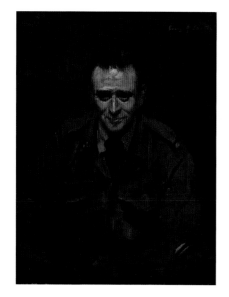

George Coates
Will Dyson (Sketch Portrait) AGNSW

George Coates
Head of a Lady V&A

Hilda Rix Nicholas
*Mrs George Matson Nicholas,
Self Portrait of the Artist* BVRG

which called itself the 'Prehistoric Order of Cannibals', included brothers Percy, Lionel and Norman Lindsay; Will and Ted Dyson, also brothers; Ray Parkinson; Myer Blashki; and Max Meldrum. These men may have devoted more energy to partying than to painting, but Coates had a serious and conscientious streak that allowed him to achieve, by application and hard work, a level of success that came more easily to some of his peers. Portraits were his strength. Coates married another artist, Dora Meeson, whose diligence and ambition complemented his own capacity for hard work. They were a power couple whose interests extended beyond painting to social and political issues.

It was not a dedicated painter, but a cartoonist, who became Australia's first official war artist. Will Dyson, who had been one of the Cannibals, had risen to fame in London as a newspaper cartoonist with a cutting and sarcastic touch at the time he was appointed to the role, late in 1916. A degree of controversy surrounded his appointment.

Hilda Rix achieved recognition and acclaim that many of the other artists would have envied for paintings she made in Morocco and northern France in 1913 and 1914. The war intervened cruelly in her life, but it would take more than a world war to repress the spirit of this remarkable woman.

George Lambert's paintings matched his engaging and mercurial personality. The joy and wonder that he found in the events of daily life found their way onto the canvas. For all his eccentricities, he was a brilliant technician, a master drawer, and a hard worker to boot.

While many of Australia's finest artists were in England during the war, Grace Cossington Smith painted the home front from the cultural wastelands of Turramurra on Sydney's North Shore. The small group of paintings and drawings she made of the war at home demonstrated a mastery of painterly technique and a level of flair and elan that belied her age – she turned twenty-five in 1917.

George Lambert
Self Portrait with Gladioli NPG

Grace Cossington Smith
Study of a Head: Self-Portrait NGA

1   BEING AUSTRALIAN

*T*wenty-sixth January 1888 was the centenary of the establishment of the colony of New South Wales. Whatever the anniversary meant for New South Wales, it meant little to the other self-governing colonies of Australia. They had few reasons to celebrate the establishment of their bumptious elder sister.

For bumptious New South Wales truly was. In 1887, Premier Henry Parkes proposed to celebrate the centenary by changing the name of the colony from New South Wales to Australia. In the resulting uproar, Premiers of the other colonies wrote indignantly to the Colonial Secretary in London. They complained that Parkes was stealing a name that right ly belonged to the entire continent. With the help of Lord Carrington, the Governor of New South Wales, and the promise of a knighthood, the Colonial Secretary persuaded Parkes that the name Australia was not his to appropriate.[1]

The episode begged the question: what, pre-Federation, was Australia? That question carried with it many others. Who qualified to be Australians? If the English migrants who had settled in the Australian colonies qualified to be Australians, were they also British at the same time? And, if they were at once Australian and British, what conflicts did that involve? In short, what did it mean to be Australian at the turn of the twentieth century?

Banjo Paterson made Clancy of the Overflow and the Man from Snowy River Australian heroes. His city readers were happy to accept that 'the drover's life has pleasures that the townsfolk never know'. They could be touchy, however, when it came to the reputations of their cities:

A visiting journalist from England … summed up the three chief cities in Australia in the words, 'Sydney for pleasure, Melbourne for business, Adelaide for culture'. This little epigram made him unpopular in all three cities. It was not what he credited each of them with, but what by implication he excluded. Each city thought itself entitled to honourable mention in all three categories.[2]

In sport, there was a choice between being Australian and being British. The first cricket Test was played in Melbourne in March 1877. The game was billed as a match between 'All England' and 'All Australia'. Within a few short years, Australia had England on the ropes. In 1882, the obituary of English cricket appeared in the *Sporting Times*:

IN AFFECTIONATE REMEMBRANCE
OF
E N G L I S H   C R I C K E T
WHICH DIED AT THE OVAL
ON
29TH AUGUST, 1882
DEEPLY LAMENTED BY A LARGE CIRCLE OF
SORROWING FRIENDS AND ACQUAINTANCES.
R.I.P.
N.B. – THE BODY WILL BE CREMATED AND
THE ASHES TAKEN TO AUSTRALIA.[3]

All Australia took inordinate pride in beating All England. *Plus ça change*.

Dame Nellie Melba achieved fame in the opera houses of London, Europe and the United States, but she stressed the importance she attached to being Australian: 'If you wish to understand me at all … you must understand first and foremost, that I am an Australian'. Born Helen Mitchell, she took her patriotism so far as to adopt a new name that was a contraction of the word 'Melbourne'.[4]

A new pride in things Australian emerged as the push for the colonies to federate intensified. In 1893, Sir William Sowden, a founder of the Australian Natives' Association, wrote that:

It [was once] the fashion to belittle everything Australian. Our wealthier men boasted, when they gave a dinner to their friends, that there was nothing Colonial upon their tables. Colonial wine was sour; Colonial ale was watery; Colonial cheese was rancid; Colonial preserved fruits were pulpy; Colonial waiters were clumsy; the Colonial sun had a sickly glare; the Colonial firmament was an exceedingly poor and shockingly burlesque copy of the dear old original heavens canopying the dear old original Mother Country! ...

But now great changes have occurred. Australian patriotism has been aroused. Instead of speaking of our national productions with shamefacedness ... we begin to boast of them; and even in such matters as public banquets, the ambition is to supply the tables entirely with local products.[5]

At Federation debates, speakers warned delegates to prepare for the changes to come. Tasmanian Treasurer Bird told delegates he wanted to 'forget that I am Tasmanian', and to feel instead that he was Australian, whilst Sir William McMillan, a Treasurer of New South Wales, told delegates that, proud as they were to be British subjects, 'bit by bit, the name of Britain must in their hearts go down before the more homely name of Australia'.[6]

At Federation, the Commonwealth of Australia continued to be a British colony.[7] Its citizens continued to be British subjects. At the ceremony to mark Federation in Sydney's Centennial Park, a choir of 10,000 schoolchildren sang 'Rule Britannia' and 'Advance Australia Fair'.[8] The songs reflected the nation's split personality.

More than 16,000 Australians volunteered to fight for the British Empire in the Boer War in South Africa. Most fought as light-horsemen. Their skills ranged from the rugged skills of the bushman to the dark arts of the horse thief. British cavalry regiments kept a close eye on their horses when Australians were around, and with good reason. When General Plumer's horse went missing, he immediately searched the Australian lines, where he soon found his horse, badly disguised and plainly recognisable.[9] The thief embodied an Australian paradox – he was equally prepared to pinch a British general's pony as he was to die defending the Empire. In Australian eyes, he was a larrikin with a heart of gold; in English eyes, once a convict always a convict.

At the turn of the twentieth century, Australians were British, but they were different from the British. They were citizens of a new country, but they were British subjects. As members of the British Empire, they felt the ties of the mother country at the same time as they felt the stirrings of an independent Australian spirit.

2 PAINTING AUSTRALIA

IN WHICH TOM ROBERTS, ARTHUR STREETON
AND CHARLES CONDER PIONEER AN AUSTRALIAN
WAY OF PAINTING, ACHIEVE SUCCESS AND ACCLAIM
IN AUSTRALIA, AND LEAVE FOR EUROPE IN SEARCH
OF SUCCESS AND ACCLAIM ON THE WORLD STAGE.

For those who would paint in the Western tradition, Europe was the centre of the art world. Young artists in Europe could see the works of the masters in the great galleries of Europe, not only in Paris and London, but also in Madrid, Amsterdam and Florence. They could see for themselves the great European buildings, the great European landscapes and the great gardens of Europe. They knew firsthand their artistic heritage.

Young European artists could be part of the latest developments in the art world. They could see the current exhibitions. They could follow the controversies and scandals. If they could not afford a Grand Tour, most could manage a trip to London, or Paris, or Venice. That, by itself, gave them a huge advantage over their Australian counterparts.

Young Australian artists had no option but to follow current developments in newspapers, books and journals. Book learning is no substitute for seeing, feeling and experiencing, but the problem went further. The quality of the images in the books and journals was so poor that it was impossible to get a good sense of the paintings they illustrated. There were no good reproductions from which the students could draw inspiration.[1]

The first Impressionist exhibition opened in Paris on 15 April 1874. Rejected by the French Salon, artists including Claude Monet, Edgar Degas, Pierre-Auguste Renoir, Camille Pissaro and Paul Cézanne staged a renegade exhibition. It passed more or less unnoticed. The few critics who reported the exhibition scorned it, using the title of one of Monet's works – *Impression, Sunrise* – to mock the collection as nothing more than impressions. The Salon saw the renegades as second-raters, whose work had been rejected for good reason. As the standard-bearer of the

French art establishment, the Salon stood firm against the interlopers.

The rift between the Impressionists and the Salon should have been bread and butter for every young artist of the day – whether painting in Europe or Australia. Short of travelling to Europe, however, there was no way for Australian artists to see the contentious paintings. And without seeing the paintings, it was difficult to understand the new artistic approaches, or to try them. As long as they remained in Australia, young painters were largely quarantined from anything causing excitement in London and Paris.

James MacDonald trained as an artist at the National Gallery Art School in Melbourne from 1892 until 1898. Afterwards, he trained and worked in Paris, London and New York, before becoming director, first, of the National Art Gallery of New South Wales, and, then, of the National Gallery of Victoria. He had firsthand experience of the dilemma facing young Australian artists:

[There] was mighty little in the way of examples to inspire a painter … The wealthier class of Melbourne, who aspired to culture by way of pictures, bought examples which make us wonder. What *could* they have seen in them? There were almost *no* good pictures here … Copies of paintings of aforetime existed; but they were mostly after second-rate Italians and Dutchmen. English painting was loyally, and badly, represented by early and mid-Victorian stuff; the worst type of subject-picture that an industrial era could produce … All of this rubbish – or most of it – found favour. Much of it was done by Royal Academicians of the day, and, those who owned it rammed it down others' throats, as good … One wonders how our pioneers got a start.[2]

Tom Roberts was a case in point. Born in England in 1856, Roberts migrated to Australia with his widowed mother when he was thirteen years old. He studied under Louis Buvelot at the National Gallery School, but returned to London in 1881, where he entered classes at the Royal Academy. In 1883, he left London to travel through Spain in company with John Peter Russell, an expatriate Sydney artist. In Granada, they met two Spanish artists, Laureano Barrau and Ramon Carbo Casas.

At this meeting, Roberts was bitten by an impressionist bug. The following account is given in William Moore's 1934 *Story of Australian Art* and repeated in the 1935 biography of Roberts written by his friend, Robert Croll:

The story of how Tom Roberts introduced impressionism in Australia begins in Granada, in Spain, in 1883. Here he met two clever artists named Barrau and Casas. Barrau, who was a pupil of Gérôme, told Roberts that his master encouraged his pupils to paint a direct sketch every day and just go for the effect of colour. 'When you draw,' he said, 'form is the important thing, but in painting, the first thing to consider is the general impression of colour.' Casas, who was a pupil of Carolus-Duran, had no theories to offer, but his brilliant sketches showed, even better than those of the other artist, what effects could be obtained in this way. It was the chance meeting with these painters, together with the *plein-air* movement in force at the time, that prompted Roberts to take up impressionism; and it was the sketches he brought back to Australia in 1885 that put Streeton and Conder in touch with the new method.[4]

Roberts' meeting with Barrau and Casas was hardly a brush with mainstream Impressionism. Barrau had been a student at the *Académie Julian* in Paris, where Gérôme had taught. Carolus-Duran had his own school, where Casas had been a student. Neither the teachers nor the pupils were at the forefront of the Impressionist movement. But Roberts made no claim to have met or fallen under the sway of the French impressionists. He visited Paris only briefly, although he probably met Gérôme during his visit.[5] Nor did Roberts attribute his conversion to painting impressions to anything he had seen or to anyone he met in London. Indeed, according to MacDonald, Roberts was not an Impressionist:

He held no brief for any single aspect of impressionism, but urged using one's eyesight; discarding shibboleths and recipes, and painting what one saw. In the works of his disciples there is no evidence of his having inculcated following the Luminists; Monet, Sisley, Pissaro and their likes; at any rate, as far as the *methods* of those painters went.[6]

One of the sketches that Roberts brought back was 'a vivid and extremely interesting portrait of Roberts as a young man'. The portrait was signed 'R. Casas, Granada, 83'.[7] Roberts kept it for the rest of his life.

Casas' portrait of Roberts was more than an aide mémoire of the encounter in Granada; it was a painting that pointed to new ways of doing things.[8] It was avowedly an impression. It gave an effect, not an exact likeness. It is easy to see how it sparked an epiphany in Roberts. Croll identified a second factor in Roberts' conversion to painting impressions – the *plein air* movement, in which artists took their easels outside to paint what they saw directly from nature.

Ramon Casas
Tom Roberts NGV

Having come under the spell of painting impressions, Roberts was zealous in recruiting disciples to follow him. The first was Arthur Streeton. When Roberts returned to Australia in 1885, Streeton was studying at the National Gallery School. He was working under George Folingsby, an Englishman who had recently arrived in the colony. Folingsby 'painted well and from that his students benefited, but he had the bad European habit of bitumen and red paint for "laying-in"'.[9] Streeton described how meeting Roberts caused him to doubt the Folingsby orthodoxy:

The impressions brought out by Roberts had the fresh air, true-tone-in-values idea which was in conflict with the academic training at the National Art School under Folingsby. I was painting a head after the manner of Roberts, when Folingsby said, 'Don't paint like that, put in the subject first with bitumen and vermilion' ... I didn't argue with him, but left the school and worked again with Roberts.[10]

Roberts met Charles Conder in a wine shop in Sydney's Mosman in 1887. Conder's biographer, John Rothenstein, gave this account of Conder's conversion:

Tom Roberts had an imposing presence, his harsh but not unkindly voice and decisive gestures carried conviction. To him belonged the quality of leadership ... Dour on occasion, aloof generally, the man who talked to Conder in the Mosman wine shop talked with missionary eloquence. A revelation had been vouchsafed to him, and he expounded it to someone who understood his meaning instantly – the kind of listener to fire a missionary ...

It was the Impressionist vision that Roberts imparted to Conder ... Before many months had passed [Conder] had left Sydney and gone to Melbourne to join Roberts and his friend Arthur Streeton.[11]

Like MacDonald, Rothenstein saw that Roberts had not 'received the full force of the fructifying impact of Impressionism', but Streeton and Conder made the most of the diluted form of the disease that Roberts had passed on to them.[12] In this, they were joined by a fourth artist, Frederick McCubbin.

The four worked together: sometimes in Melbourne; sometimes in the bush, near Box Hill, Heidelberg and Eaglemont; and sometimes on Port Phillip Bay, at Mentone and Beaumaris. Following the gospel according to Roberts, they often painted *en plein air*. They did not reject the teachings of the National Gallery School – McCubbin had taken up an appointment as drawing master there – but they did take charge of their own artistic development. Their easy camaraderie was reflected in the nicknames they gave to one another. Roberts was 'Bulldog'; Streeton was 'Smike'; Conder was 'K'; and McCubbin, naturally enough, was the 'Proff'.[13]

Roberts painted *A Summer Morning Tiff* and *Allegro con Brio: Bourke Street West*; Streeton painted '*Still Glides the Stream, and Shall For Ever Glide*'; Conder *A Holiday at Mentone*; and McCubbin *Gathering Mistletoe* and *Lost*. The paintings had in common a diffuse quality that prompted James Smith, a Melbourne art critic, to write in the *Argus* newspaper on 11 September 1888:

Mr Tom Roberts, Mr F. McCubbin and Mr Arthur Streeton, who may be grouped together on account of the similarity of their procedure in landscape painting, seem to be falling more and more under the influence of the French impressionists; leaving so much unexpressed in their representations of nature and avoiding lucidity of statement, and delineation of detail, as if both these aims were against the canon of art.[14]

When Smith accused Roberts, McCubbin and Streeton of falling under the influence of the French Impressionists, he meant to insult. His disdain for Impressionism not only followed that of the French Salon, it echoed conservative artistic opinion. WP Frith, a realist painter and a member of the Royal Academy, represented the conservative viewpoint in Britain:

A new style of art has arisen which seems to gratify a public ever craving for novelty. Very likely I am posing as an old-fashioned Academician, who declines to acknowledge that eccentricity is a proof of genius, or audacity an evidence of power; and I may be justly, or unjustly, accused of unfairness when I declare that the *bizarre*, French 'impressionist' style of painting recently imported into this country will do incalculable damage to the modern school of English art.[15]

Undaunted by the tut-tutting of old men, Roberts, Streeton and Conder staged an exhibition. The *9 by 5 Impression Exhibition* opened in Melbourne on 17 August 1889. The front cover of the catalogue for the exhibition, drawn by Conder, was deliberately provocative. It showed 'Convention' as a puzzled woman, her clothes in disarray. Inside was a mini-manifesto of the Roberts philosophy:

EXHIBITION OF IMPRESSIONS

'When you draw, form is the important thing; but in painting the *first* thing to look for is the *general impression* of colour.' – Gerome

TO THE PUBLIC

An effect is only momentary: so an impressionist tries to find his place. Two half-hours are never alike, and he who tries to paint a sunset on two successive evenings must be more or less painting from memory. So, in these works, it has been the object of the artists to render faithfully, and thus obtain first records of effects widely differing, and often of very fleeting character.[16]

Roberts' philosophy dictated that the exhibition was not an Impressionist exhibition, but an exhibition of impressions.[17] It took its name from the fact that many of the paintings were painted on 9 × 5 inch cigar box lids. The impressions were a mix of colour and spontaneity. They might be general impressions of colour (courtesy of Gérôme), or they might be first records of fleeting effects.

James Smith was not impressed. He wrote that something like four-fifths of the exhibits were:

a pain to the eye. Some of them look like faded pictures … others suggest that a paint-pot has been accidentally upset over a panel nine inches by five; others resemble the first essays of a small boy … whilst not a few are as distressing as the incoherent images which float through the mind of a dyspeptic dreamer.

He ended by saying that the exhibition would cause him and the other good citizens of Melbourne 'to despond with respect to the future of art in this colony, did we not believe, with Mr WP Frith, R.A., that "Impressionism is a craze of such ephemeral character as to be unworthy of serious attention"'.[18]

For young artists eager for publicity, Smith's review was a gift beyond words. The city's leading reviewer was playing the role of Conder's 'Convention', and doing it free of charge in the city's major newspaper. Roberts pinned the review in pride of place in the gallery. Keen to maximise the publicity, Roberts, Streeton and Conder wrote to the *Argus*, agreeing that their exhibition was, indeed, about the future of art in the young colony: 'In the formation of taste in this new country where art is so young and so tentative, every public expression of opinion and every show of works must have a more or less strong influence in the making of that taste'.[19]

It was a debate that would never have taken place in Europe. French artists of the late nineteenth century did not need to develop a French style of painting. It already existed. The same could be said for all of Europe, and for England. Over centuries, artists had developed recognisable idioms for painting the landscapes of their countries. Rembrandt, Velasquez and Turner were not only different from one another; they were identified with the artistic traditions of their countries. Moreover, the traditions of their countries differed appreciably from one another.

The colony of Victoria was barely fifty years old. It was yet to establish an artistic tradition. Roberts, Streeton and Conder told the *Argus* that they were developing their own idiom for painting the colonial landscape:

Let us try to state our case or the principles upon which we have worked, and as well as we can put them in writing. They are these:- That we will not be led by any forms of composition or light and shade; that any effect of nature which moves us strongly by its beauty, whether strong or vague in its drawing, defined or indefinite in its light, rare or ordinary in colour, is worthy of our best efforts and of the love of those who love our art. Through and over all this we say we will do our best to put only the truth down, and only as much as we feel sure of seeing: and it is here that many will say, 'Give us work done faithfully according to such principles, and surely we are ready and willing to admire'.[20]

This was more than misty-eyed idealism – it was a declaration of artistic independence. For Roberts, Streeton and Conder, the landscape of Victoria was something new, waiting to be discovered and painted. A new landscape demanded new techniques to paint it. European ideas and approaches would not necessarily work in Victoria. It would take time, experimentation and patience to discover what would work.[21]

The light in Australia was brighter than in northern Europe. Horizons shimmered in the heat and humidity. Colours were different. The pasture was yellow, or blue or grey – seldom green. The trees were evergreen, not deciduous. The sea could be a bright blue, not grey, or green. The sun shone bright and fiercely – it was rarely muted. Roberts, Streeton and Conder saw that painting styles developed in Europe and North America gave few precedents that suited Australian conditions. They had to work out their own approaches:

we believe it is better to give our own idea than to get a merely superficial effect, which is apt to be a repetition of what others have done before us, and may shelter us in a safe mediocrity, which, while it will not attract condemnation, could never help towards the development of what we believe will be a great school of painting in Australia.[22]

Smith dismissed Roberts, Streeton and Conder as pretentious posers:

a few young artists … have formed themselves into a Mutual Admiration Society, and cherish the deplorable delusion that the greatest landscape painters the world has ever seen were not only blind to the majesty and loveliness of nature, but were completely ignorant of the true method of interpreting her; while it seems to be believed that a little coterie of painters, in one corner of Australia, is about to revolutionise the entire theory and practice of landscape art.[23]

Smith was to Melbourne what the Salon was to Paris and the Royal Academy to London. Roberts, Streeton and Conder were sharing the pain of like-minded painters in Paris and London. Smith added one thing to the mix – the colonial inferiority complex. Questions of painting technique were settled by looking at the great artists of the Old World. Australian artists who thought they knew better were rising above their station.

The colonial inferiority complex dictated that success in Australia, no matter how great, counted less than success overseas. Dame Nellie Melba subscribed to this view. She lived outside Australia from 1886 until 1902. For the rest of her life, she lived in Australia when her engagements overseas permitted. She wanted, first and foremost, to be Australian, but her ambition told her that she could only achieve her potential by leaving Australia and performing on the world stage.

Paris and London cast a similar spell for Australian artists. It was there, in the French and English art schools, that the latest developments could be studied. It was there, in the galleries, that the works of the masters could be seen. Australia could not pretend to match Paris or London. It was only natural that ambitious Australian artists would want to be there.

After the *9 by 5 Impression Exhibition*, Roberts, Streeton and Conder took a cottage near Heidelberg, east of Melbourne, where they painted together for two years. The name, 'Heidelberg School', was first used in a review of an exhibition by Streeton and Melbourne artist Walter Withers in July 1891. Written by Sidney Dickinson, the review struck a more encouraging note than James Smith's review of the *9 by 5 Impression Exhibition*:

It would be quite impossible to find, in any part of the world, more striking effects than are found ready to the artist's hand in the Australian landscape at certain seasons of the year. The golden glory of English wheat-fields cannot excel the splendour of the wide wastes of grazing land under the dry sky of an Australian summer …

Works like these justify a hopeful augury for the future of Colonial art, and some of them at least, will surprise by their excellence many opinions that have been formed of its present condition.[24]

The review was positive, but the colonial inferiority complex was still evident. Dickinson felt the need to persuade his readers that the colonial landscape could be compared with the English. Equally, he was tentative in his claim that colonial art might have a future. Yet, in naming the

Heidelberg School, and in stating what it stood for, he went some way towards identifying an Australian style of painting.

Ironically, the founders of the Heidelberg School were already going their separate ways even before the name was coined. Conder sailed for France on 26 April 1890. Roberts and Streeton left for Sydney in 1891. Only McCubbin, recently married, remained in Melbourne.

In Paris, Conder based himself in Montmartre. Moving to London in 1900, he lived in Chelsea, on and off, until his death in 1909.

Sydney gave Roberts and Streeton an abundance of challenging subjects. Streeton painted *Cremorne Pastoral*; Roberts *Mosman's Bay*. These gave an idyllic view of the harbour. Roberts' *Sydney Harbour from Milson's Point* showed the harbour as a working port. Roberts and Streeton joined the community of artists then camped in Mosman. 'Curlew Camp', in Little Sirius Cove, near the current site of Taronga Zoo, was their base.[25] They often painted *en plein air*.

The camping life was hardly strenuous. The artists chipped in to pay for manservants to do the cooking, and to shine their shoes. There was a separate dining tent. The sleeping tents were furnished with beds, chairs, tables and chests of drawers. One tent, called the 'tabernacle', boasted a billiards table.[26] In the warmth of a Sydney afternoon, the artists enjoyed the harbour at its carefree best. As Streeton enthused:

Hundreds and hundreds of yachts are coursing over the purple sea (it is as wine). The brilliant white sails cutting finely against the soft summer sky. Ferryboats puff and paddle along crowded with the pleasure-loving folk – the youth of Sydney in bright flannels hang out to windward, their bronze limbs all aglitter with the spray of the salt waves – in every nook and bay are numbers of boats full of gay costumes and laughter – some parties are singing in chorus others cooee and listen to the echo across the bright bay. The air is warm and soft like unto a drooping crimson poppy … Around the tent climb the Begonia and Clematis and Sarsaparilla the rough winds broken for us by an exquisite fusion of tender gum leaf – Honeysuckle (like the trees of old asters). Cotton plants heath and a wild cherry (bright green at our tent door) and the beautiful flood beneath.

All is splendid.[27]

Roberts travelled in country New South Wales. Reflecting the wealth that was coming from the wool boom, he painted *Shearing the Rams* in the Riverina and *The Golden Fleece* at Newstead, a property near Inverell. At Newstead, he also started on *Bailed Up*, a monumental painting of a stagecoach robbery remarkable for the total absence of tension. In what would normally be considered an occasion of stress, the bushrangers in *Bailed Up* were models of serenity. Roberts did not complete the painting until almost thirty years later. These paintings were so pictorial as to belie the Impressionist label. Bernard Smith, whose *Place, Taste and Tradition*, published in 1944, broke new ground in Australian art criticism, saw them as 'important historical records; they show an important aspect of Australian life during a significant phase of its development'. Smith was not happy labelling Roberts an Impressionist, believing that 'The phrase, "frontier painters," [was] a better description of the genre work of Roberts and McCubbin'.[28]

In 1891, Streeton painted *Fire's On! Lapstone Tunnel*. The painting took the *plein air* method to extremes – Streeton painted it from the vantage point of a rock overlooking the mineshaft, and a man was killed in an explosion in the mine as he painted.[29] Among many favourable reviews of the painting, one critic went so far as to say that it 'would take pride of place in any gallery. The painting is free and masterly, but it is the qualities of light and air the artist has infused into the picture that give it pre-eminence'.[30]

Streeton made a series of paintings of the Blue Mountains and the Hawkesbury River in 1896, among them *The Purple Noon's Transparent Might* and *Grey Day on the Hawkesbury*. He took them to Melbourne, where he held Australia's first one-man art show. Unable to resist teasing the Melburnians,[31] he called the show *Streeton's Sydney Sunshine Exhibition*. The Melburnians responded in good part. They made the show a huge success. Even the Victorian gallery came to the party, paying £150 for the *Purple Noon* painting.[32] Streeton wrote to Roberts: 'A year or two & I may be lying on a lovely balcony or housetop gazing with half closed eyes at my blue Mediterranean'.[33] Who could blame him? Not yet thirty, he was riding the crest of the wave. In January 1897, he left Melbourne for London.

In Sydney, Roberts married Lillie Williamson. They settled in Balmain where their son, Caleb, was born. Roberts was enjoying the success of his shearing paintings, but now he had a family to feed. He turned increasingly to portraiture, painting celebrities such as Sir Henry Parkes, Edward Ogilvie and Major General Hutton. A few years of painting society portraits produced the desired income, but left Roberts feeling that his career had reached a dead end – that there was nothing left for him to achieve in Australia. It was 1900. Roberts wrote:

There seemed so little in front of us, and I felt the need of seeing the fine workers and their work in our art, and having saved a little money, we got our things together to leave Sydney … and stay a while at Melbourne, and do some work there on the way to Europe.[34]

As the artists of the Heidelberg School worked to create a great school of painting in Australia, the vast majority of Australian artists were unaffected by their concerns and aspirations. These were the hundreds of men and women who worked as commercial artists making the illustrations and drawings that appeared in newspapers, magazines, advertising and signage across the country. Known as black and white artists, they produced the spectacular array of images that appeared in books, magazines and newspapers every day of the week.[35]

The black and white artists included many cartoonists whose work appeared in newspapers and in periodicals, including the *Bulletin*. Among the leading cartoonists were Hop, Phil May, Norman Lindsay, Low and Stan Cross. They were the doyens of the black and white artists. Their fame stood in contrast to the obscurity of the vast majority of black and white artists, most of whom toiled unheralded and poorly paid.[36]

The Commonwealth of Australia was inaugurated on 1 January 1901, the first day of the twentieth century.

Inauguration was one thing, but as Sir Robert Garran, one of the founders of Federation, observed: 'It takes more than a day to create a Commonwealth'. Creating a Parliament from scratch was breaking new ground. The sequence of events began with the designation of Lord Hopetoun as the first Governor-General of Australia. He arrived in Sydney Harbour on board HMS *Royal Arthur* in December 1900. His first act as Governor-General was to choose a Prime Minister. The choice fell on Edmund Barton, who formed a Cabinet in the absence of an elected Parliament.

Garran described what happened next:

On the appointed day, 1st January 1901, at a brilliant ceremony in the Centennial Park, the Commonwealth was established, Lord Hopetoun assumed office, and his Ministers were sworn in. The same day the first meeting of the Executive Council was held, at which seven Departments of State were created, and portfolios were allotted, so technically the Commonwealth was in being, but actually, little change was observable … The Governor General was there, the Executive Council of Ministers was there, but as yet they had little to administer … The next step was to create a Commonwealth Public Service … [and the next job after that] was to arrange the elections for the first Federal Parliament.[38]

The elections were held in March. The Parliament of Australia was ready to open for business on 9 May 1901. It met in Melbourne.

There was a gala ceremony to mark the opening of the new Parliament, even though the nation was in mourning for Queen Victoria, who had died on 22 January 1901. The venue was the Royal Exhibition Building, in Carlton, a pavilion large enough to hold the 12,000 guests.[39] The guest list was a rollcall of the great and good. The colonies – which became states under the new Constitution – sent governors, politicians, judges and other dignitaries to Melbourne for the occasion. Bishops, foreign envoys, and leaders of business and commerce attended. The guests took their places in the presence of the Duke of Cornwall and York. King Edward VII had acceded to the throne on the death of Queen Victoria. The Duke of Cornwall and York, his son, was now heir to the throne.[40] The Duke had with him his Duchess and a retinue of fashionable young people from London, including a 'glittering group of officers'.[41]

The orchestra played 'God Save the King'. The Clerk of the Parliament read the letters patent commissioning the Duke to open the Parliament. Psalm 100 was sung. Lord Hopetoun said the Lord's Prayer. The newly elected members of Parliament assembled. The Duke – a small, bearded man in an admiral's uniform – stood on a raised platform to deliver a message from the King. The message gave the King's explanation of the significance of the day:

His Majesty has watched with the deepest interest the social and material progress made by his people in Australia and has seen with thankfulness and heartfelt satisfaction the completion of that political union of which this Parliament is the embodiment.

The King is satisfied that the wisdom and patriotism which have characterised the exercise of wide powers of self-government hitherto enjoyed by the colonies will continue to be displayed in the exercise of the still wider powers with which the united Commonwealth has been endowed. His Majesty feels assured that the enjoyment of these powers will, if possible, enhance that loyalty and devotion to his throne and Empire of which the people of Australia have already given such signal proofs.

It is His Majesty's earnest prayer that this union so happily achieved may, under God's blessing, prove an instrument for still further promoting the welfare and advancement of his subjects in Australia, and for the strengthening and consolidation of his Empire.[42]

With this reminder that the citizens remained subjects of the King, and Australia a part of his Empire, the Duke declared the Parliament of Australia open.[43]

Roberts and his family arrived in Melbourne on 5 May 1901, in time to take part in the celebrations.[44] Roberts intended to do some painting there before heading on to London, but fortune intervened to keep him in Melbourne longer than he planned.

A group of entrepreneurs saw a chance to profit from the opening of Parliament. They formed a company to commission a noted artist to paint the opening ceremony. Their scheme was not to sell the painting, but rather to make 500 engravings from the painting, and sell them.

Their first choice of artist was portraitist and landscape painter, JC Waite.[45] He declined the commission. The promoters then approached Roberts, who accepted. A formal agreement was drafted under which Roberts was commissioned to make a painting that included 'correct representations' of the Duke and Duchess, the Governor-General, the governor of each state, the members of both Houses of the Parliament and other distinguished guests 'to the number of not less than 250'. The promoters promised to pay a flat fee of £1000, plus expenses, plus a guinea for each recognisable face. The agreement specified that the painting had to be at least 10 feet high and 16 feet 8 inches wide. Roberts agreed to sign all 500 reproductions of the painting.[46]

The deal had its critics. In fact, it was a very twenty-first century debate. The critics claimed that the history of the Parliament was a national treasure too precious to be outsourced. The promoters – free market men – replied that the deal was a win-win proposition. It was generous to Roberts. He would earn a fat fee; he would reap the rewards that came from rubbing shoulders with the Duke, the Duchess and the other famous subjects; and 'the sheer merit of his work [would] make him famous'. The promoters stood to make a profit, of course, but the up-front cost was significant. The *Bulletin* agreed. It wrote that 'their patriotism may at least be valued at £3,000, the actual cost of giving the nation this historical record, and their treatment of the artist is claimed [by them] to be – well, "fair"'.[47]

Roberts was at the opening. He saw 'that immense gathering of people from all Australia, and from so many parts of the world. It was very solemn and great. The heads on the floor looked like a landscape stretching away'. And Roberts painted the scene as though it were a landscape. He placed the Duke on red carpet in the left centre of the painting, with the Duchess near him. They were lit by a shaft of sunlight streaming into the building, as if God were blessing the nation at the moment of its birth. Roberts painted a sea of heads stretching into the distance.

Roberts called it the *Big Picture*. He had a long list of important people whose heads had to be painted. If Roberts expected to find them reluctant to sit, he was wrong. The opportunity to be painted in the same painting as the royal couple was all but irresistible. Roberts eventually included more than 250 recognisable faces, but it was hard work. Arranging the sittings and devoting the time to do justice to each recognisable face was a logistical nightmare.

The job of painting the opening of the Parliament was an assignment of national significance. It involved dealing with the crème de la crème

Tom Roberts
Opening of the First Parliament of the Commonwealth of Australia by HRH The Duke of Cornwall and York (Later King George V) May 9, 1901
PHAC

of Australian and English society. It was to be the principal record of the moment the nation was created. Failure was unthinkable. Roberts may have been the only artist in Australia with the painterly ability and the personal presence to carry it off.

But the *Big Picture* meant more to Roberts than simply a feather in his cap. He planned to paint most of the work in Melbourne before completing it in London. It was to be his entrée to the art world of London. Roberts would arrive in London as the artist chosen to paint the Duke of York, now appointed the Prince of Wales, and his entourage. It was a royal endorsement beyond the dreams of common colonials.

3 FROM HEIDELBERG TO LONDON – OR PARIS

IN WHICH A SECOND WAVE OF ARTISTS
FROM MELBOURNE DEPARTS FOR EUROPE.

*I*n Melbourne, the Heidelberg School was not the only game in town. The National Gallery of Victoria produced many fine students. For example, Bertram Mackennal, the sculptor, studied there before he left Australia for London in 1882.[1] The painter, Rupert Bunny, was also a student. He left for Europe in 1884.[2]

George Folingsby, the painting master, persuaded the gallery to institute a Travelling Scholarship to send young artists to Europe.[3] The winner received £150 per annum over three years. The scholarship was first awarded in 1887 and every three years after that. Scholars were required to make copies of two Old Masters and give them to the gallery, along with one of their own paintings. Most scholars stayed in Europe after their three years expired.

John Longstaff won the first Travelling Scholarship. He was Folingsby's favourite student.[4] He travelled to Paris. On the advice of John Peter Russell (who had accompanied Tom Roberts to Granada), Longstaff studied at Cormon's *atelier*, where Russell had studied. Russell introduced Longstaff to Monet, Rodin and van Gogh. Moving to London in 1894, Longstaff's good looks, engaging personality and refined manners eased his way in London society. The same attributes equipped him to be a portrait painter.[5] When he returned to Melbourne in 1895, he continued to paint portraits, including those of Sir Edward Knox, the businessman; Sir Arthur Snowdon, the Lord Mayor of Melbourne; Sir Frederick Darley, the Chief Justice of New South Wales; and Henry Lawson, the poet. Longstaff's portraits all featured thick, expressive paintwork *à la mode française*.[6]

It was, however, Longstaff's landscape work that took him back to

London, courtesy of the trustees of the National Gallery. The Gillbee Bequest endowed the trustees to commission pictures of scenes from Australian history. The catch was that the pictures had to be painted in England, a requirement that presented no hardship for Longstaff. In 1900, the trustees commissioned him to paint the *Arrival of Burke, Wills and King at the Deserted Camp at Cooper's Creek, Sunday Evening, 21st April 1861*. With the advance from the trustees, Longstaff took his wife, Topsy, and their fourth son to London, arriving there in 1901.[7]

Other winners of the Travelling Scholarship were James Quinn, who won in 1893, and George Coates, who won in 1896.[8] Quinn used his scholarship to go to Paris. He studied at the *Académie Julian* and at several other art academies, before moving to London in 1902.[9]

George Coates was Melbourne's version of a Renaissance man. He was an accomplished weight-lifter; he was so good at boxing that his trainer urged him to turn professional; at cricket, he was good enough to play for Australia; he was a swimmer and high diver at the St Kilda Baths; he painted superbly; and, for good measure, he was 'a beautifully built lad'.[10]

Coates was the 'King' of the Prehistoric Order of Cannibals.[11] Percy, Lionel and Norman Lindsay, Will and Ted Dyson, Ray Parkinson, Myer Blashki and Max Meldrum were the Cannibals. There were no female Cannibals. The younger Cannibals found Coates a 'delightfully simple character. He asked from life but his bread, art and a cigarette … [When] he rolled a cigarette and lit up after a meal, he would say with a smile … "Is there anything in the world so good as tea and tobacco?"'[12]

The Lindsay brothers and Will Dyson were close. They called each other 'Joe'. This confused the uninitiated, but never any of the Joes, who knew by instinct which Joe was being addressed. They led a carefree lifestyle in the cheap cafes and chop-houses of Melbourne. Will Dyson and Norman Lindsay were especially close, sharing a similar sense of humour and a disdain for popular morality. The Cannibals wore a lapel-badge in the shape of a small red artists' palette with a skull painted on it. Their meetings were blokey occasions – opportunities to smoke pipes, drink rum and swap yarns. Dyson, in particular, was a fine raconteur.[13]

The Cannibals saw themselves as following in the footsteps of Roberts, Streeton and Conder. At Heidelberg, they took a 'big stone house' called Charterisville, not far from Eaglemont, where Roberts, Streeton and McCubbin had painted. Lionel Lindsay lived at Charterisville for several years. He wrote that:

Such a place is an incentive to the next generation. The very air is hallowed by the memory of the artists who worked here, and just as the spirit of Constable haunts the Stour, so will the name of Arthur Streeton forever possess these gentle slopes that fold upon the winding Yarra.[14]

Sunday was a special day at Charterisville. George Marshall-Hall, an Englishman who was professor of music at Melbourne University, had taken one of the studios and installed a piano there. After a hot summer's day, the Cannibals lay on the hillside, smoking, while Marshall-Hall serenaded them with Schubert lieder – mixing culture and cannibalism.[15]

George Coates won the Travelling Scholarship from a stellar field that included Hugh Ramsay, Portia Geach and Dora Meeson. Ramsay was a brilliant painter who died young and tragically. Geach, a successful artist who worked in London, Paris and New York, is remembered today in the Portia Geach Memorial Award for portraits by Australian women. Dora Meeson was the daughter of a wealthy English family. She trained at the Slade School of Fine Art in London, before she came to Melbourne with her family. Recognising her ability, Bernard Hall, the director of the National Gallery of Victoria and head of its Art School, sent her straight to the painting class, without first serving time in the drawing class, as was normal for newcomers. This caused friction. Other students thought that she '*must* imagine herself superior to colonial students'.[16] She and Coates were rivals. Dora beat George for first prize in a poster competition, but George beat Dora for the Travelling Scholarship. There was some justice in the result – Coates lacked the means to travel abroad, whereas Meeson was shortly to return to Europe with her family. Their rivalry grew into friendship. As they waited for the judges to announce the decision on the scholarship, George asked Dora to sit for a portrait. Dora wrote that, during the sittings, 'a close friendship was formed … and we agreed to meet on the other side of the world'.[17]

Coates sailed to London in 1897. After a few days exploring the London galleries, he visited Charles Conder in Dieppe, on the northern coast of France, before travelling to Paris to take up his studies at the *Académie Julian*. George was reunited with Dora when she arrived in Paris in 1898. At *Académie Julian*, her work outshone his, but their romance intensified. They wandered the streets of Paris together. They explored the countryside nearby. They visited galleries, admiring the works of Fantin-Latour, Puvis de Chavannes, Renoir, Sisley, Monet and Rodin. They mixed with James Quinn, Charles Conder, James McNeill Whistler and a number of other American artists. They met Oscar Wilde.[18]

Coates and Meeson were enthusiastic adopters of the French style. For George, 'it was a privilege to have been in Paris at a period when art was at its zenith, if not just passing it – when such men as Puvis de Chavannes, Monet, Manet, Renoir, Degas, Jean-Paul Laurens, and Dagnan-Bouveret were still living, and to have come under their influence'.[19] Dora, who later wrote a biography of George, told how: 'we both favoured a very full brush and were never, either of us, accused by the French of what was known in those days as *"la peinture anglaise,"* viz. thin, smooth, chalky painting'.[20]

Dora's family spent the summer of 1899 in Brittany. George followed on a bicycle: 'George rode over on the week-ends, and it was there that we settled that, as we had been so long fellow-students, we would run together for the rest of our lives'.[21] For the moment, they kept their engagement secret. Dora's father would never allow her to marry an artist. Not only did George have no income to speak of, he had yet to start on his scholarship picture. The secret lovers were separated once more the next winter, when Meeson *père* took his family to Menton, in Provence, for the winter, leaving Coates in Paris alone, lovelorn, poor and cold. When Coates fell ill, Dora had the cure: 'As I knew that my family would shortly be returning to London, I wrote from Menton urging him to go [to London] to paint his scholarship picture'.[22]

It was all the incentive Coates needed. He arrived in London in 1900.

Meanwhile, members of the Dyson and Lindsay families embarked on a series of romances that fuelled family feuds for years to come.

Lionel Lindsay and Jean Dyson led the way. They met in Florence in 1902, when friends introduced them. They fell in love. Within a fortnight, they were engaged. They returned separately to Australia, Lionel arriving in Sydney before Jean returned to Melbourne in 1903. As soon as they could, they married. They remained married until Jean died in 1956, leaving Lionel devastated.[23] The conventionality of their relationship defied family standards.

On his return to Sydney, Lionel found his younger brother, Norman, working as a commercial black and white artist on the *Bulletin* and living in a rented house in Northwood.[24] Norman was married to Katie, the sister of another Cannibal, Ray Parkinson, but Katie had returned to her family in Melbourne for the birth of their second child. At the same time, Will Dyson arrived from Melbourne to work as a cartoonist. The three men shared the Northwood house.

Keen to show Dyson a good time, Norman introduced him to his favourite model, Rose. Rose was cheerful, outgoing, cockney and curvy, with the trademark shape of a Norman Lindsay model. After making the introduction, Norman had second thoughts. He set to work wooing Rose himself, in competition with Will.[25] Norman emerged victorious from the contest that followed.[26]

Will returned to Melbourne, somehow retaining his affection for Norman. He wrote to Norman:

[Dear] good kind Joe you may have done me for the girl but I love you and if you and me wasn't born to be pals well then I am not the handsome honourable young fellow I know I am not. Well the unblessed Trinity was a happy and gay little trinity while it lasted.[27]

When Katie Lindsay, now with two children, returned to Sydney, she found Norman living in the Northwood house with Rose.[28] Norman rented a house for Katie and the children across the harbour in Waverly. He made infrequent visits there, spending most of his time with Rose. She was now his sole model. The elevation in Rose's status caused consternation in the Lindsay family – and among the wives of Northwood.[29]

In Melbourne, Will Dyson turned his attention to Norman's younger sister, Ruby. Many people regarded Ruby as the beauty of her age. Like most of the Lindsays, she was an accomplished artist. She was studying at the National Gallery School. Posing as the trusted friend of her elder brother, Will tried to take Ruby under his wing, but Ruby was a step ahead of him. 'The foolish child resents me advising her,' he wrote to Norman. 'She has had so many of these young pricks taking on themselves the airs of guardianship that she resents my attempt to direct her faltering footsteps – I, who am a truly great man'.[30]

Dyson returned to Sydney to work. Dyson needed somewhere to live, so Norman suggested he stay at the Waverly house with Katie and the children. Shortly afterwards, Norman went to Melbourne for Christmas. On his return, his son Jack – three or four years old – innocently told him that 'Will Dyson slept in Mummy's bed',[31] provoking a confrontation between the two men.

Ruby Lindsay SLNSW

Norman was in no position to lecture Will about morals – he had abandoned his wife and young family for a bosomy model. For his part, Dyson may have slept with Norman's estranged wife, but he was still carrying a torch for Norman's sister. Further, having moved out of the Waverly house, Will saw Norman and Rose every day, and remained friendly with them.

Dyson returned to Melbourne where he worked with his brother Ambrose and Ruby Lindsay supplying illustrations for a magazine called *Gadfly*. Ruby was as unconscious of her good looks as she was devoted to her work. She was becoming a fine illustrator, publishing under the name 'Ruby Lind'. In 1906, she provided illustrations for Steele Rudd's stories of Dad and Dave, *On Our Selection*, as well as supplying illustrations for many magazines.[32]

Dyson's career was also taking off. His political cartoons, sharp to the point of being biting, were in demand. A committed socialist, he was more adept at pinpointing the quirks of others than at pinpointing his own.[33] He criticised anyone who fawned to the English. In October 1908, he went so far as to publish a cartoon mocking artists who left Australia for England, even though he was dreaming of doing exactly the same thing. Just like those he criticised, Dyson wanted to try his luck in London.[34]

His plans to go to London brought forward the question of marriage. Money was a problem until May 1909, when he sold all 182 drawings he offered at a one-man show of his work.[35] Ruby and Will married on 30 September 1909.[36] A week later, they sailed for London on board the *Osterley*. Norman sailed with them, leaving Rose behind in Sydney, promising she could join him later.[37]

George Bell, a shy and conscientious artist, did not fit the Cannibal mould. He took classes at George Coates' studio before entering the National Gallery School in 1896. He studied there until 1901, following the 'dogmatic, academic teaching of Bernard Hall, where the emphasis was placed on Royal Academy and Paris Salon standards of excellence'.[38] Bell travelled to London in 1904, spending six weeks there before crossing to Paris. He entered the *Académie Julian*, where the teaching took a similarly academic approach.

Bell rejected the academic approach. He wrote that his time in Paris caused him to reorganise his 'whole outlook on painting'.[39] He struck out on his own, spending a summer in Étaples, an artists' colony on the northern coast of France, and a year at St Ives, in Cornwall, where artists also congregated.[40] At Étaples and St Ives, he worked to develop an approach of his own. It involved concentrating on the subject to the exclusion of other motifs or themes. Bell's idea was that 'the subject should justify itself solely as something fine to look at. Any literary or metaphysical significance it may have is a very secondary consideration'.[41]

Hilda Rix's mother was a painter. Her father was an inspector of schools. Educated at Merton Hall, a Melbourne private school for girls, Hilda studied with McCubbin at the National Gallery School from 1902 until 1905. 'Her earliest student efforts displayed something of the spirited independence of outlook that was later to become the outstanding feature of her work.'[42] Her father died in 1906, leaving the family with sufficient funds for Mrs Rix to take Hilda and her sister, Elsie, on an extended painting trip to London and Paris. In London, Hilda studied at the New Art School in Kensington.[43]

4 SYDNEY FOLLOWS MELBOURNE

IN WHICH SYDNEY ARTISTS FOLLOW
THE MELBURNIANS TO EUROPE.

*T*he art scene in Sydney fell short of that in Melbourne. There was an art gallery, but it lacked the generous funding of the National Gallery of Victoria. One visionary, Julian Ashton, stood out as the leading advocate of the artists seeking to develop an Australian style of painting.

Ashton was born in England of an American father and a Sicilian mother. Having trained in London and Paris, he lived first in Melbourne, before moving to Sydney in 1883. From his time in France, he was an enthusiastic *plein air* painter.

In Melbourne, he found that *plein air* painting was unknown and that Victorian artists preferred to do careful drawings in the open and return to the studio to turn them 'into dull uninspiring pictures'.[1] Things were no better in Sydney. The work displayed at the exhibition of the Art Society of New South Wales in 1883 was so bad that Ashton thought it 'impossible that a collection of such indifferent work could have been publicly displayed'.[2]

One artist, however, who did impress Ashton in his early days in Sydney was Henry Fullwood. Born in England in 1863, Fullwood travelled to Sydney in 1881, aged seventeen. He was a fine illustrator. For three years, he worked as a black and white artist for the *Picturesque Atlas of Australasia*, travelling as far afield as Darwin, the Torres Strait, Port Moresby, and New Zealand in the process. He impressed Ashton with his studies of bush scenery.[3]

When Streeton and Roberts came to Sydney, Ashton, Fullwood and William Lister Lister (another Englishman) came under their influence. They found Streeton's work more compelling than Roberts'.

Lister Lister wrote that, 'As a result of our English training, Ashton, Fullwood and myself were painting in low tones, but, after seeing Streeton's work, we began to observe that the colour and atmosphere of the landscape were brighter than we had previously realised'.[4]

Ashton painted an imposing portrait of Sir Henry Parkes, the Premier of New South Wales, resplendent with white mane and beard. On showing the picture to a minister in Parkes' government, the minister gasped: ''Tis a wonderful portrait. You've got the honest, straightforward look in the old man's eyes'. On showing it to Mr Dibbs, the Leader of the Opposition, Dibbs commented: 'Splendid portrait, Ashton. You've got the foxy look in the old rascal's eye when he has something up his sleeve'.[5]

When Ashton criticised the trustees of the National Art Gallery of New South Wales, Parkes – a noted stirrer – appointed him to the board of the gallery, to the irritation of the incumbents.[6] As a trustee, Ashton favoured the emerging *plein air* artists, whilst his colleagues preferred old-style Academy paintings. It was thanks to Ashton that the New South Wales gallery bought Streeton's '*Still Glides the Stream and Shall For Ever Glide*' from under the nose of the Victorian gallery in 1890. The Paris Salon gave its imprimatur to the purchase in 1892, when it hung Streeton's *Golden Summer, Eaglemont* on the line (that is, in pride of place, at eye level), but that was not enough to convince the conservative trustees. Ashton had to go in to bat again in 1893 to persuade them to buy another of Streeton's paintings, *Fire's On! Lapstone Tunnel*.[7]

Ashton was an inspiring teacher. Among his students were George Lambert and Thea Proctor.

George Washington Thomas Lambert was born in St Petersburg on 13 September 1873. His father, an American engineer, died two months before he was born, leaving his widow to make her way in her father's household. The father moved the family first to Germany, then to England, before migrating to Australia.

In Australia, a generous great-uncle welcomed Lambert to his sheep station, Eurobla, near Nevertire in north-western New South Wales. He left Lambert free to roam the property and learn the ways of the stockmen, the sheep, the horses and the cattle. Lambert already had 'this desire to do Art'. Eurobla gave him his 'first real fill of Nature'. Aged thirteen, he was on course to become an artist, but his grandfather thought shipping was the right career. Two stints as a shipping clerk proved that George did not suit the office. He returned to Eurobla, to sketching and drawing.[8]

It was not until 1896, when Lambert was twenty-three, that his skill at drawing led him to Julian Ashton's art school. Lambert worked as a grocer's clerk during the day and attended classes with Ashton at night. From the outset, he demonstrated precocious talent. His first task was to draw a head of Apollo from a plaster cast. Ashton said that, when it was drawn, he would hold the drawing against the cast to see if it was the same size. To Ashton's surprise, the drawing was close to perfect in size and execution. When Lambert insisted that he had no previous experience, Ashton asked him if he thought the drawing was the right size. 'No. It's a quarter inch too small,' replied Lambert. 'Not half an inch?' asked Ashton. 'No, sir, not quite'.[9]

Lambert was, at once, aloof, attractive and fascinating to women. At the Ashton school, he met his future wife, Amy. She found him 'tall, fair-haired, blue-eyed, broad-shouldered, and extremely swift in all his movements'.[10]

In 1899, Lambert won the Wynne Prize, which the New South Wales gallery awarded annually for the best landscape painting of Australian scenery. Lambert won with a painting of horses: *Across the Black Soil Plains*. The prize was £27. Better still, the New South Wales gallery bought the picture for 100 guineas.

The next year, the New South Wales Society of Artists awarded its first Travelling Scholarship. Each entrant submitted three paintings – all anonymously. The judges – Frederick McCubbin, Emanuel Phillips Fox and John Longstaff – all came from Melbourne. In a contest of scrupulous fairness, Lambert won. He sold his winning entry for £50, but was left with a bad case of seller's remorse when he learned that the New South Wales gallery paid £200 for the second-placed painting.[11]

Lambert's future looked rosy. As he made plans, Longstaff took him under his wing, advising him how to make the most of his opportunities in Paris, and arming him with introductions.

One detail remained to be settled – Amy. Lambert made her an ultimatum: 'Well, I am going to London and Paris, but not without you'. The caveman approach worked. George and Amy married on 4 September 1900. Two days later, they boarded SS *Persic*, bound for England. Hugh Ramsay joined the ship in Melbourne. Having missed out on the Victorian gallery's Travelling Scholarship for 1899, he was travelling under his own steam. As both men intended to study in the same *ateliers* in Paris, they had a lot in common. Hugh, George and Amy became friends as the ship made its way north.[12]

In February 1901, Ramsay and the Lamberts crossed to Paris. Hugh and George enrolled in the *Académie Colarossi* and later at the *Académie Delécluse*. Lambert struggled to graduate from black and white work to painting. He had to work hard on drawing, on composition, and on the techniques of applying paint.[13]

Painting came more naturally to Ramsay. His work was consistently rated above Lambert's. In 1902, the Salon accepted four of his paintings, and hung them together – a rare honour for an unknown artist. But Ramsay paid a heavy price for his stay in Paris. He succumbed to tuberculosis. Amy Lambert attributed the disease to the unsanitary condition of his lodgings. After two years in Paris, Ramsay returned to Australia, hoping against hope that the warmer climate would improve his health. Sadly, it did not. He died in 1906, aged twenty-nine. George Lambert's 1902 portrait of Ramsay showed a handsome man with a strong jaw and a firm gaze. Ramsay's own paintings showed a delicate touch, his paintings of women being especially *simpatico*, and reminiscent of Conder's.[14]

After two years in Paris, the Lamberts, now with a young son, Maurice, returned to London.[15]

Thea Proctor joined the Ashton school in 1896. She came from a well-to-do family, although her parents lived apart. Her father, a lawyer, lived in Sydney's Hunters Hill. Her mother lived in Bowral. Thea was sent to boarding school in Armidale in northern New South Wales. She was not the first artist in her family – her great-uncle was the ubiquitous John Peter Russell. Her mother encouraged her in the vocation. She was an immediate success at the Ashton school. According to Ashton, she 'was a charming, amiable youngster and a favourite with everyone in the school, where she remained until she was about twenty; then she entered upon the usual pilgrimage to London'.[16]

In fact, Thea Proctor was twenty-four when her mother took her to London in 1903. She studied at the St John's Wood Art School.[17]

Led by Roberts, Streeton and Conder, a strong contingent of Australian artists established itself in England and France. To those already mentioned, may be added the names of several more pilgrims.

Henry Fullwood, the illustrator whose skills had impressed Julian

Ashton, left Australia in 1900 with his wife, Clyda, and two sons, bound for London, via New York. In 1902, they settled in Chelsea.

Harold Septimus Power was born in New Zealand in 1877. A country boy, he developed an interest in painting horses. In 1900, Power moved to Adelaide where he worked as a cartoonist and illustrator. He met the great South Australian painter, Hans Heysen, and painted with him in the Adelaide Hills. The trustees of the Art Gallery of South Australia gave him 100 guineas to paint an animal picture. The result – *After the Day's Toil* – was of two boys on draught horses leading other horses. In September 1904, Power married Isabel Butterworth, and, on their long honeymoon, they travelled to Paris, where he studied at the *Académie Julian*.[18]

Fred Leist worked as a black and white artist for the *Bulletin* and the *Sydney Mail*, before taking his wife and daughter to London in 1908. In London, he turned to oil painting with some success, exhibiting regularly at the Royal Academy of Arts.[19]

Charles Bryant was educated at Sydney Grammar School before starting work as a clerk in the Bank of New South Wales. To overcome this unpromising start, his parents gave him art lessons with William Lister Lister, who was a family friend. Living in Manly, Bryant developed an interest in painting seascapes, ships and coastal scenes. He went to London in 1908.[20]

Other artists who travelled to Europe included Harold Parker,[21] Benjamin Minns,[22] Girolamo Nerli,[23] Iso and Alison Rae,[24] Jessie Traill,[25] Bessie Davidson,[26] Stella Bowen,[27] William Hardy Wilson,[28] Grace Cossington Smith[29] and Margaret Preston.[30]

5 LIFE IN LONDON

IN WHICH AUSTRALIAN ARTISTS
LIVE THE DREAM IN CHELSEA.

Arthur Streeton arrived in London in June 1897. He and Charles Conder spent a riotous night on the town in the course of which Conder, 'half-cornered', invited Streeton to share his studio. In the sober light of day, Streeton realised that he could not live up to Conder's pace.[1]

Streeton knew only two other people in London – Mackennal, a sculptor, and Minns, a watercolourist. He had one letter of introduction. Younger artists working in the schools and *ateliers* had a ready-made circle of friends in the other students. Streeton was left to work on his own. He took a small studio in Joubert Mansions, Chelsea. He was lonely. In October 1897, he wrote:

I pass about 20 of the 24 hours in this studio it is workroom, bedroom and all. I have a visitor to see me about once a fortnight, and the caretaker brings in my breakfast of a morning. Man is naturally a gregarious beast, but here in London (London is cruelly large), the millions herd along all on their own and not caring for their neighbours and suspicious of the stranger … You see when painting's done for the day, you eat your dinner at a restaurant (if you have the money), then walk about looking at the people.[2]

Streeton missed McCubbin. He longed to 'hear just once more his healthy laughter with its ponderous echoes … How I'd love to take him for a stroll round Piccadilly and hear his laughter at the Dingbats'.[3]

He missed Roberts, too. Streeton was in London for six years before Roberts joined him. Streeton learned the hard way how much of his success in Melbourne had been due to Roberts' genius for marketing. Without Roberts as his ideas man, Streeton found it difficult to make progress. His marketing plan was: 'I'll send in to shows as they come along – It seems everybody has to serve a terrible apprenticeship to London – especially unbusinesslike devils like me'.[4] Subtler approaches were foreign to him. Conder called him 'Innocent Streeton', a description that was harsh, but fair.[5]

Streeton's fame in Australia had come from the success of his large-scale landscapes. He was good at painting the Australian bush. He struggled to find an English subject that equally suited his style of painting. Towards the end of 1897, he spent several days working on a 'little decorative picture of Ariadne'. It was a bizarre choice of subjects. Ariadne was the daughter of Minos, King of Crete, famous from the Greek tale of Theseus and the Minotaur. Streeton painted her with 'a lovely background of gum trees and quiet harbour water' on a small canvas, 5 × 14 inches.[6] A Sydney audience might conceivably have recognised the background, but there was nothing in the painting for a London audience. It was as though Streeton was deliberately playing to his own weaknesses.

Success in Australia was no guarantee of success in London. If that was not already obvious to Streeton, it was proven by the response to a major exhibition of Australian art in the Grafton Galleries in April and May 1898.

The selection committee for the exhibition included Roberts, Streeton, Fullwood and Ashton. They chose 371 works. Unsurprisingly, all of the selectors were well represented. Julian Ashton had 19 paintings; Henry Fullwood 17; William Lister Lister 14; Tom Roberts 13; Arthur Streeton 9; George Lambert 6; Frederick McCubbin 5; Walter Withers 4; and James Quinn and Charles Conder, 2 each. Sixty-one paintings came from the Sydney gallery. Nine came from the Melbourne gallery. The exhibition was a good cross-section of colonial art.

The colonial inferiority complex was on display once more. The catalogue for the exhibition was self-conscious, as though the authors were uncertain whether to boast about Australian art, or to apologise for it. Noting that 'All the Pictures exhibited were painted *in Australia* by Australian Artists', it continued:

The Trustees of the National Art Gallery of New South Wales have been pleased to undertake this project, which seeks to obtain a more extended attention to Australian Art beyond the Colonies ... The Trustees recognise that the Artists of Australia, availing themselves of this opportunity, have done their best to represent their Art, the result being this collection submitted to the judgment of connoisseurs outside of Australia.[8]

RAM Stevenson, an art critic and a cousin of Robert Louis Stevenson, wrote that: 'This exhibition proves that French art, which has swept the European Continent, has almost conquered Australia'. Stevenson's point of comparison was an exhibition of Australian works in 1886, which he had found to be a pale imitation of English fashions, mostly devoid of artistic talent. In the current show, he thought that Roberts' *Golden Fleece* showed:

an excellent power of drawing, much careful observation of certain types of men and the business like packing of a picture that goes to make good illustration. When you have seen it, you will know how sheep shearing takes place in Australia; you will know the type of man produced by the country, his tallness, leanness, wiry activity and hard intelligence. But you will know little of Mr Roberts or his way of seeing.

He singled out Streeton's *Early Summer* as the 'cleverest, the most brilliant, the highest toned work in the show'.[9]

Writing in *The Times*, another critic, Sir Thomas Ward, thought the exhibition was of unusual interest:

One is tempted to assume in a general way, that colonial art cannot be very good; that the country is too young, and that the talents of its sons generally find other outlets. But in point of fact, the last 20 years have wrought a great change in Australia, and the practice of art has thriven there ... These galleries show it, and they show also that the impulse, or at least the mode of expression, has to a great extent come from Paris, through English and Australian teachers who had first learned what the Paris *ateliers* had to teach them.[10]

Ward acknowledged that the French techniques had been adapted to Australian conditions:

In this bright and pleasant display there is very little that recalls anything English; the broad summary treatment, the firm and yet careful drawing, the manner of laying on paint are in origin French, though they have become in a measure transformed by transplantation.[11]

He admitted that he was judging the paintings for their likeness to a landscape he had never seen:

Mr Streeton claims our gratitude for giving us impressions of landscape which seem to be distinctly Australian; his 'Hawkesbury River' and 'Still glides the stream, and shall for ever glide', albeit a little too much composed, could hardly represent anything in any other latitude.[12]

Ward's conclusion was as favourable as the New South Wales gallery trustees could have expected: 'This Australian exhibition is worth seeing. The subjects are fresh, and in technique the average work of Chelsea or Clichy is certainly no better'.[13] If the work of the Australians measured up to the standards of London and Paris, Australian art had, indeed, come a long way.

Dugald MacColl, who later became keeper of the Tate Gallery, gave a different view of the exhibition:

There is no Australian art. There are a number of young men who would like to be artists and who do their best to create art on the basis of the illustrated paper and such popular pictures as find their way to Australian public galleries, but there is no evidence of their having ever seen a good picture … They have the instinct of art, vague information about its nature, the most misleading examples, and they struggle to produce they know not what.

Conder was an exception. He 'was in Australia for a few years in extreme youth, but was lucky enough to escape'. Streeton might conceivably be another Conder. When allowances were made for his colonial background, his pictures showed 'no little talent, but a talent how badly served by models of the poorest modern French drawing'.[15]

MacColl was the son of a Scottish Presbyterian minister. Drawing on the deepest well-springs of Presbyterian charity, he found something good to say about Australia: 'The importation of Australian meat and wine has its excuse, for those things, though not the best of their kind, are cheap and not unwholesome; but for the importation of the existing brands of Australian painting and sculpture there can be no excuse whatever'.[16]

The exhibition was not all bad news for Streeton. The generous reviews of Stevenson and Ward counted against McColl's boorish rant, yet Streeton was losing confidence. When the Academy rejected one of his paintings a month later, he wrote to Roberts that it 'did not hurt my vanity very much for I was quite prepared. Still it would have helped considerably to have been [selected]'. Streeton grumbled that the Academy had 'an inartistic atmosphere'.[17]

He told Roberts that seeing the great galleries of London had persuaded him to change his techniques:

I feel convinced that my work hereafter will contain a larger idea & quality than before – After seeing Constable, Turner, Titian, Watts & all the masters … I'm evolving & should I return I'd never paint Australia in exactly the same way – by

Gad I'll do one or two great things if I get out there again – I know more now –
& would touch it more *poetically*.[18]

It made perfect sense for Streeton to choose JMW Turner as his exem-
plar. Turner's later paintings – for example, *Rain, Steam and Speed – the
Great Western Railway, Wrecked Coast of Northumberland* and *The Fighting Temeraire Tugged to her Last Berth to be Broken Up* – were years ahead
of their time. Their misty, spiritual qualities were more in tune with the
work of the French Impressionists than with mannered English styles.
If there was an artist who embodied what it meant to paint *poetically*, it
was Turner.

Back in Australia, Roberts could be forgiven if he was scratching his
head. After Stevenson's criticism that *The Golden Fleece* said little about
Roberts or his way of seeing, now Streeton was telling him to paint more
poetically. Interviewed in 1899, Roberts said that Streeton was 'under-
going a whole revolution … England, it seems, has set his notions of art
and technique a-ferment, and when Streeton comes out of the chaos –
well, he will not be the Streeton we are accustomed to. Who knows but
he will want to burn that *Hawkesbury River* before he is 5 years older?'[19]

Unlike Streeton, Longstaff took London in his stride. He adapted so well
to English society that Streeton called him 'Lord Longstaff'.[20] Longstaff
deferred his Gillbee Bequest painting of the explorers Burke and Wills,
while he finished portraits of King Edward VII, Queen Alexandra, and
the Prince and Princess of Wales. To his royal subjects, Longstaff added
an impressive stream of commoners: Sir Edmund Barton, Australia's
first Prime Minister; the Countess of Darnley; the wife of South African
diamond merchant, Louis Breitmeyer; the wife of JC Williamson, the
Australian theatre impresario; and the Countess of Eldon in her Coronation robes.

Success bred success. Longstaff was invited to dances, dinners and
weekends away at English country houses. His contacts produced a
healthy flow of commissions. With the income from the commissions,
Longstaff left Chelsea for posher surrounds in St John's Wood. He did
not complete the *Arrival of Burke, Wills and King at the Deserted Camp
at Cooper's Creek, Sunday Evening, 21st April 1861* until 1907.

Longstaff returned to Australia to visit his ageing parents in 1910. So
prosperous was he that he took a nine-room stateroom on the German

liner in which he sailed to Melbourne. On arrival at his parents' home town of Shepparton in country Victoria, a cheering crowd met him at the train station; the town band played Handel's *See, the Conquering Hero Comes*; and the shire president made a speech of welcome to which Longstaff replied:

Am I glad to be home again? I cannot tell you how glad. The Australian landscape has always seemed to me the most beautiful in the world as well as the most mysterious. When I first saw the brown, hot earth from the ship's decks at Fremantle I cannot tell you the emotion it gave me – after all that confounded sappy English green.[21]

That was Longstaff's strength – he knew how to play to the crowd.

Chelsea was a bohemian district on the left bank of the Thames. Streeton's hero, JMW Turner, lived in Cheyne Walk, as did the artists, James McNeill Whistler and Dante Gabriel Rossetti; the politician David Lloyd George, who later became Prime Minister; Ralph Vaughan Williams, the composer; and Sylvia Pankhurst, the suffragette. Cheyne Walk was favoured because it was on the Embankment. Its houses had views across the Thames to Battersea.

Conder and his wife lived at 14 Wellington Square, Chelsea. Streeton spent the Christmas of 1902 with them. In his bachelor days, Conder's eye for the women had been so well developed that his biographer called it 'an infirmity', but marriage had curbed his more flamboyant ways.[22] Streeton wrote to Roberts that Conder's wife, Stella Maris, was 'a good sort & very sensible – & he is now a steady going married man. It's made a wonderful improvement in him'.[23] Stella also had an income of £800 a year, sufficient to keep the dissolute Conder in a style to which he had never been accustomed.

In 1904, the Conders moved to 91 Cheyne Walk, a beautiful eighteenth-century house overlooking the river. Here, on 18 February 1905, they held a famous costume party. Conder painted the invitation, with the instruction: 'Disguise Imperative'.[24] All the great artists attended. Augustus John, a Welsh painter with an eye for the women to rival Conder's, went as a Bohemian. Conder was a gypsy organ grinder. The women, vying for the prize of a Conder fan for the wearer of the most beautiful dress, could not match Madame Errazuriz, 'a dazzling South American', who took the prize with ease.[25] In 1938, John Rothenstein

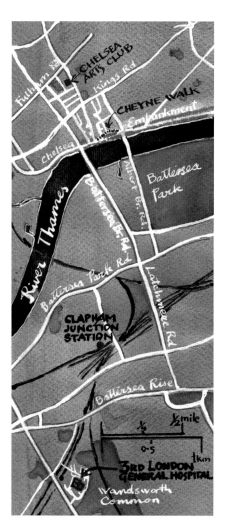

Walter Di Qual
London Showing 3rd London General Hospital, Wandsworth, & Chelsea Arts Club

wrote that the party 'was memorable enough to be talked of to this day'.[26] Thea Proctor was still talking about it when she painted Barry Humphries' wife and daughter in Sydney's Double Bay many years later in 1966.[27]

Cheyne Walk was the expensive end of Chelsea. Most of Chelsea still offered cheap rents. The general rule was: the further away from the river, the cheaper the rents. Streeton paid £75 a year for a studio at 59 Glebe Place. His studio was 150 metres from King's Road and 300 metres from the river. Within a hundred metres, there were the studios of at least thirty other artists. Streeton was happy in this studio – it was comfortable, dry, warm and hearty.[28] George and Dora Coates paid £50 a year for their studio in Trafalgar Studios, a set of purpose-built artists' studios in Manresa Road.

The artists drank at the Chelsea Arts Club.[29] The Chelsea Arts Club had been formed in 1890 as a club for architects, engravers, painters and sculptors. Whistler was a founding member. The club was (and still is) in a large building in Church Street, complete with a garden, bowling green and flowerbeds. It served breakfast, lunch, tea and dinner every day, as well as maintaining a well-stocked bar. The atmosphere of the club was relaxed and informal, indulging the eccentricities of its members. The subs were kept low – around 30s a year – indulging the fickle incomes of its members.[30] All the Australian artists seemed to be members – Streeton, Mackennal, Longstaff, Fullwood, Quinn and Lambert among them.[31]

The English members included Frederick Brown, Henry Tonks and Philip William Steer, all teachers at the Slade School of Fine Art and influential in the direction of English art. Other painters, such as Walter Sickert, Albert and William Rothenstein, John Singer Sargent, William Orpen and Augustus John, were also members, as was Dugald MacColl, the acerbic Scot who had so rudely reviewed the Australian exhibition of 1898.[32] Francis Derwent Wood, the English sculptor, was popular with the Australian members. He was married to the Rockhampton-born soprano, Florence Schmidt.[33]

Streeton thought the Chelsea Arts Club was the most artistic club in England.[34] The other contender for that title was the New English Art Club. Many artists belonged to both – including John, Orpen, Singer Sargent, Steer, Sickert and Tonks. The New English Art Club was more edgy than the Chelsea Arts Club. The New English attracted young artists, trained in France, whose paintings the Academy often rejected on the grounds that they were too 'French'. The young artists, in turn, thought that the values of the Academy were too 'English'. It was uncertain whether the Chelsea Arts Club or the New English Art Club was the surer path to fame. Many artists believed it was essential to join the Chelsea Arts Club to become a member of the Royal Academy. Others 'held the narrow door of the New English Art Club to be the only gate to Heaven'.[35]

Roberts landed in England in April 1903. He could have joined Streeton in Chelsea, but, instead, rented a flat in Putney. If Chelsea was considered out of town, Putney was a few kilometres further on. It still had market gardens and open fields. Living there, Roberts was isolated from the Chelsea arts scene. He rode a bicycle, but it was a fair ride to Chelsea – and, although Roberts could cycle there, his wife and young son could not.

The promoters were applying pressure for him to finish the *Big Picture*. A lot remained to be done. Roberts was relying on the English celebrities to sit for him. In addition to the Duke and Duchess (now the Prince and Princess of Wales), Roberts hoped to paint Sir Arthur Bigge, the Prince's private secretary and Sir Charles Cust, the Prince's equerry. All of his subjects claimed they were too busy to sit, which they probably were. Cust added that it was pointless working to perfect the minor faces because 'They [the viewers] only look at the two principals'.[36]

A standard studio would not do. Roberts had to find accommodation big enough to fit the giant canvas, and comfortable enough for the celebrity sitters. The Imperial Institute, a body dedicated to promoting the interests of the British Empire, came to the rescue. It gave Roberts the South Africa Room in the Institute Building in South Kensington. At 12 metres long and grandly decorated, the room was good for the canvas and the sitters.[37]

By hard work and perseverance, Roberts completed the *Big Picture* in November 1903. The promoters gave the painting to the Commonwealth of Australia, which re-gifted it to the King.[38] The King lent it to the Royal Academy, which hung the painting, more out of deference to the King, than in admiration of Roberts' work. The painting received lukewarm reviews, praising the scale of the work and the skill with which Roberts had captured the occasion, but stopping short of acclaiming it as a great work of art. The engravings, when they came, were disappointing. Lacking the colours of the original, they dulled the painting down.[39]

Roberts now looked for new opportunities. He painted river scenes near Putney, including *Putney Bridge, London* and *The Towpath, Putney*. These, too, were disappointing. They lacked the clarity and light of his Australian landscapes.

Roberts thought the *Big Picture* would win him commissions for portraits of historical significance. The Art Gallery of South Australia commissioned him to paint the Governor-General, Lord Hopetoun (now the Marquis of Linlithgow). Roberts showed the Marquis in all his military finery, but the portrait lacked qualities that would single it out. When the Royal Academy refused to hang it, Roberts was disappointed, but not surprised. It was not a breakthrough painting.[40] This was the first of a series of rejections by the Royal Academy. Roberts was not alone in being rejected, or 'biffed', as the Australians called it, but he did have to endure the humiliation, year after year, of the Academy biffing him, whilst accepting works from Australian artists whom he regarded as his inferiors.[41]

Isolation remained a problem for Roberts. Things improved when Henry Fullwood took digs downstairs in the same block of flats as the Roberts, and James Quinn took a terrace house nearby.[42] Roberts went with Fullwood to London to see the Turners, admiring them as much as Streeton did.[43] In May 1905, Roberts moved to a new studio in South Kensington. Closer to town, he had more visitors in a day in South Kensington than in a month at Putney. He worked happily there, keeping the studio until 1910.[44]

Roberts later called the years from 1904 until 1910 'the black period of his painting'.[45] The English landscape did not offer him the same opportunities as the Australian landscape. Commissions for portraits did not come freely to a painter who shunned high society. Moreover, Roberts copied Streeton's mistake of turning to mythology for inspiration. It was not a move to make the most of his talents. He painted a work now lost, *The Sleeper Awakened*, based on *The Arabian Nights*. Roberts had doubts about the painting, and returned to it over and again.[46] In 1907, the Royal Academy biffed *The Sleeper Awakened* and a second entry – a sculpted bust of his son – whilst accepting paintings from nine other Australian artists. The Academy rejected Roberts again in 1908, this time accepting paintings from twenty-one other Australian artists.[47]

The proud leader of the Heidelberg School was struggling for recognition. Roberts complained that 'England doesn't really *want* anybody … She has the whole world to draw upon … The only thing is to make her want you, and that is difficult, for she really only wants the exceptional in any line'.[48] He travelled to Holland, but the idea of painting in France, where the landscape and the light might have suited his style of painting, does not seem to have occurred to him. As his artistic fortunes languished, Roberts took a greater interest in the activities of the Chelsea Arts Club, becoming a regular attender at the smokos and a member of its committees. In 1908, the club held the first of the fancy dress balls for which it became famous. Roberts went dressed as a sundowner.[49]

It was not until 1910 that the Academy accepted two of his paintings – *April Girl* and *Mme Hartl as La Tournabuoni*. As if to make up for grievances past, the Academy hung *Mme Hartl* on the line.

George Lambert was tall, slim and athletic. He had red hair, which he accentuated by affecting a Vandyke beard and a waxed moustache. He was a forceful man, a boxer in his youth, and energetic and outgoing as an adult.

He was entertaining, amusing, and the life of the party. As his wife, Amy, said: '[T]here was something exhilarating in his appearance'. Going on a Sunday walk with him was like 'being attached to a comet'.[51] Yet he was sensitive, and Amy thought his outgoing manner covered 'what might have been considered an inferiority complex, which occasioned a certain aggressiveness in speech, that was more of a justification addressed to himself than a challenge to others'.[52]

The same observation could be made of his many self-portraits. Most are painted from a low angle, looking up at Lambert, who is posed to emphasise his flamboyance, eccentricity and whimsical qualities. He dressed to similar effect, wearing dapper suits and shirts and flowing gowns, even in the studio. If he presented himself as a showman, that was not to cover up a want of application to his work. On the contrary, he was conscientious to a fault, with strong motivation, and a healthy streak of self-criticism.

When the Lamberts returned to London from Paris, they established themselves in a small studio in the Rossetti Studios, in Chelsea. The apartment was crowded with furniture, especially after Constant, a second son, was born in 1905. Spurred on by apprehended poverty and the need to feed his family, Lambert's output was prodigious. He saved on the cost of models by painting Amy, the children, and himself.

When Thea Proctor arrived in London, the Lamberts helped her find a flat in Oakley Street, Chelsea. Thea not only drew and painted with George; she sat as an extra model, often in paintings with Amy and the children. George painted *Miss Thea Proctor*, on page 48, in 1903. In it, Thea wore an elegant, flowing dress of dark blue, patterned with understated purple polka dots, and a large picture-hat. At twenty-five, she was at the peak of her beauty – at once handsome, languid and stylish. The manner of the painting, reminiscent of Hogarth and Rubens, was safe enough for the Royal Academy to hang the painting on the line.[53]

Lambert was to paint Proctor over and over – and always as an object of veneration: aloof, handsome and strikingly patrician. This would have excited lesser wives, but Amy kept her cool. She wrote:

Thea Proctor featured in many paintings – *The Bathers, The Mother, The Blue Hat* and so on, for she was a daily visitor at both studio and home; at the former as student and model. The friendly interchange was of mutual benefit, as Lambert gained the services of an exceptionally graceful and artistic model, and Miss Proctor's drawings strengthened in line and directness of approach, and she rarely considered any design complete before it had been passed by Lambert.[54]

It is not so much that Thea Proctor featured in so many of Lambert's paintings, as the way that he painted her that raises speculation about the nature of their relationship. So tender is the painting of *Miss Thea Proctor* that it seems natural, and not prurient, to draw the conclusion that there was an intimate connection between the sitter and the artist.

The Bathers shows Amy taking the children to an English beach. Maurice leads the way, naked and carrying a towel, while Amy follows along carrying Constant, by then a big baby, in her arms. Thea, tall, aloof, and elegantly dressed, makes a striking contrast to Amy's maternity. *The Mother* shows the same subjects. Again, Amy's maternity contrasts with Thea's elegance, although the sense of that painting is that the two women were close. The contrast between elegance and maternity is absent from George Bell's 1910 painting, *The Conversation*, which shows George Lambert with Amy Lambert and Thea Proctor. In Bell's rendering, there is little to choose between Amy Lambert and Thea Proctor in looks, elegance or style.

Lambert was fond of using Proctor's elegance as a counterpoint in his paintings. *Lotty and a Lady* places Proctor, aloof as always, at a table with Lotty – a fishwife about to gut a fish on the table. *The Sonnet* makes another puzzling contrast. In the foreground, Thea Proctor looks out,

aloof again, and seemingly unaware of the scene behind her, in which a naked beauty luxuriates next to Arthur Streeton. Streeton pays her no attention – he is giving his full attention to a book of sonnets.

The Sonnet attracted controversy whenever it was hung. Amy wrote that it was 'never exhibited without evoking outcry and letters asking for an explanation of its meaning'.[55] This was understandable. It must have been some sonnet for Streeton to ignore the beauty at his side. And how aloof was Proctor, that she could ignore what was going on (or not going on) behind her? Possible interpretations abound.

It is, of course, a gross presumption to infer from the way Lambert painted Proctor that they were lovers. His and her friends and family were divided on the subject,[56] leading Lambert's biographer to conclude that the exact nature of their relationship 'was inaccessible to say the least'.[57] Neither Lambert nor Proctor ever admitted an affair. Moreover, Amy Lambert remained close to Thea Proctor after George Lambert died. In 1946, she gave *Miss Thea Proctor* to Miss Thea Proctor.

George Lambert
Miss Thea Proctor AGNSW

George Lambert
The Sonnet NGA

With his outgoing nature and flamboyant character, Lambert was a natural for the Chelsea Arts Club. He involved himself in the club's pageants, appearing in elaborate costume as Lord Thomas Seymour in a pageant commemorating Princess Elizabeth Tudor. He helped organise the Chelsea Arts Club balls. The club also provided George with an outlet for the manly side of his nature. He and Augustus John – a kindred spirit among the English artists – demonstrated their masculinity by boxing one another in the street outside the club. Lambert had the better of the bout, knocking John to the ground.[58]

Lambert was painting well. In Chelsea, he found a home that allowed him to meet the best English and expatriate artists in congenial circumstances. His work was favourably reviewed, but critical success was not translating into cash. His young wife, concerned for her two boys, wrote ruefully that 'Lambert always suffered from a reputation disproportionate to his means, which were very fluctuating, and generally insufficient to cover his combined expenses of makeshift studio and extremely modest home, and sometimes non-existent'.[59]

George Coates arrived in London with an introduction to an American, Dr Henry Williams, who was producing a 25-volume set called *The Historian's History of the World*. Dr Williams employed Coates to copy old prints and make drawings from specimens in the British Museum. When Dora Meeson and her family came to England, they settled in Rye. George joined the family, sending a package of pen and ink drawings to Dr Williams each week. Dora helped George with the drawings.

Their secret engagement was a source of worry. Dora's father came from the old school. He did not want Dora to marry at all, 'least of all to an impecunious artist, he had a rooted objection to artists, and declared they were the most brainless of all the men he had ever met'.[60] Against these odds, George asked Dora's father's permission to marry his daughter. The father agreed, but gave himself a lifeline – the marriage could not take place until George was making a steady income. He may have thought this would never happen.

According to Dora, she and George had an idyllic romance. Together they walked and sketched the length and breadth of the Romney Marshes: 'George used to say, it was there he escaped from the sense the English country always gave him of being enclosed in a tidy garden.

Particularly at Rye Harbour, he felt the openness and big distances as in Australia'.[61]

In 1902, Dora's family moved to Wimbledon. Dora had a studio in the garden. As they were now officially engaged, Dora's father allowed George to work together with Dora in her studio. This was a racy privilege, given that Dora and George were only thirty-three.[62]

Dora joined George on Dr Williams' staff. With two incomes – £6 a week – they were on track for marriage, but Dr Williams chose this moment to shelve his project and return to America, sacking all the staff. George and Dora kept the reversal a secret. That deception allowed them to be married on 23 July 1903.[63]

After honeymooning at Rye, Dora and George took rooms in a cottage in Ealing. Later, they moved to a photographer's studio. It had a glass roof, which made it unbearably hot in summer. To escape their cheap digs, they spent time with Dora's parents, even though Dora's father reminded them constantly that they only had themselves to blame for rushing into marriage without sufficient means.[64] It was humbling for the one-time King of the Cannibals.

George worked hard on a picture of Mary Magdalene at the foot of the cross, but the Royal Academy would not hang it. In 1908, the Paris Salon accepted a picture of children, *The Children's Orchestra*, but the English would not hang it. George and Dora were discouraged. It seemed there was little they could contribute to the art world. Their income came from teaching a few pupils each week.[65]

They decided to move to Chelsea. After beginning in cramped accommodation in Cheyne Row, they rented an unfurnished studio at No 9, Trafalgar Studios, for £50 a year from Augustus John. That left them £10 a year, plus whatever they might earn, on which to survive.[66]

They made their own furniture. They lived on oatmeal, herrings and flank of beef. When friends were kind enough to invite them for a good meal, they could only accept if the friends lived within walking distance. Mr and Mrs Elmslie Horniman invited them to parties at nearby Elm Park Gardens, where they met other artists. When the Hornimans held a ball at Chelsea Town Hall, George impressed with his waltzing.[67]

George painted the portrait of Miss Jessica Strubelle, an American singer. It was painted in a muted style, reminiscent of Conder's work. Roberts liked the painting. Seeing that the style of the painting was more appealing to French eyes than to British, he advised George to submit it to the Paris Salon, where it received a *mention honorable*.[68]

Like Streeton, George and Dora were reluctant to market themselves. According to Dora, 'George always said: Let the work speak for itself'. He resented the role of the entrepreneur in the world of art. Gradually, they learned the black arts of self-promotion.[69]

Trafalgar Studios, a building of three storeys, was home to many artists. A Dutch artist, Maurice de Groot, and his wife held parties in their studio on the same floor as the Coates. Tom Roberts often dropped in during the evening. A friend lent Dora a piano. She played Beethoven, Chopin, Mozart and Bach, while Roberts and George listened.[70]

Conder had a studio at No 6, Trafalgar Studios, although George and Dora seldom ran into him. Condor was dying of syphilis. In his glory days in Australia, twenty years before, Conder had fallen behind with the rent. When he confessed to the landlady that he had no money, the landlady replied: 'There are other ways of settling debts'.[71] What looked like an easy way out of a liquidity problem became a life sentence. Unaware of the details of Conder's illness, Dora wrote that he 'shut himself in, often till very late at night, was said to be ill, and in a pitiable state, through the influence of a drug, and died shortly after'.[72]

Florence Haig, a Scots portraitist, lived at No 4, Trafalgar Studios. She was a member of the militant Women's Social and Political Union. Between 1908 and 1912, she was gaoled three times for her activities as a suffragette, the last time for breaking the windows of the DH Evans department store in Oxford Street. When in prison, Haig joined a hunger strike.[73]

Encouraged by Florence, Dora joined the suffrage movement. George followed dutifully, by joining the Men's League for Women's Suffrage. 'Although he himself cared little for politics, he was keen on fair play and believed in granting the same facilities to women as to men to further their natural abilities, and he had a very human wish to support anything that would improve the condition of the masses.' He marched in the suffragette processions, which was an ordeal for him, not because of the threat of police violence or reprisals, but because he 'hated publicity and crowds'.[74] George and Dora together carried a banner, painted by Dora, in the Women's Suffrage Coronation Procession held on 17 June 1911.[75] The banner urged Britain to trust women with the vote, as Australia had done in 1902.

Dora was not prepared to risk a spell in gaol. The worst she did – in company with George – was to paste notices on public hoardings and pillar-boxes. George was unusual among the male artists of Chelsea in

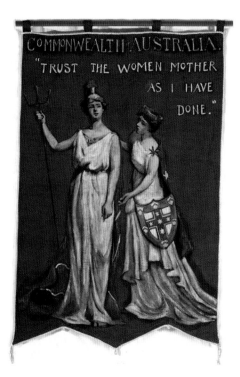

Dora Meeson
The Women's Suffrage Banner: Trust the Women … PHAC

supporting the suffrage movement. According to Dora, the male artists were always conservative and not partisans of the movement, adding the whole-of-gender rebuke that 'In this they did not differ from the average male'.[76]

The Coates made many friends through their involvement in the suffrage movement. They lent their studio for suffrage meetings. At one meeting, they met Emily Ford, an artist who also designed stained glass, who had a cottage and studio at 44 Glebe Place, Chelsea. Another friend was Edith Elder, Dora's contemporary at the Slade, who invited George and Dora to her home at 101 Cheyne Walk. Edith introduced George and Dora to many members of the New English Art Club.

George joined the Chelsea Arts Club in 1905. At the club, he might have reverted to his role as King of the Cannibals, but Dora kept him on a tight leash:

[George] did not frequent [the club] much, except for an occasional smoke and chat before dinner, or a game of snooker or billiards, of which he became quite a good player. The convivial evenings there did not appeal to him. Though by no means a teetotaller, he had not the head nor the taste for much strong drink. I only once saw him intoxicated, and that was about this time, after one of these jovial evenings, from which he returned very late. I was so distressed that he never again allowed himself to get into this condition.[77]

The Coates suffered a setback one evening when they were downstairs having tea with Florence Haig. Hearing noises coming from their studio, they ran upstairs to find it full of flames. There were no telephones, so George ran for the fire brigade, which arrived in time to save the building, but too late to save George and Dora's paintings, many of which were destroyed.[78]

Florence Haig was friendly with Arthur Walker, the sculptor, whose major works included statues of two strong women: one of Florence Nightingale, and the other of Emmeline Pankhurst. In 1912, the Royal Academy accepted George's *Arthur Walker and his Brother Harold*, along with two other canvases. The painting of the Walker brothers, remarkable for catching the family likeness, was well received. John Longstaff wrote to Coates: 'Want to tell you how much I appreciate your picture of the two Walkers. Amongst all the banalities in portraiture it stands out as something real and vital. Good luck to you. *Continuez, mon ami*'.[79]

Dora's work was equally well received. Meeting the famous teacher, Henry Tonks, who had taught her years before when she was a student at the Slade, she invited him to visit their studio. This was a brave move – Tonks had a formidable reputation for outspoken criticism.[80] Having looked at her work and at George's, Tonks pointed to one of Dora's landscapes and said: 'Send that along to the New English [Art Club], but we don't want anything of your husband's'.[81]

George did, however, reap a dividend from his abstemious behaviour at the Chelsea Arts Club. When the Scottish artist George Henry visited the Coates' studio, he took Dora aside to tell her how nice and quiet George was: 'Not like most of the other Australians at the Club, noisy, blatant fellows'.[82]

Two noisy, blatant fellows arrived from Australia in December 1909: Norman Lindsay and Will Dyson. Arthur Streeton took them to a welcome dinner at the Chelsea Arts Club. Lambert proposed the toast and Dyson replied. Their next outing to the club was the annual dinner of the Australian artists. One of the toasts was to the new arrivals. Dyson's reply was a 'rattling performance'.[83] The club was more Will's domain than Norman's. Norman distrusted it, calling it a place where 'the frenzies of jealousy are excited and ambition stimulated'.[84]

Will and Ruby Dyson were on their honeymoon, but, so far, it was not much of a honeymoon – Norman was sleeping on the couch in their flat. They also needed work; Ruby was anxious for financial security. The financial problem was soon solved. Will, a committed socialist, put Ruby's needs ahead of his own beliefs. He found work as a cartoonist on Lord Northcliffe's *Weekly Dispatch* – overlooking the fact that the Northcliffe press was renowned for its right-wing stance on nearly everything.[85]

Solving the Norman problem was more difficult. For Norman, the trip to London had been a convenient way of ditching Katie and the boys, but he was missing Rose. To make matters worse, he was hearing rumours that Rose was not letting the grass grow under her feet, but was seeing BR Wise KC, a New South Wales barrister and politician. Norman asked his brother Lionel to find Rose and send her to London on the next boat. Lionel told Norman his meeting with Rose was 'an uncle's talk with her about the rumours'.[86] Rose told Norman that Lionel 'asked me *ever* so seriously if I had been unfaithful to you and heaps of things of a private nature … such as did I want it'.[87] In due course, Lionel escorted Rose on board the SS *Ophir*.

Rose arrived in London in March 1910, where Norman was waiting to confront her about her 'past four months of gadding'. Rose wrote that

Norman 'hammered' her 'about everything', giving a 'sort of jury sum-ming-up' of her conduct. 'The verdict? Guilty.' It came as no surprise to Rose – she more or less entered a plea of guilty – but she was remorse-ful about the punishment: 'The constant nagging and the cold weather made me wish that I had never left Sydney'.[88]

With the arrival of Rose, Norman moved out of the Dysons' flat, but that was not the end of the troubles. Ruby was angry that her brother was setting up home with an old flame of her husband, and refused to acknowledge Rose's presence in London.[89] The row spread from London to embrace every branch of the Lindsay and Dyson families. Ted Dyson sided with Will and Ruby. Lionel Lindsay sided with Norman and Rose. Lionel's wife, Jean (Dyson), sided with Will and Ruby. Jean's disapprov-al of Rose forced Lionel to keep secret his visits to Norman and Rose. Daryl, the youngest Lindsay brother, called Rose 'a common harlot'.[90]

There were other reasons why Norman and Rose were unhappy in London. Norman had gone to London to sell a set of illustrations he had produced for an edition of *Casanova*, believing that they would launch him on the world stage. However, they were poorly received. Another set of illustrations, based on the *Satyricon*, met with an equally cool reception.

By contrast, the English loved Dyson's cartoons. British politics were in a state of upheaval, providing plenty of good material. Dyson saw the inequality in the battles between the bosses and the workers. He delighted in portraying capitalists as fat and rapacious, and workers as bravely combating hopeless odds.

But Dyson was not always on the side of the disenfranchised. He scorned the suffragettes, portraying them as shrill and discordant.

At the end of 1910, Norman and Rose returned to Australia. Norman was glad to be home, away from 'the disruptive effect that Europe has had on so many Australian artists'.[91] Will and Ruby stayed on in London. Norman, who had enjoyed success in Australia, struggled in London. Will, who had struggled in Australia, succeeded in London.[92]

In September 1907, the Rix ladies moved to Paris where they took rooms in Montparnasse. Hilda studied at the *Académie Delécluse* and at the *Académie de la Grande Chaumière*, working on drawing, before turning to oil painting. In April 1908, the trio travelled to Italy, reaching as far south as Amalfi, before returning to Paris in July the same year.

Will Dyson
Labour Wants a 'Place in the Sun'!

LABOUR WANTS A "PLACE IN THE SUN"!

CAPITAL (deeply shocked at Labour's efforts to emerge): "Back to your abyss, Sir! As it is already there is scarcely enough sun to go round!"

They spent the summer of 1910 in Étaples where Hilda took a studio among the artists. The Rixes enjoyed Étaples and the company of the other artists who lived there, among them Iso and Alison Rae. The Rixes stayed in Étaples for the rest of 1910 and made painting trips there every year until war broke out.[93]

While at Étaples, Hilda Rix began to achieve serious recognition. In 1911, the Salon accepted her painting, *Retour de la Chasse*, painted at Étaples, and hung it on the line. *Retour de la Chasse* was painted with a palette of lighter colours. Another work, *Grandmère*, demonstrated the sensibility that Hilda brought to painting French women in their own milieu. *La Robe Chinoise*, one of Hilda's finest paintings, showing Elsie Rix in a splendid Chinese gown, also dates from this period.

In 1912 and, again, in 1914, Hilda and Elsie visited Morocco. Tangier was a revelation: 'So much like an extraordinarily beautiful dream that I'm afraid to wake up in the morning and find it all gone … There is such a quantity and richness of wonderful picturesqueness every way one turns the head there is a new picture'.[94] If Rix found the markets of Tangier threatening, her work did not show it. *Grand Marché, Tangier, Arab Sheep Market* and *Negro Boy, Morocco* (in pastel) displayed her confidence as an artist and her comfort with her subjects. Rix's Moroccan paintings were a sensation when she exhibited them in Paris in 1912.[95] The work more than justified Hilda's exuberance: 'I love, love, love this place – there's not one moment when one's imagination is not touched There's a flavour everywhere and for anyone who has a passion for colour, why it is a veritable paradise'.[96] In 1912, the French nation bought *Grand Marché, Tangier* and hung it in the *Musée du Luxembourg*, which then housed the nation's collection of contemporary art.[97] If the Australian artists went to Europe in search of success and acclaim on the world stage, Hilda Rix reached the goal. When the French nation bought her *Tangier* painting, she achieved a level of acclaim of which Tom Roberts could but dream, but the occasion passed unnoticed in Australia. In Tangier, the Rixes met Rupert Bunny and his wife, Jeanne Morel. Bunny, too, was well established in French artistic circles, painting in Étaples, as well as in Morocco. By 1914, Bunny's reputation and acceptance in Paris exceeded that of any other Australian artist.[98] Like Rix, his success was all but ignored in Australia, as the art journal, *Art in Australia*, acknowledged when it wrote in 1918 that 'There are few Australian painters with a greater international reputation than Rupert CW Bunny, although there are many painters whose work is better known in Australia than his'.[99]

Hilda Rix
La Robe Chinoise AGWA

Other Australian artists were also achieving success.

George Bell moved from St Ives to Chelsea in 1908, eventually settling in Cheyne Walk. Critical acclaim in England brought him a steady flow of commissions and a measure of prosperity. Bell adapted readily to the life of a Chelsea artist. He was a member of the Chelsea Arts Club. He indulged his taste for music, often attending concerts with George Lambert. He took in a few students, without the need to depend on teaching for an income. He was on friendly terms with George and Amy Lambert, with George Coates and Dora Meeson, with Will Dyson and Ruby Lindsay, and with Fred Leist, as well as with many English painters.

Septimus Power spent two years in Paris from 1905 until 1907. He studied under Jean-Paul Laurens at the *Académie Julian*, perfecting his technique as a painter of animals. When Power and his wife crossed over to London, he established himself as a specialist painter of animals, in which niche he enjoyed the approval of the English traditionalists, and made a good living.

James Quinn, who spent eight years in Paris after winning the 1893 Travelling Scholarship, arrived in Chelsea in 1902. He made a career painting celebrity portraits, including those of Joseph Chamberlain, the Duchess of York and the Duke of Windsor. He was accepted at the Royal Academy. In Paris, *Mère et Fils*, a portrait of his wife and son, was commended at the Salon in 1912. He painted many self-portraits. Once again, the formula of a safe pair of hands, painting in traditional style and concentrating on portraits, brought a steady income and the acceptance of the English art establishment.

Henry Fullwood spent the early part of the century travelling the world, living in New York, London and Cape Town, before settling in Chelsea. He, too, joined the Chelsea Arts Club and took on the life of a Chelsea artist. Although he had lived for many years in Australia, he was born in England. His English birth gave him a foot in the English camp, as well as the Australian. He could paint well – his work was accepted at the Royal Academy and in Paris – but he worked mainly as an illustrator, doing black and white work.

Charles Bryant, the Manly boy with a love of the sea, found his way to coastal St Ives when he went to England in 1908. There, he learned marine painting, working with Julius Olsson and William Ashton. In London, he, too, fell in with the Australian push, taking the standard membership of the Chelsea Arts Club.[100]

English writer Arthur Ransome lived in Chelsea. He had the English capacity for multi-tasking in unusual ways: he was, at once, the author of a famous series of children's books, *Swallows and Amazons*, and a spy who worked in Bolshevik Russia. In his first major work, *Bohemia in London*, written in 1907, he captured the life of a Chelsea painter in the years before the Great War:

When it grows too dark for painters to judge the colours of their pictures, they flock out from the studios, some to go up to Soho for dinner, some to stroll with wife or friendly model in the dusk. Their favourite promenade is along Cheyne Walk, where the lamps shining among the leaves of the trees cast wavering shadows upon the pavements. Only the black and white men, working against time for the weekly papers, plug on through the dark … The painter might go to [a club]; or else, after a supper in Soho, or in one of the very few little restaurants in Chelsea, he might spend the evening in someone else's studio, perhaps in the same block of buildings as his own, for few of the studios are isolated, and there are often three, five, eight, or more under a single roof. The studio life is like that of a university, with its friendliness, its sets, and their haughty attitude to each other … The men of each set have a habit of dropping in to talk away their evenings in particular studios … About nine o'clock the painter, if he has not gone to a club, will arrive, without particular effort, at one of these more popular studios. Perhaps there will be a piano in a corner … Perhaps there will be a witty little model telling stories and keeping everybody laughing. Perhaps there will be no more than a couple of friends, who no longer find talk necessary for intercourse, but can be perfectly contented in tobacco smoke and each other's silence.[101]

The Australian artists were far removed from the bush, the beach and the harsh light of the Australian sun. Some prospered – Longstaff, Bell, Quinn and Power found acceptance and a ready demand for their work. Some followed the French path – Conder, Bunny and Russell preferred France to England, and developed styles of painting that English traditionalists condemned as 'French'.[102] Hilda Rix found success in France without fully embracing French techniques. Some floundered – Streeton and Roberts found it all but impossible to find subjects that suited their styles of painting. But most loved the excitement of living in Chelsea – Lambert, Coates, Meeson, Dyson, Ruby 'Lind' (Lindsay), even Conder, for the short time he was there and well, revelled in the combination of a congenial working environment and an engaging social scene.

6 WAR

IN WHICH WAR COMES AS A SHOCK, MANY OF THE ARTISTS LEARN THEY ARE TOO OLD, OR TOO UNFIT, TO DIE FOR KING AND EMPIRE, AND LOOK FOR OTHER WAYS TO CONTRIBUTE TO THE WAR EFFORT.

*T*he summer of 1914 was balmy and warm, ideal for tennis, cricket and fox-hunting. George and Dora Coates were staying with a friend, Mollie Moorhouse, in the country near Newbury. Towards the end of June, Mollie brought them a black-edged newspaper carrying the news that Archduke Ferdinand and his wife had been assassinated. Mollie said: 'This will mean a European war'. No one else in the group had an inkling of war. They thought Mollie was wrong. Dora wrote: '[W]e were too wrapped up in our own doings to be at all over-anxious about events in the Balkans, which seemed almost as remote as happenings in China'.[1]

War broke out a month later, on 4 August 1914.

Streeton was in Australia when war was declared. His pockets were full after successful exhibitions in Melbourne and Sydney, but he was keen to return to London to be with his wife, Nora, and their young son, Oliver. He wrote to Nora:

I wish to heaven I were there with you & Oliver. But if I left tomorrow in the first steamer I could not arrive till (at earliest) mid-September, when it – the possible tragedy of European war – is practically over. It is too costly to last more than 2 or 3 months.[2]

Roberts chose the moment of crisis for a European vacation. He took the boat train from Charing Cross, bound for Lake Como. He crossed France with difficulty, battling railway schedules disrupted by the mobilisation of the French army. He arrived at Lake Como just as war was declared. For six weeks, he remained in Italy, watching Italian soldiers take up positions on the Austrian frontier, and reading newspaper accounts of the first weeks of the war.[3]

The Germans began well, sweeping through Belgium and into France. Unable to stop the German advance, the Allies fell back on Paris. By the first week of September, the Germans were 80 kilometres from the city. The situation was so bleak that the French government fled to Bordeaux, and the Military Governor of Paris was ready to blow the bridges over the Seine, and even the Eiffel Tower. The French made a stand on the Marne. The battle proved decisive. By 9 September 1914, the Germans were retreating. When the Germans arrived at the river Aisne, both sides were exhausted. They took to the shovels, and dug in.

It was then that Roberts decided to return to London. The closer he came to Paris, the more chaos he found. The trains were a shambles. Soldiers were everywhere. Many Parisian shopkeepers had fled the city, leaving their shopfronts boarded up. Roberts took the train from Paris for Calais. Normally a day-trip, the journey took almost a week. The Channel ferry had a destroyer escort. Landing in Folkestone, Roberts found wartime security arrangements in place. For the first time in his life, he had to show a passport to enter the country of his birth.[4]

The success of the German advance shocked Britain. It proved the weakness of the French army and the inadequacy of the British. When Lord Kitchener joined the Cabinet as Secretary of State for War, he warned his colleagues that a long road lay ahead. Churchill, then First Lord of the Admiralty, wrote that:

on almost the first occasion that he joined us, and in soldierly sentences, [Kitchener] proclaimed a series of inspiring and prophetic truths. Everyone expected that the war would be short; but wars took unexpected courses, and we must now prepare for a long struggle. Such a conflict could not be ended on the sea or by sea power alone. It could only be ended by great battles on the Continent. In these the British Empire must bear its part on a scale proportionate to its magnitude and power. We must be prepared to put armies of millions in the field and maintain them for several years. In no other way could we discharge our duty to our allies or to the world.[5]

From July spent carefree to August looking down the barrel of a German gun, the transformation was dramatic. Dora Coates was an anxious observer:

Never shall I forget how suddenly Chelsea seemed to become an armed camp. Soldiers were bivouacked in Ranelagh Gardens and the Royal Hospital grounds, army motor lorries were rattling noisily along the usually quiet Embankment,

Dora Meeson
Leaving for the Front AGB

and those hot nights we lay awake listening to the heavy, ominous rumble of laden troop trains, all night long, slowly steaming out of Victoria Station. It was a heartbreaking sight to see the young men of all ranks going up the steps into Chelsea town hall to enlist or, even worse, to see squads of them in civilian clothes marching down Whitehall in charge of a sergeant. There was no elation, only a grim, set look on their faces, a determination to do their duty, for they had no real desire to fight.[6]

The glory days of the Chelsea art commune were over.

In the series of shocks that followed the outbreak of war, the first reaction of the artists was to volunteer. This brought another shock – volunteering was a young man's sport. Lambert was forty-one, Coates and Quinn were forty-five, Streeton forty-seven, Fullwood fifty-one, Longstaff fifty-three, and Roberts fifty-eight. They were all too old. To serve at the front, a soldier had to be between nineteen and thirty-eight years of age.

Some of the younger artists were unfit for military service. Septimus Power was thirty-seven. He volunteered, but was rejected because he was deaf.[7] George Bell was thirty-six. He volunteered, but was rejected because of a deformity in his feet. He tried to work in a munitions factory, but the factory, too, rejected him as unfit. He taught maths and coached cricket in a school in Hampshire in 1916, until he finally found work as a fitter in a munitions factory in 1917.[8]

With so many young men dying at the front, art was too frivolous an activity to indulge. In a total war, the nation could not afford to support activities that made no contribution to the war effort.[9] Painting was a luxury that could be targeted in the name of wartime austerity. In any event, buyers deserted the art market, with the morbid exception that there was a boom in portraits of young men in khaki.[10]

It took time for the artists to understand that there were ways in which they could contribute to winning the war. At thirty-four, Will Dyson was young enough to volunteer, but he continued to work as a cartoonist, drawing cartoons that ridiculed the Kaiser and German militarism. In January 1915, he published *Kultur Cartoons*, a book of twenty cartoons that lampooned the German war machine.[11]

Norman Lindsay was thirty-five when the war broke out, but the long illness that began when he returned from England left him unfit for war service.[12] Unable to enlist, he was drawing cartoons for the *Bulletin* in Australia that were similar in appearance and message to those of Will Dyson in Britain.

In addition to cartoons, Norman painted recruiting posters, but his work did not measure up to the exacting standards of the Lindsay family. His brother, Daryl, gave a lukewarm report:

In 1914 Norman was caught up with the war fever of the day and from his hand came powerful cartoons for the *Bulletin* and recruiting posters for the Government. But strong and bitter as they were, they lacked the biting sarcasm of his brother-in-law, Will Dyson, who was working in London.[13]

THE GOOSE STEP, OR THE MARCH OF CIVILISATION

Will Dyson
The Goose Step, or the March of Civilisation

Norman Lindsay
Australia Answers the War God's Call

The recruiting posters tapped into sentimental themes, but Norman was not proud of his work: 'This stuff is not art and its sole intention is to stir up the slack to a sense of what this war means'.[14]

When Norman talked of stirring up the slack, he was talking about 'slackers' – citizens who refused to do their wartime duty.[15] One solution to the problem of slackers – attractive to some politicians – was conscription. In Britain, Prime Minister Baldwin led the debate over conscription. The debate ran throughout 1915 and was resolved by the introduction of conscription in January 1916. The Australian debate came later. It was led by Billy Hughes, who became Prime Minister in October 1915, in a deal that saw his predecessor, Andrew Fisher, resign the prime ministership and take up the role of Australian High Commissioner in London. As Prime Minister, Hughes led the Australian debate over conscription. It ran throughout 1916 and 1917. It was resolved by the defeat of two conscription referenda. The debate in both countries was willing. Supporters of conscription portrayed themselves as patriots and their opponents as disloyal. Opponents claimed that it was possible to support the war effort without supporting conscription.[16]

Will Dyson was a staunch opponent. Unlike many socialists, he supported the war, but his support did not extend to conscription, which he saw as a means of suppressing the working class. In September 1915, the London *Herald* published *Conscript 'Em!*, which it described as 'A collection of Will Dyson's striking cartoons sent forth by "The Herald" to assist in combatting [sic] the vicious conscriptionist campaign'.[17] One cartoon showed capitalism as a fat man aiming to 'Conscript everybody in low places'. Another asked: 'Why these unfounded working-class suspicions of Conscription?', as the fat capitalist fired off a machine gun that used twenty-year-olds – young men born in 1895 – as bullets.

It was a debate of some subtlety. Norman Lindsay drew cartoons that pilloried slackers because they refused to do their wartime duty. Conscription would certainly force slackers to do their wartime duty. But it did not follow that Norman Lindsay supported conscription. It was logically possible to be anti-slacker and anti-conscription at the same time. Norman may well have agreed with Will.

The debate over conscription was personal for Dyson in a way that it was not for Norman Lindsay. Lindsay was unfit for military service. Dyson was young, fit and not in uniform. He chose not to enlist, and remained, instead, in his well-paid job as a cartoonist. He was just the sort of person who might be called a slacker. This was, after all, a time when young men were given white feathers if they were not in uniform.[18]

THE MAN BEHIND CONSCRIPTION

" Why these unfounded working-class suspicions of Conscription? "—" National Service " plaint.

Why did Dyson not volunteer? He was not a pacifist.[19] Ross McMullin wrote two highly partial biographies of Dyson.[20] In the first biography, McMullin offered no explanation for Dyson's failure to volunteer. In the second, he wrote: 'Dyson apparently made inquiries about enlisting in the AIF [Australian Imperial Force], but this was impossible in England'.[21] It is true that it was not possible to enlist in the AIF in England, but it was a simple matter to enlist in the British army. Dyson did not enlist in the British army and McMullin (although addressing the issue of Dyson's attempt to enlist in the AIF) made no suggestion that he attempted to enlist in the British army. In the mood of the time, Dyson's failure to enlist was a fact that required explanation.[22]

Rupert Bunny
Waiting to be X-rayed AWM

In Chelsea, meanwhile, the older artists were concerned not to be labelled as slackers. They looked for ways to contribute to the war effort.

Lambert believed he was fit enough to serve in France, but his age was against him. He was held back for work on the home front, where 'he assisted in the training of men of military age, teaching riding, in which he was an expert, and collecting with some pride the testimonials his pupils gratefully sent him when they put his instructions to the test'.[23] Despite the praise, Lambert was not satisfied with his contribution. Through a contact, he found work he thought was more useful – producing timber in Wales. As a divisional works officer, he took on a management role in a timber-cutting operation in forests between Aberystwyth and Haverfordwest. Timber was needed for the war effort.

The work was tough and demanding, and the bureaucracy was stifling, yet Lambert was happier because the work made a genuine contribution to the war effort. He worked in Wales until the end of 1917.[24]

Rupert Bunny, who was fifty when the war broke out, volunteered to serve in the American Hospital, in Paris. His duties were menial – they included 'carrying patients to and from wards, operating rooms and X-ray plants, up and down many flights of stairs, and the carrying of patients in their beds to and from the terraces'.[25] Bunny found the work stressful; according to his niece, 'the physical and emotional strain of the work and especially his involvement with amputations [had] a deep effect on him'.[26] His painting of the radiology department of the hospital, made in 1915, had a depressing air, as a wounded man is prepared for X-ray, watched by other wounded men waiting in line for their turn at the machine.

The British army had a tradition of 'Pals battalions', in which men with common interests formed their own regiments. There were local battalions – the Birmingham Pals and the Glasgow Pals; sportsmen's battalions – the Football Battalion and the Scottish Sportsmen's Battalion; and battalions for trades and professions – the Glasgow Tramways Battalion and the Stockbrokers' Battalion. There were even old school tie battalions – the Public Schools Battalion and the Cambridge Battalion.

Francis Derwent Wood, the sculptor, approached the War Office, asking permission to establish the Chelsea Arts Club Corps. The War Office refused on the grounds that the Territorial Force already had a unit that catered for artists – the Artists Rifles. First established in 1860, the Artists Rifles was a volunteer light infantry regiment, based in London, that drew its membership from painters, sculptors, engravers, musicians, actors, architects and others involved in creative endeavours.[27] The Artists Rifles became the unit of choice for the artists of Chelsea. The younger members of the Chelsea Arts Club joined the Artists Rifles. They used the club garden as a parade ground.[28]

George Coates joined the Artists Rifles, but he felt that drilling with them was not enough. He learned to drive, hoping to offer his services as an ambulance driver. When the special constabulary was established, he joined, working as a policeman guarding electricity-generating stations and patrolling the streets of Chelsea against threats that were more imagined than real. As might be expected, George found the work of a policeman dull, and questioned whether he was making any worthwhile contribution to the war effort.[29] Dora went to work helping refugees.

Many Belgian refugees found their way to London. Dora worked to find them food, accommodation and medical treatment.[30]

Roberts, the father of the group, was more accepting of the *Dad's Army* role than the others. He called his fellow warriors the 'last ditchers', but he did not shrink from the physical demands of his service, which were considerable. Other men of fifty-eight would have objected to a 30 kilometre route march each weekend, but Roberts undertook it without complaint.[31] When Streeton returned to London early in 1915, he, too, joined the Territorial Force, and drilled with the old stagers.

For all their hard work, the older artists were frustrated. Nothing they were doing inflicted pain on the Germans, or hastened victory. They continued to meet each night at the Chelsea Arts Club, but it was not the same as before the war. With the young members at the front, the club was home to a collection of increasingly bitter old men. If only they could find a better way to contribute to the war effort.

Total war demanded hospitals on an industrial scale.

If Britain were drawn into a Continental war, her existing hospitals could not cope with the flood of casualties that might be expected. The British army had plans to establish new hospitals in London upon mobilisation for a European war. Until mobilisation, the hospitals existed as paper entities only, waiting for the call to arms. They had a skeleton staff, but they had no buildings, no wards, no beds, and no operating theatres.[33]

One of the theoretical hospitals was the 3rd London General Hospital, commanded by Lieutenant Colonel Harry Edwin Bruce Bruce-Porter. Within minutes of the declaration of war, Bruce-Porter received a telegram: 'Mobilise, act accordingly'.[34] At 6 o'clock the next morning, 5 August 1914, Bruce-Porter and his men occupied the building that was designated as their hospital. It was the Royal Victoria Patriotic Asylum, an imposing nineteenth-century mansion, complete with witches'-hat turrets, located near Clapham Junction on the edge of Wandsworth Common, about an hour's walk from Chelsea.[35]

The building was an orphanage. Bruce-Porter's first task was to re-house the orphans. He then had to turn the orphanage into a modern hospital of 520 beds.[36] The Victorian building only had room for 200 beds. For the rest, huts were built on the common behind the building, each hut accommodating twenty patients. The huts also housed an operating theatre, a sterilising room, a post-mortem room and a mortuary. In the main building, the school hall adjoining the entrance was set up as

a reception ward to process new patients and draft them to the wards.[37]

By 26 September 1914, all 520 beds were made up, ready to receive patients. It was an impressive achievement. When the representatives of the *British Journal of Nursing* took a guided tour, they found a hospital 'fitted up with everything brand new and spick and span, waiting and crying out for the patients to arrive'.[38] There were handsome buildings and spacious grounds. There were medical, surgical and ophthalmic wards. There was even a bronze statue of Lord Kitchener. Ominously, 'countless drums' of sterilised dressings were also in readiness, and the nurses waited apprehensively for what they were about to experience:

There was a homely and welcoming air about [the wards] that will make them indeed a haven to our wounded soldiers, after the stress and horror of War. We were on the other hand shown a padded room; some of us have no doubt seen in the Press that there are cases of insanity reported among the troops. What wonder?[39]

In a European war, winter makes fighting impossible. The fighting season starts in spring and runs through to late autumn. By the spring of

Victoria Patriotic Asylum, Wandsworth, AWM

1915, the 3rd London General Hospital had 1500 beds ready for the spate of wounded men who were expected to arrive with the thaw.[40]

The army plans originally envisaged that the hospital would serve overseas, so Bruce-Porter had selected only A-class men – those young enough and fit enough for overseas service – to serve as orderlies in the hospital.[41] When it became apparent that the hospital would remain in London, Bruce-Porter wanted to release the A-class men for service overseas. With the expansion of the hospital, the staff of orderlies had grown to 204 non-commissioned officers and other ranks.[42] Before Bruce-Porter could release them, he had to work out a way of replacing them. Where would he find men who were willing to perform the arduous duties of a hospital orderly and yet were too old, or not fit, for service at the front?[43]

Bruce-Porter found his solution at the Chelsea Arts Club.[44] Derwent Wood led a delegation of artists seeking employment at Bruce-Porter's hospital. Bruce-Porter recounted what happened:

One morning I had shown into my office a group of rather elderly men, as judged by war standard. They said they had come to enlist in order that they might do what they could for their country.

They were members of the Chelsea Arts Club, and not a few of their names were to be found in *Who's Who*. I asked: 'How old are you?' The answer was: 'How old may we be?'.

Amongst them was my friend, as he afterwards became, George Coates. His companions were, among others, the late Alfred Withers, Tom Roberts, Derwent Wood, and Fullwood. They were soon joined by a number of their friends and were numerous enough to fill a twenty-one-bed hutment.[45]

Bruce-Porter jumped at the chance of accepting the 'rather elderly men'. Red tape stopped them serving at the front, but there was nothing to stop them serving as orderlies. Far from being slackers, they would be making a contribution to the war effort, not least by freeing up A-class men to serve at the front. In order to serve as orderlies, the artists had to enlist in the Territorial Royal Army Medical Corps. Tom Roberts, the oldest, forgot several birthdays when he filled in the enlistment form.[46] Dora Coates recalled that George 'strode into the studio and flung an army kitbag on the table. "Well! I've done it. I'm in Derwent Wood's contingent for the duration."'[47]

It was 24 April 1915. At dawn the next morning, British troops went ashore at Gallipoli.

7 GALLIPOLI

IN WHICH AUSTRALIA HAS HER BAPTISM
OF FIRE AND FAILS TO MAKE A WORTHY RECORD
OF HER ACHIEVEMENTS AND SACRIFICES.

*I*n March 1915, rumours began to circulate of a landing at Gallipoli. CEW Bean, Australia's official war correspondent, became concerned that he lacked the accreditation necessary to go with the men to land on the beaches. When he was appointed, Bean, a 34-year-old journalist, had been given the status, but not the rank, of captain. General Bridges and Colonel Brudenell White did that deliberately so that Bean would be in a position to produce an eyewitness account of the war, free – to the extent possible – from military censorship.[1]

Obsessive about secrecy, British admirals and generals were trying to silence Bean. When, finally, they agreed that he could go, it was on condition that he report nothing without their permission, which permission they withheld until 2 May 1915, a full week after the landing. In the meantime, they allowed their own journalist, Ellis Ashmead-Bartlett, to despatch his report on 29 April 1915, giving him the scoop over Bean.[2]

Not for the last time, British authorities left Australian parents waiting anxiously and needlessly for news of their sons at the front.

The British adhered to their mania for secrecy throughout most of the war.[3] The urge to censor extended not only to reporters, but also to photographers, artists and soldiers – indeed, it extended to every citizen. *The Defence of the Realm Act 1914* empowered the Crown to make regulations 'to prevent persons communicating … information … calculated to jeopardise the success of the operations of any of His Majesty's forces or the forces of his allies or to assist the enemy' and to 'prevent the spread of false reports or reports likely to cause disaffection to His Majesty or to interfere with the success of His Majesty's forces by land or sea' and 'otherwise to prevent … the successful prosecution of the war being endangered'.[4] The Crown exercised the power freely, making many repressive regulations.

In the *Official History*, Bean wrote:

In most modern wars preceding that of 1914, artists and photographers were sent to the front, in the same manner as war correspondents, by the enterprise of newspapers or news agencies. In the Great War, however, the issues dependent upon the maintenance of secrecy were enormous, and the penalties for any indiscretion which lifted the curtain veiling the front were instant. The journalists and photographers who managed for a few adventurous days, to avoid arrest during the retreat from Mons and the weeks following it were quickly and unsparingly routed out of France.[5]

Quite why the British were at such pains to prevent journalists and photographers from reporting the Great War is a mystery. Journalism had been part and parcel of the Boer War, where Britain's most famous journalist had been none other than Winston Churchill, now First Lord of the Admiralty, and architect of the Dardanelles campaign.

The official censorship regime did more than preserve the secrecy of operations; it facilitated cover-ups. At Fromelles, on 19 July 1916, the AIF fought its first battle in France under the command of the English General Haking. Thanks to his impetuosity and ineptitude, the 5th Australian Division suffered 5533 men killed or wounded in a single day. Under the censorship regulations, all that appeared in the British press was: 'Yesterday evening, south of Armentières, we carried out some important raids on a front of two miles in which Australian troops took part. About 140 German prisoners were captured'.[7]

In the *Official History*, Bean told the story of the cover-up without comment, save to say that the suppression of the shocking truth was 'in accordance with the policy at this time adopted by GHQ [General Headquarters]'.[8] Censorship denied the public the explanation it deserved; it allowed General Haking to escape much of the criticism he deserved. But it did not stop the diggers giving Haking a nickname he was never able to shake off: 'Butcher' Haking.[9]

At Gallipoli, censorship applied to all means of recording events. According to the *Official History*:

Sketching and the taking of photographs – except by officers or men on some special duty of survey – were entirely prohibited, and the staff permitted no cameras to be carried within the British area, except under its direct control.

When, therefore, in 1915, it became clear that, mainly for purposes of propaganda, photographs of the British front must be furnished to the press, the supply was provided by official photographers, who were appointed and maintained as officers of either the British or the Canadian Army.[10]

This meant there was no Australian photographer or artist whose task it was to record the exploits of the diggers at Gallipoli. This had unsatisfactory consequences. In Bean's words:

For photographs, therefore, of the Gallipoli campaign in 1915 the Australian War Museum, which houses the Australian collection, is dependent upon those taken by the Official War Correspondent [Bean] and by officers and men, who in consequence of the non-enforcement on the Peninsula of the order against photographers, were enabled to carry their cameras.[11]

In short, Australia's official record of the Gallipoli campaign only exists because of the Australian penchant for ignoring inconvenient British orders. Amusing or ironic as that may be, it also means that the contemporary record of the campaign at Gallipoli is deficient. It was one thing to smuggle a small camera to the front. It was quite another to smuggle a decent box of paints and canvases. Paper, pens, ink and pencils were all in short supply. Would-be artists had to improvise, using the equipment at hand – pencils, pen and ink, even iodine brushes.[12] The result is that there are few contemporary drawings, sketches or paintings of diggers at Gallipoli.

Signaller Ellis Silas was born in London in 1885. He came from a wealthy family. His father was a landscape painter, his mother an opera singer. He was educated at home before training as an artist under Walter Sickert. Silas travelled to Australia in 1907. When war broke out, he was working as an artist in Western Australia. He was thirty years old when he enlisted in the AIF on 16 October 1914. Appointed to the Signals Corps, he joined the 16th Battalion.[13]

Silas and the 16th Battalion landed at Gallipoli on the first day. They were involved in heavy fighting at Bloody Angle. After signalling continuously for several days, Silas was found unconscious and delirious. He was evacuated from the Peninsula on board the hospital ship SS *Galeka*. On 28 May 1915, he was admitted to the 1st General Hospital in Heliopolis, where he was diagnosed as suffering from neurasthenia.[14] Later, he developed typhoid. In August, he was taken on board SS *Demosthenes*

Ellis Silas
The Landing, AWM

Ellis Silas
In the Trenches, Quinn's Post
AWM

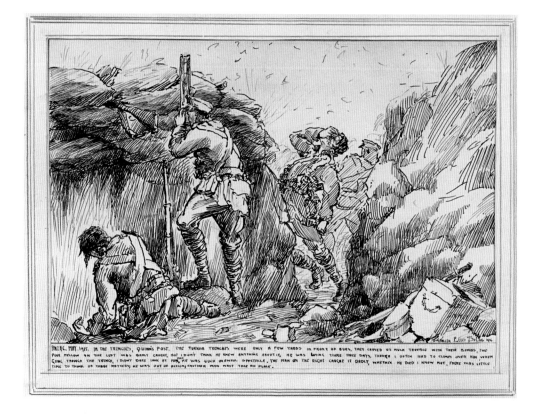

for transfer to England. On 21 December 1915, a medical board listed his symptoms as: 'loss of memory; confusion of ideas; becomes talkative and excited if overworked; heart rapid and irritable; hands tremulous'. The board certified him as permanently unfit for active service, but fit for home service. On 17 August 1916, he was discharged in England as permanently unfit for active service.[15]

Silas made sketches of his time in the AIF, beginning with the convoy travelling to the Middle East and covering his exploits in Egypt early in 1915.

Frame by frame, his pen and ink sketches unfolded his story: the sea voyage; the landing; the dead and wounded; the fighting at Bloody Angle; the carnage after the battle; the stretcher-bearers and the wounded; a field dressing station; Quinn's Post, the most advanced Anzac post; a field hospital; evacuation to the beach; then to *Galeka*; then to a hospital train; and, finally, to a hospital bed in Cairo – 'Heaven!'[16]

Silas published the sketches in London in 1916, in a book called *Crusading at Anzac, AD 1915*. General Birdwood, commander of the Anzac force, wrote an introduction for the book, calling it 'an excellent record of the life spent by [the Australian] troops during the months they and their comrades at Cape Helles and Suvla were upholding the honour of the British Flag in that part of the world'.[17]

Unlike fellow British generals, Birdwood lacked the instinct to censor:

I heartily wish Signaller Ellis Silas all success with his book, and trust that, before the war is finished, his health will enable him to rejoin the troops, and that he will find opportunity of giving us yet further proofs of his ability as an artist, in showing us something of the life of the troops in other theatres of war.[18]

Silas did recover. He lived into his late eighties. The Australian War Memorial bought three oils that he painted after the war: *Roll Call; The Attack of the 4th Brigade, AIF, at Bloody Angle*; and *Digging in at Pope's Hill: End of a Great Day*. Silas worked briefly as a black and white artist in Sydney in the 1920s, before returning to London in 1925. He enjoyed a long career as an artist in many different genres, going so far as to paint murals in ocean liners.[19]

George Benson was another digger who sketched Gallipoli in defiance of the ban. He trained at the National Gallery School of Art under Bernard Hall and Frederick McCubbin. He enlisted at Victoria Barracks in Melbourne on 8 September 1914, when he was twenty-eight years old. On enlistment, he was sent to the artillery where he proved to be

Ted Colles
Something to Remember Us By! AWM

David Barker
At the Landing and Here Ever Since
AWM

a good soldier. He was promoted to corporal in the field for good service. Corporal Benson was mentioned in divisional orders for 'acts of conspicuous gallantry or valuable service during the period 6 May 1915 to 2 September 1915'. Benson was evacuated from the Peninsula, ill, on 8 September 1915, but did not recover in time to return to Gallipoli.[20]

Benson made sketches of Gallipoli in a 56-page notebook. The first was a reconnaissance sketch drawn on 22 April 1915, three days before the landing. The sketches included a pencil sketch of the landing itself, an ink wash sketch of a sentry at the water point at the foot of Victoria Gully, and a pencil sketch of a digger on water fatigue.[21]

Major Leslie Francis Standish Hore was a Tasmanian barrister. He served on Gallipoli with the 8th Light Horse Regiment. He spent two spells on the Peninsula. The first ran from 26 May 1915 until 7 August 1915, when he was wounded and evacuated to Cairo. The second ran from 28 September until 19 December 1915, when he was again evacuated, this time suffering from jaundice.[22] He kept a diary of his time on Gallipoli which he illustrated with hand-coloured pen and ink sketches. The diary is now held in the Mitchell Library in Sydney.[23]

The Anzac Book was the outstanding contemporary Australian record of Gallipoli. It was produced by the diggers themselves. Most of the work was done by an editorial committee of CEW Bean; his batman, AW Bazley; and five artists serving in the trenches: Privates Frank Crozier, Ted Colles, David Barker, Otho Hewett and Cyril Leyshon-White.[24] The committee began work on 14 November 1915, calling for contributions from all the men at Gallipoli. Many men sent in contributions, but most of the drawings in the book came from the five artists on the committee. The Royal Engineers and the Royal Navy helped 'with some drawing paper, ink and paints, and the Photographic Section with some excellent panoramas; but for the rest, [the contributors] had to work with the materials at hand: iodine brushes, red and blue pencils, and such approach to white paper as could be produced from each battalion's stationery'.[25]

The paintings, drawings and sketches reflected the circumstances in which they were made. Frank Crozier, who studied at the National Gallery School from 1905 until 1907, produced sketches with sentimental and historical themes. Ted Colles, a cartoonist, made caricatures of Turkish soldiers, showing them as fat, bloated and primitive.

David Barker and Cyril Leyshon-White drew cartoons highlighting the quirks of the diggers. The artists added colour using iodine brushes, or the red and blue pencils scrounged from the intelligence units.

Otho Hewett closed the book with two cartoons: the first showed different types of rations; the second, in the form of a standard black and white cartoon, showed the grim reaper in military uniform, taking a shell in the back.

Outside the editorial committee, William Eltham made pencil sketches, on page 78, of the landscape of the Peninsula.[26]

The Anzac Book was a compilation of written pieces, drawings, paintings and photographs, almost all made in the trenches. It had the feel of a school yearbook, bristling with private jokes that only the diggers would understand. In his introduction, General Birdwood described the work as a book of reminiscences: 'In days to come I hope this book will call to the minds of most of us incidents which, though they may then seem small, probably loomed very large before us at the time, and the thought of which will bring to mind many a good comrade'.[27]

There were many attempts at humour, some successful. More serious articles drew on official records of the fighting, quoting General Sir Ian Hamilton's dispatches and setting out many significant orders, including the orders for the landing, the August offensive, and the evacuation. The book included maps of the battlefield and photographs taken by the official photographer, Lieutenant Brooks; by the Royal Engineers; and by Bean.

Gallipoli was evacuated before the book was finished. The editorial committee moved from a trench on the Peninsula to the army base on the island of Imbros. They finished work on 29 December 1915. The evacuation removed the need to censor the book in case it fell into enemy hands. It also changed the emphasis of the book, altering it from a Christmas magazine for the troops, to a souvenir of the entire campaign. The book was finished in London, with help from Captain Henry Smart, an Australian journalist working as a publicity officer in the office of the Australian High Commissioner.

The Anzac Book was a substantial volume. Cassell and Company, a major London publishing house, published the book. It sold for 2s 6d, the proceeds going to the Anzac Patriotic Funds.

Cobbled together in less than a month, *The Anzac Book* boasted neither deathless prose, nor outstanding art. It was a good amateur production, without being first-class. Given the circumstances under which the book was produced, the results were superb.[29] For all its good qualities,

Cyril Leyshon-White
Kitch AWM

Otho Hewett
Finis AWM

– North flank –
Suvla from Anzac.

South Flank –
Gaba Tepe from Anzac.

however, *The Anzac Book* was not a worthy record of the achievements of the Australian army during its first major campaign.

For want of someone better placed to do the job, Bean had taken charge of *The Anzac Book*. In difficult circumstances, he made a good fist of it, but his work was no substitute for an official record. In submitting to the censorship of British officers with a mania for secrecy, the Australian army ignored its own responsibilities. But for the initiative (and disobedience) of a few men in the trenches at Gallipoli, who drew the battlefields despite the ban, there might have been no contemporary images of the campaign at Gallipoli.

It was time to create a proper, historical record of the Australian war effort. Gallipoli had transformed the diggers from a scratch group of volunteers into an army with its own ethos and traditions. The diggers who returned to Egypt from Gallipoli thought of themselves as members of an Australian army, separate and distinct from the British army. At home, Gallipoli was seen as signifying that Australia had a future as a nation in her own right. Independent nations owed it to themselves to record and preserve their myths and legends – to take control of their history.

Moreover, it was obvious that the war would not end any time soon. Sixteen months of warfare had produced a stalemate on the Western Front and defeat at Gallipoli. The Australian army was about to move from the sideshow in the Dardanelles to the main game on the Western Front. It was one thing to take a piecemeal approach to making a record of a short, sharp campaign. A war of indefinite duration demanded a more permanent solution.

William Eltham
North Flank, Suvla from Anzac AWM

William Eltham
South Flank, Gaba Tepe from Anzac AWM

8 THE 3RD LONDON
GENERAL HOSPITAL

IN WHICH THE ELDERLY ARTISTS SHOW
THEIR METTLE AS HOSPITAL ORDERLIES.

*T*he artists who volunteered to serve in the 3rd London General Hospital during the Great War enlisted as members of the Territorial Royal Army Medical Corps. As private soldiers, they were subject to all the rigours and inanities of military discipline. Although they could have walked from their homes in Chelsea to the hospital at Wandsworth, they were required to live in huts at the hospital.

Hut 6 became home to the artists. In addition to Francis Derwent Wood, the contingent of English artists included Alfred Withers, FC Mulock, Stephen de la Bere, WB Fagan, Noel Irving, Paul Kirk, William Stott, CRW Nevinson and JH Dowd, a *Punch* cartoonist. The Australians were Coates, Fullwood, Roberts and Streeton. Myer Blashki, now known as Miles Evergood, a cartoonist and painter who had been a member of the Prehistoric Order of Cannibals, also signed up.[1]

One non-artist was admitted to Hut 6 – Ward Muir. He was a mere author, but the artists were generous enough to treat him as a kindred spirit. Muir wrote a series of books about his experiences at the 3rd London General Hospital.[2] He also acted as lead editor of the hospital magazine, the *Gazette of the 3rd London General Hospital*.[3] Together, Muir and the artists made a comprehensive record of life at the hospital.

The hospital had sixty wards. Most of them were in the huts that sprawled behind the main building, connected by covered walkways. Fullwood painted a 'balloon view' of the hospital, showing the train line in the foreground, the main building in the middle ground, and the city of huts trailing away into the distance.

There were thirty beds to a ward, fifteen on each side of the room.[4] Beside each bed was a small locker. The nursing sister's writing table was in the centre of the ward. There were two coke-burning stoves and a

number of potted plants. The floors were bare, and highly polished. The windows had special window sashes that admitted light and fresh air, but kept out the rain and draughts. At one end of the ward, there was a covered veranda. Inside the huts were a kitchen, bathroom, lavatories, an isolation room for the sicker patients, a linen room and a storeroom.

Hut 6 was different from the hospital wards. It had twenty-one beds and one coke-burning stove. A continuous shelf ran along the wall where each orderly kept a greatcoat, water-bottle and mess-tin. Under each bed was a box for other belongings. The boxes were aligned neatly with the owner's boots, to a military pattern. There were two electric lights. The only luxuries were a couple of chairs and a table, and a strip of linoleum on the bare boards down the centre of the hut.

Each man's bedding consisted of a mattress, a pillow and three army blankets. The patients had sheets; the orderlies did not. The mattress had to be rolled up each morning, with the pillow inside the roll, and the blankets folded in approved military fashion. Greatcoats, too, had to be folded. There was a daily inspection to ensure that the orderlies maintained the required standards.

The obsession with uniformity extended to the hospital as well. In the wards, the mouths of the pillowcases had to point the same way, and the sheets and blankets had to be folded identically.

The daily routine was arduous.[5] Each morning, the orderlies rose at 5.15 in time to shave, dress and do the necessary folding before the first

Hut at Wandsworth AWM

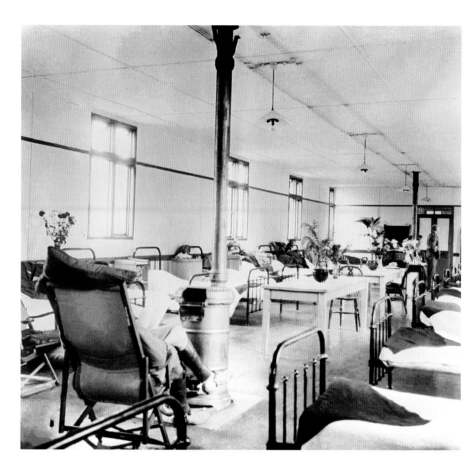

Hut at Wandsworth AWM

parade at 6 am. On parade, they were given the day's orders before being sent off to work. Their first job was to clean up the mess that had accumulated in the wards overnight, before heading to the steward's store to collect milk, butter and ten loaves of bread. Back at the ward, the orderlies cut and buttered the bread and boiled eggs, before going to the kitchen to collect the tea. At 7.45, they had their own breakfast, often in a rush, because at 8.30 there was a second parade at which the commanding officer inspected the men and their kit.

After the second parade, the orderlies collected sheets and towels for the laundry, being careful to deliver and receive in exchange the correct number of each item. They had to ensure that the ward had adequate supplies of eggs, milk, soda water, jam, sugar, floor polish, metal polish, cleaning rags, matches, soap, lint, bandages, carbolic lotion, methylated spirits and all the other needs of a pyjamas.

At midday, they served dinner – the main meal of the day. They collected the food from the kitchen in a large tin, plated and served the meal, washed the plates, washed the tin and returned it to the kitchen.

After the midday meal, they helped the wheelchair patients to dress, and wheeled them into the garden or onto the veranda, before finding time to have their own dinner at 1.15.

At 2 pm, there was another parade, followed by more work in the ward – seeing to the patients, mowing the lawn near the hut, cleaning, taking patients to other wards for treatment, collecting drugs from the dispensary, or taking patients to the recreation room. At 4.45 or 5 pm, there was time for the orderlies to have a cup of tea. The ward orderlies alternated, working afternoons from 2 pm to 5 pm one day, and evenings from 5 pm to 8 pm the next. Those working the evening shifts had to fetch and clean up the evening meal.

The orderlies were all things to all men – a combination of 'parlour-maid, waitress, charwoman, messenger, bath-chairman, barber, bootblack, window-cleaner, bath-attendant, gardener, valet, washer-up, and odd-man'.[6]

Wounded men were delivered to the hospital, literally, by the trainload.

The wounded were inducted into the hospital system at the front. There, they were tagged with large labels that described their wounds.[7] So tagged, they were loaded onto purpose-built hospital trains, each carrying 396 patients. In times of crisis, the hospital trains travelled on a continuous loop from the front line to the Channel ports – Dunkirk,

Calais and Boulogne – and back. At the ports, the wounded were embarked onto hospital ships that took them across the Channel. In England, they were loaded once more onto hospital trains. These trains took the men bound for the 3rd London General Hospital to Clapham Junction, the station nearest the hospital. The trains arrived at all hours of the day and night. So efficient was this system that it was possible for wounded men to be in hospital in London 36 hours after they were wounded in France. Most, however, had spent anything from a day to a few weeks in hospital in France before being sent home.

When a train was due at Clapham Junction, the hospital buglers sounded bugles and the sergeant majors blew whistles to raise a party of orderlies to march to the train station and unload the train.[8] Whatever the weather, the party lined up and marched the mile to Clapham Junction station. For most of the march, the orderlies followed the lesser standards of drill for which the Territorial Force was famous, singing songs and smoking cigarettes. When an officer came into view, the singing stopped, the cigarettes were hidden and the party attempted the Eyes Right salute. For the last few hundred yards to the station, the party smartened up, putting on a display for locals. Invariably, the party arrived an hour before the train, so the men had to cool their heels and stand, waiting, on the platform. The trains always seemed to arrive at mealtimes.

The trains came from all the great railway lines of England. South Western, North Western, Great Northern, Midlands, Great Central, Lancashire and Yorkshire. Each coach was painted with a red cross. The trains had a coach or two of ordinary carriages for the walking wounded. The rest of the carriages were set up to carry stretcher-cases. Access to these carriages was by a pair of sliding doors in the centre of the carriage.

Unloading began as soon as the medical officer on the train had checked his paperwork with the medical officer on the platform. Sometimes, Lieutenant Colonel Bruce-Porter himself went to the station to check the unloading. First came the walking wounded. They hobbled and shuffled along the platform. In wet weather, the uniforms of those coming from France were often still covered in the mud of the trenches. Volunteer drivers transported the walking wounded from the train to the hospital in motor cars, sweeping them off, five or six at a time.

For the stretcher-cases, a different set of volunteers, called 'bluebottles' for their blue uniforms, took stretchers onto the train, lifted patients onto the stretchers, and carried them off the train. On the station, the hospital orderlies took over – four men carried each stretcher along the platform and up the iron stairs to a waiting ambulance. The orderlies had to be careful to keep the stretchers horizontal as they climbed the stairs. If the convoy was a large one, as happened when there was an offensive at the front, it was arduous work, dashing back to the station to collect yet another patient.

Once the train was unloaded, the party of orderlies was lined up and counted, ready for the march back to the hospital. The hospital being strictly teetotal, some orderlies took a well-earned drink in the station bar. With the drinkers back in line, the party marched back to the hospital.

At the hospital, the receiving ward became the centre of activity.[9] The walking wounded arrived ahead of the ambulances. Within ten minutes of arriving, they found themselves drinking a cup of cocoa, and giving their particulars to a triage nurse, who noted their details on an index card and allocated them to a ward. They were given a package containing the royal blue hospital pyjamas. The paperwork over, they picked up the package and the mugs of cocoa and made for the change rooms. Here, their khaki uniforms were taken, ticketed and sent to the fumigators to kill the lice and other bugs that came with them from the trenches. Next came the luxury of a hot bath, before the wounded men dressed in their hospital pyjamas and made their way to the wards.

When the stretcher-cases arrived, orderlies carried them from the ambulances to the receiving ward. At the door of the receiving ward, a doctor briefly looked at the patient, checked his label and assigned him to a ward. The attendant sergeant then picked a metal ticket from a rack, and laid it on the stretcher. This ticket gave the patient his ward and bed number.

More serious cases were taken directly from the front door to their ward. Less serious cases were taken into the receiving ward and transferred from the stretcher to a bed. The stretcher-cases gave their particulars, which were entered in the index. They were given blue pyjamas and cigarettes, before being put on trolleys and wheeled to the wards, where they received a blanket bath and a meal, and were examined by the ward sister.

Each morning, an 'Empty Bed' list was compiled, indicating where the hospital had capacity, and where it was filling up, ready to receive the next trainload. A new trainload arrived practically every day. If a train arrived unexpectedly, leave for the orderlies could be cancelled without notice. Noel Irving noted that:

The horrors of war were never far from us. Frequently, on returning on 'late pass' to the hospital, orderlies were greeted with a telephone message from the main hall to the guard on the gate: 'Stop the next four late orderlies: send them to ward so-and-so: case number xyz has "gone west." They are to move the body to the mortuary'.[10]

A death meant a funeral. Men who died at the 3rd London General Hospital were buried with full military honours, with the orderlies acting as pallbearers. Coates and Irving, being the same height, were often paired for funeral duty.[11]

It is an hour's walk from Wandsworth to Chelsea. The artists could have walked from Chelsea to the hospital and back each day, but the army made them live at the hospital in boarding school conditions. They were allowed to go home for the afternoon every second Monday (2–10 pm) and for a sleepover every second weekend (from 2 pm on Saturday until 10 pm on Sunday). Their wives could come to the hospital to visit them during visiting hours.

It was discipline for the sake of discipline. The artists were volunteers, working at the hospital out of a sense of duty. Confining them to barracks was a needless burden.

The artists had no choice but to conform. To make things worse, many of the ward sisters ruled with an iron fist. When Coates first entered a ward, he hung his jacket and cap inside the door. The sister growled: 'Not there, orderly, take your coat out into the kitchen and hang it up where the chars hang theirs'. Fullwood struck worse trouble. When the sister told him to make a ward full of beds, he said: 'But, my dear girl, I never made a bed'. The sister exploded before he could finish his sentence.[12]

The discipline – both military and hospital – was unrelenting. Not only did the artists have to learn to work as labourers, they had to subject themselves to the rigours and inanities of hierarchical discipline – and, in many respects, hospital discipline was more inane than military discipline. For men unaccustomed to lifting anything heavier than a paintbrush, learning to be labourers was a hardship. For men whose idea of discipline was to be out of bed before 10 o'clock in the morning, learning to jump to orders was all but impossible.

When George Lambert painted Arthur Streeton in his orderly's

George Lambert
Arthur Streeton AWM

uniform, he captured the sense that the artist orderlies were fish out of water. He painted Streeton as a corporal, but gave him the imperious air of a general. It was classic Lambert.

No sooner had the artists signed on as orderlies, than they heard the news of the slaughter at Gallipoli. Men who had been wounded in the Dardanelles – many of them Australian – soon began to arrive at the hospital.

Trooper Oswald Walker made the journey from Gallipoli to Wandsworth.[13] Twenty-five years old, and a station manager by occupation, he joined the 6th Light Horse, in Sydney in January 1915. He landed on Gallipoli in May. On 7 September 1915, he contracted dysentery. He reported to the casualty clearing station, from where he was transferred to Mudros and, from there, to Malta. For a month, he was a patient at the Floriana Hospital, one of many hospitals established on Malta to receive casualties from the Dardanelles. Making little progress in his recovery, Trooper Walker was certified 'For England' and embarked on SS *Dunluce Castle*. It was a four-day voyage from Malta to Gibraltar, and five days from Gibraltar to Southampton.

Trooper Walker had his first glimpse of England as the ship passed the Isle of Wight. He could see fields, and cottages nestled in the hills. He was admitted to the 3rd London General Hospital on 19 October 1915. Walker described the final stage of the journey in an article in the *Gazette of the 3rd London General Hospital*:

In the morning we were alongside the wharf in Southampton. Southampton made no other impression on me than that it was cold, damp and smoky. We were a motley crew when we disembarked – Australians, New Zealanders and Tommies from almost every unit, some on crutches, some on stretchers, men with empty sleeves, and others – walking-cases – showing the ravages of dysentery and fever on their thin faces and wasted frames.

After various delays, waiting for the men to be sorted out to their different destinations, we were at last put on a very comfortable hospital train and made a start on our two hours' journey to Clapham Junction. Being now a walking-case, I was able to secure a seat near a window, hoping to get a glimpse of the country now and again. I was richly rewarded. One often hears about England's unrivalled rural beauty, but one never gets a true conception of it. One cannot, of course, see the best from a fast-travelling train, but what I saw eclipsed my ideal. Now that the autumn leaves were falling and all the crops were gathered in, one was seeing it perhaps at a disadvantage. But what a sight for sore eyes to see green grass again; and such a green, too!

The journey was soon over, and we caught sight, for the first time for many months, of men in uniform other than Khaki, namely, the men of the British Red Cross Society, who looked very spick and span in their dark blue uniforms. It was not long before we were run up in the motor ambulances and had a good hot drink of cocoa (real cocoa made with milk), and were allotted to our wards. After having a hot bath and getting dressed in our hospital blues, we waited beside our ward stove for some tea before going to bed.

Square Dinkum, it was cold.

With all the warm things available, with my dressing gown on and my feet resting on top of the stove, I still felt cold. It was not till after being put in a warm bed with a hot-water bottle at my feet for a few hours that I at last felt warm again.[14]

George Coates made a watercolour sketch of the arrival at Wandsworth of diggers from Gallipoli. *The Arrival of the First Australian Wounded from Gallipoli at the Third London General Hospital, Wandsworth*, on page 90, showed a patient in the receiving ward at Wandsworth. He was evidently in a bad way. His right arm was bandaged. His head was bowed. Two sisters and two nurses were caring for him. The sister in the foreground had a domineering air – perhaps Coates was taking a shot at one of the bad-tempered sisters. The background of Coates' sketch was the distinctive minstrel gallery at the north end of the receiving ward. The minstrel gallery is shown in the photograph of the receiving ward on page 91, as is the sheet-folding prowess of the hard-working orderlies.

In all, more than 12,000 Australian soldiers were evacuated from Gallipoli to the United Kingdom.[15] Many found their way to Wandsworth. Bruce-Porter put the number of sick and wounded Australians treated at Wandsworth throughout the war at more than 17,000.[16] During the summer of 1915, arrivals from Gallipoli were so common that 'the entire staff of orderlies had to roll up, again and again, for stretcher carrying, both by day and at night'.[17]

Lieutenant Hugo Throssell, who won the Victoria Cross for valour at Gallipoli, recovered from his wounds at Wandsworth. Like Victoria Cross winners today, Throssell was something of a celebrity. During a spell of light duties, Tom Roberts was detailed to act as unofficial batman for Throssell, showing him the sights of London. They formed an enduring friendship. When Roberts returned to Australia after the war, he visited Throssell and his wife during the ship's stopover in Perth.[18]

George Coates
*The Arrival of the First Australian
Wounded from Gallipoli at the
Third London General Hospital,
Wandsworth* AWM

Nurses with starched uniforms and capes feature in many photographs of Wandsworth. The stripes on the sleeves of the nurse in the photograph with Lieutenant Hugo Throssell VC indicate she was a nursing sister.

In time, Roberts rose to be the dental nurse at Wandsworth, 'patching up poor fellows with face wounds'.[19] His job had many aspects: he was the messenger boy; the cleaner; the steriliser of instruments; and the valet. He kept the appointment book and the records of treatment; he helped with the anaesthetics; and he sponged the faces of the patients, whose courage taught him 'not to think quite so much of one's own importance'.[20] But courage was relative. The finest soldiers could be terrified of the dentist's chair, and it was Roberts' job to calm them: 'The "dodge" was to get an officer into the chair first; of course he had to remember he was both

The receiving ward at Wandsworth

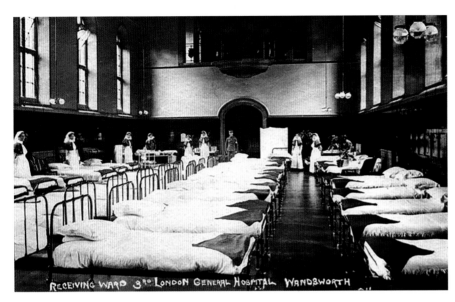

an officer and a gentleman, and that gentlemen didn't yelp. With this to keep up the morale, the yelping would decrease'.[21]

Some of the nursing sisters at Wandsworth treated the artist orderlies as underlings,[22] but Lieutenant Colonel Bruce-Porter was astute enough to let them contribute according to their own lights. After beginning as ward orderlies, or as members of the 'chain gang' that worked in the grounds and gardens, Bruce-Porter encouraged the artists to take on roles that better suited their talents and temperaments.

In September 1915, he asked Coates (now a lance corporal), Withers and Streeton to take charge of the recreation room. They put on an art exhibition. They turned the recreation room into a picture gallery, decorating it with 'plants, dark red draperies, Persian rugs and carpets'. They hung more than a hundred paintings and drawings, most of them made by the artist orderlies.[23] Among the artists who lent paintings were Sergeant Withers, Corporal Evergood, Lance Corporal Coates, and Privates Fullwood, Roberts and Streeton. Sergeant Wood upstaged the painters by lending an entire collection of bronze statuettes.[24]

Patients used the recreation room to play billiards, cards, dominoes and other indoor games. There were desks to write letters. Concerts, plays and charades were performed three or four times a week. Streeton and Roberts became the art department. They painted the advertising flyers, the scenery and the backdrops. They even designed the costumes.[25] The audience of patients made their way to the recreation room as best they could: some on crutches; some in wheelchairs; some

Lieutenant Hugo Throssell VC recovering at Wandsworth AWM

Arthur Streeton
Concert by Miss Hullah AWM

The art exhibition in the recreation
room at Wandsworth AWM

George Coates
A Hero from Mons CAGHM

on trolleys. The men from the eye ward formed a line, the one-eyed men leading the blind in a vision-impaired conga line that wound along the corridors to the concert.[26]

Bruce-Porter encouraged the artists to sketch, paint and sculpt. Coates drew scenes of the recreation room for the *Gazette of the 3rd London General Hospital*. In *The Light that Failed*, a wounded soldier read to two blind comrades. In *Ready for the Concert*, a man in a blue uniform and cap sat in a wheelchair, waiting for a push. JH Dowd's *Sister and her 'Boys'* showed a sister sitting among a group of invalids, some limbless, some in chairs, some bandaged, all enjoying the concert. Coates also painted many of the patients and staff of the hospital. One of his subjects, a young boy, recovered from his wounds sufficiently to return to the front, where he was killed. Coates gave his portrait to the boy's mother.[27]

Bruce-Porter was not just giving the artists a break when he asked them to supervise the recreation room. He knew that they would make a contribution to the recovery of patients. He wrote:

It was essential for the comfort of the patients as a whole that the atmosphere of the [recreation room] should be a good one, and that patients could find sympathetic men to whom they could unburden their minds and ask advice on the variety of worries which beset these young soldiers far from home and who had no relations or friends within reach.[28]

Coates was a natural choice for the role. His charm, his sporting prowess and his authoritative bearing combined to encourage the young soldiers to discuss their problems with him.[29]

George Coates
Portrait of a Soldier AWM

Coates painted a life-size portrait of Bruce-Porter. He made sketches
in Bruce-Porter's office as Bruce-Porter went on with his day's work, one
of which is reproduced above. He finished the painting in his new 'studio'
– a small alcove, curtained-off from the recreation room stage. The Royal
Academy accepted the finished portrait, hanging it in the principal room
at Burlington House. Coates gave the painting to Bruce-Porter.[30] In 1917,

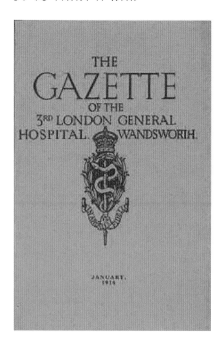

Cover of the *Gazette of the 3rd London General Hospital, Wandsworth*

he painted a second portrait of Bruce-Porter, this time placing him in the hospital garden.[31]

Derwent Wood sculpted a bust of Bruce-Porter. It stood in the recreation room.[32] Coates persuaded his sculptor friend, Arthur Walker, to lend the hospital the plaster cast of his statue of Florence Nightingale that stood in Waterloo Place.[33]

It was Bruce-Porter's idea to establish the *Gazette of the 3rd London General Hospital*.[34] He asked Ward Muir to be general editor and Noel Irving to be art editor.

Ward Muir was 'a writer, journalist, and photographer. He suffered from TB and he was continually volunteering for dangerous service and being turned down. His lungs had collapsed, his heart had moved from his left side to his right, yet he was a man of indomitable courage'.[35] Thwarted in his plans to place himself in harm's way, Muir concentrated on his role as editor of the *Gazette*. Drawing on the talents of the patients, the artists and the entire staff of the hospital, it provided an intimate view of the operations of the hospital.

The *Gazette* was published monthly from September 1915 until the end of the war. The monthly print run was 5000 copies. Each copy sold for 4d. A special edition of the *Gazette* – called *Happy – Though Wounded!* – sold for half a crown.[36]

Bruce-Porter was an active contributor, as was the matron, Edith Holden. The artists supplied sketches and drawings, the cartoonists provided cartoons, and the patients wrote articles describing their lives and experiences. Coates contributed many sketches. Private Vernon Lorimer, an Australian stretcher-bearer wounded at Gallipoli, who had worked for the *Bulletin* in Sydney, contributed cartoons of hospital life.[37] Private Stephen Bagot de la Bere, an English artist, drew cartoons showing the sister as a slave-driver and an orderly as a slave. His drawings included Heath Robinson–like machines to relieve the drudgery of the orderly's life.[38] Jimmy Dowd, in peacetime a cartoonist with *Punch*, became the regular cartoonist.[39]

The tone of the *Gazette* was always one of self-deprecating humour, gently poking fun at the quirks of the institution. Despite what might seem to have been distressing circumstances, the *Gazette* never allowed the patients or the staff to lapse into self-pity. Bruce-Porter was a true leader, who infected the entire hospital with his own sense of spirit, enterprise and optimism. It was largely due to him that the 3rd London General Hospital deserved the nickname Muir gave it – 'the Happy Hospital'.

9 THE WESTERN FRONT, 1916

IN WHICH THE ACTION SWITCHES TO THE WESTERN FRONT,
THE WAR CONFRONTS HILDA RIX, THE FIRST OFFICIAL
WAR ARTISTS' SCHEMES ARE BORN AND WILL DYSON
BECOMES AUSTRALIA'S FIRST OFFICIAL WAR ARTIST.

War on the Western Front was an entirely different proposition from war at Gallipoli.

At Gallipoli, the opposing trenches were so close that men could throw bombs between them. The risk of death was constant. All supplies had to be brought by sea and carried to the trenches. Water was short. Food was monotonous. Dead bodies were left to decompose, unburied, in no man's land. Flies were everywhere. The diggers fought as an isolated invasion force. The only infrastructure was that which they built themselves. There were no friendly locals to support them. There were few distractions, and fewer opportunities for leave away from the front.

When the diggers arrived on the Western Front, they found that the war was conducted from trenches that offered real protection from enemy fire. The opposing trenches were so far apart that trench raids were unlikely and bomb-throwing was impossible. Compared to Gallipoli, this type of warfare was a dream – less tense, more comfortable, settled and relatively safe. General Birdwood wrote that 'Going round the trenches was a much quieter business than it had ever been at Gallipoli, for here a broad expanse of No Man's Land made life far safer. Indeed, by comparison with [Gallipoli], we found it very peaceful'.[1]

The trenches seldom moved. The battle zone, including no man's land and the trenches on either side, was 5–8 kilometres wide. Although shelling could turn the battle zone into a wasteland, the visible impact of the fighting was limited to a narrow strip. A few kilometres from the front, life continued, more or less, as before the war. Farms continued to operate. Towns were busy, with shops open and an air of normality that surprised new chum soldiers. When troops were not in the trenches, they were free to relax in the French towns and countryside.

Because the front was stable, an elaborate system of supply had developed. Water came to the trenches in pipes. The men received a hot meal each night, thanks to light railways that serviced the trenches. It was a kilometre or so from the lines to the nearest *estaminets*, where beer, wine and omelettes were served. When General Monash arrived in France in May 1916, his brigade was posted close to the town of Armentières in northern France. He wrote home that:

This town is a truly astonishing place. It is within seven kilometres of our front trenches. Our artillery is on its eastern outskirts. When our guns are not making a noise we can hear the Boche guns quite plainly. Aeroplanes, both ours and enemy's, often fly overhead … Yet in spite of all this the town is in full swing and teeming with life … [It] is replete with every comfort, a plenitude of fresh eggs and butter, fruit, vegetables, fresh fish, poultry, cheese, still and sparkling wines, delicatessen of all kinds; while in the shops, there is nothing you can think of that you cannot buy … I came here expecting to find a ruined devastated country, without population, with farms and fields laid waste, buildings and churches in ruins and a population of refugees living in misery. Yet here, within four and a half miles of the German Army, I find a peaceful, prosperous … town, full of life … and a people calm, sedate, confident, and utterly unconcerned as to the terrible slaughter going on within earshot.[2]

Joe Maxwell, later to win the Victoria Cross, described his arrival in France:

We had come from months of the coppery sheen of the desert, from the land of soggy heat, flies and dust. Now we glided past French villages, bright and glowing … Green spears of poplars, red roofs, white walls, gardens aflame with colour, bubbling wine at every tiny station, decent French bread and generous welcome from French villagers. On rocked the train, around green hills, down into tranquil valleys where war seemed a remote thing, over stone bridges and across rivers and streams where gables and poplars and chimneys and a lacery of fresh smoke were mirrored.[3]

In April, diggers went into the front line for the first time at Armentières. This was a 'quiet' sector of the line, suitable to introduce the new chums to trench warfare Western Front–style.

As the diggers adjusted to their new surroundings, the British commander-in-chief, General Haig, was planning his 1916 offensive. It was the Battle of the Somme – a battle which, with that of Third Ypres, did so much to give the Great War its ugly reputation. The diggers were

Walter Di Qual
The Western Front

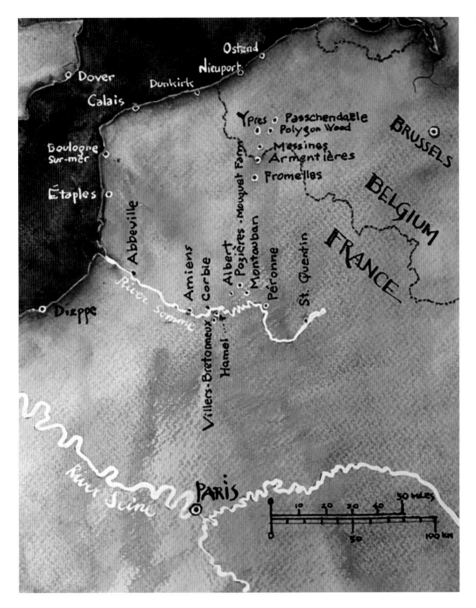

fortunate to miss the first phase of the Somme battle. They remained, for the moment, in trenches north of the Somme Valley, but their luck did not hold. First came the Battle of Fromelles. It decimated the 5th Australian Division. There were three other Australian divisions in France – the 1st, 2nd and 4th. They joined the second phase of the Battle of the Somme – the battle for the ridge at Pozières and for Mouquet Farm, on the far side of the ridge. The casualties suffered in seven weeks at Pozières and Mouquet Farm exceeded those suffered in eight months at Gallipoli.

The British sector of the front line ran from the Somme Valley in the south through Ypres to the coast in the north. Whilst the line was mostly stable, it did move – hence there is no front line shown on Walter Di Qual's map. For example, in 1917, Third Ypres pushed the front eastwards from Ypres in the direction of Passchendaele. At the beginning of 1918, the front in the Somme Valley was near St Quentin. In April, the Germans pushed it as far west as Villers-Bretonneux. By the end of the war, the line was, once again, near St Quentin.

George Nicholas and Hilda Rix at Buckingham Palace SHSM

Some of the toughest fighting on the ridge at Pozières was in the battle for two German trenches called 'OG1' and 'OG2'. By August 1916, Australian troops had taken the trenches, but were suffering casualties from a German machine gun that enfiladed OG1. Captain George Nicholas, a 29-year-old schoolteacher from Gippsland in eastern Victoria, and an officer of the 24th Battalion, was sent to reconnoitre the position.[5] According to the *Official History*:

Nicholas not only located the German machine gun post that had caused so much trouble … [he] captured the German party and came in with their gun on his shoulder. 'Just as well,' he said, 'to make certain that it won't be used again.'

For this act of bravery, Nicholas was awarded the Distinguished Service Order (DSO).[6] Later in the war, the same act would have won a Victoria Cross.[7]

Nicholas was no stranger to tough fighting. He had served on Gallipoli from 30 August 1915 until 15 December 1915, when he took a severe gunshot wound in the arm. His recuperation took him to a hospital in Étaples. There, he saw paintings by Hilda Rix. So impressed was he, that he determined to seek out the artist and meet her.[8] Now, in September 1916, he had his chance. Nicholas was sent to London to receive his medal from King George V.

When George Nicholas met Hilda Rix in London, he found her in the saddest of circumstances. On 2 August 1914, two days before war was declared, Hilda Rix, her sister, Elsie, and her mother had fled Étaples on one of the last ships to leave for England. On the trip, Elsie contracted typhoid fever. She died on 2 September 1914. Her mother was devastated. In March 1916, she, too, died, leaving Hilda alone in London.

George and Hilda fell in love. On 4 October 1916, George took Hilda to Buckingham Palace for the investiture of his DSO.

Hilda drew her lover, handsome in the uniform he now wore – that of a major. He was also wearing the red and blue ribbon of the DSO, the white over red shoulder patch of the 24th Battalion, and a red wound stripe on the lower left sleeve for the wound to his arm. Hilda also drew George's younger brother, Lieutenant Bryon Nicholas, a winner of the Military Cross.[9] He, too, was in the 24th Battalion. A third Nicholas brother, Frank, had enlisted in the ranks, at the age of eighteen years and eleven months.[10]

George and Hilda married on 7 October 1916. Three days later,

Hilda Rix Nicholas
Major George Matson Nicholas AWM

George returned to the front.[11] On 11 November 1916, he took command of the 24th Battalion. On 14 November 1916, he was killed while leading his battalion back to the front.[12]

Only five weeks after her wedding, Hilda was a widow. In her grief and solitude, she turned to painting. *Desolation* was a picture of the widow left behind, and *Pro Humanitate* a triptych examining what followed when a soldier was shot. Both paintings were destroyed by fire in 1930, but Hilda's pencil studies survive.[13] An oil of the same period, *These Gave the World Away*, also survives. It shows what was left for Hilda to paint.

Hilda wrote that 'I who was so alone painted out my heart in these big canvases'.[14] She also took out her Morocco paintings and changed the signatures to her new name: 'Hilda Rix Nicholas'.

At a point when it seemed that nothing worse could happen to one individual – that she had borne more than anyone could have been expected to bear – on 9 October 1917, a year later, Bryon Nicholas was killed in action at Broodseinde Ridge, near Passchendaele.[15] Frank Nicholas was not killed, but suffered from disabling shell shock that prevented him from returning to duty. Hilda Rix Nicholas brought Frank home with her when she returned to Australia in May 1918.[16]

The failure of the Battle of the Somme forced British politicians to rethink the balance they had struck between the conflicting demands of operational secrecy and the propaganda war.

At home, there was unrest when the government published huge lists of names of the dead and wounded, whilst at the same time suppressing news of what was happening at the front. Overseas, the Germans were winning the propaganda war. They had sent artists to the front shortly after the war began. Their work, depicting both the front line and the home front, appeared in galleries in Vienna and Berlin, and copies of artworks were seen in newspapers and magazines around the world. Far from suppressing images of the war, the Germans used them for propaganda purposes. The Germans saw that the work of their artists would foster morale and boost support for the war effort at home and in neutral countries.[17] German propaganda was particularly effective in the United States, thwarting British hopes of garnering support for their own war effort in that country.[18]

The British had established a War Propaganda Bureau in the first few weeks of the war. The Bureau had its offices in a block of flats called 'Wellington House', from which the Bureau took its popular name.[19] In

Hilda Rix Nicholas
These Gave the World Away NGA

an Orwellian twist, however, Wellington House was made to subordinate its propaganda activities to the army's demands for secrecy.

It gradually dawned on British politicians that they had to take the public into their confidence if they were to maintain morale on the home front. They could not expect the public to continue to support the war effort while they censored news of the fighting. They could not expect to win the propaganda war in the United States while they obstructed the efforts of American journalists to report the war.

The time was ripe for Wellington House to expand its role, especially if it could operate in areas that did not threaten operational secrecy. War art fitted that bill. The generals could hardly argue that an artist painting pictures at the front would compromise operational secrecy. Wellington House already used official photographers extensively, but its leader, Charles Masterman, agreed with the Germans that some things were better conveyed 'through the eye of an artist'.[20] When the opportunity came to appoint an artist to paint the war, Masterman was ready to take it.

Muirhead Bone was a famous Scottish etcher and watercolour artist. In May 1916, he received his call-up papers from the British conscription authorities. Reluctant to serve in the ranks, he was casting around for a way to avoid the draft.

The *Military Service Act 1916* called up all unmarried male British subjects aged between eighteen and forty who were ordinarily resident in Great Britain. An amendment in May 1916 extended the draft to married men. Local tribunals were established under the Act to enforce the draft. The tribunals could exempt men from the draft in cases of serious hardship, ill-health or infirmity, or conscientious objection. The tribunals could also exempt men if it was 'expedient in the public interests' for them to serve in a non-military capacity.[21] The tribunals granted exemptions quite freely. Between March 1916 and April 1917, they granted 779,936 applications for exemptions, while refusing 371,500.[22]

As Bone looked for ways to avoid the draft, he met a literary adviser to Wellington House, who suggested a plan. If he could convince Masterman that Bone would be better used painting for Wellington House than serving in the trenches, perhaps a tribunal would grant Bone an exemption on the public interests ground. Masterman agreed. With the support of the War Office, he secured Bone's exemption from military service so long as he worked as an artist for Wellington House.[23] Given the honorary rank of second lieutenant and an annual salary of £500, Bone arrived at the front in August 1916. He was Britain's first official war artist.[24]

Bone's exemption raised ethical issues. It was probably true that Bone would be better used painting for Wellington House than serving in the trenches, but the same could be said of almost every other artist conscripted to serve in the British army. Why should Bone be treated differently? And what was so special about artists? If artists qualified for special treatment, why not musicians, ballet dancers or butchers? Having abandoned the voluntary principle in favour of compulsory service, equity demanded that like cases be treated alike.

In September 1916, Dyson published another collection of cartoons: *Will Dyson's War Cartoons*. The publication of a second collection was a measure of Dyson's success in London. Here was a cartoonist at the top of his game. He mixed with the rich and famous. HG Wells wrote the foreword to *Kultur Cartoons* and called Dyson 'this extraordinary artist'.[25] Lord Desborough, the Bishop of Birmingham and GK Chesterton were among the celebrities who contributed written pieces for *Will Dyson's War Cartoons*. Chesterton described Dyson as 'the most original and penetrating English artist of our time'[26] – a big call for a black and white newspaper cartoonist.

Yet storm clouds were gathering. Dyson was a fit man of military age.[27] As a British subject, he was liable to be conscripted, like any other British subject.[28] It was only a matter of time before his call-up took effect.

Dyson had not volunteered to serve. Like Bone, he was anxious to avoid the draft. In that ambition, he found a ready ally in the Australian High Commissioner, Andrew Fisher, who opposed conscription. His opposition to conscription brought him into conflict with Billy Hughes, who, as Prime Minister, was now his boss, but Fisher was firm in his views.[29]

Fisher and Dyson joined in a scheme to save Dyson from the draft in the same way that Masterman had saved Bone. The scheme had two parts. The first was to secure the Australian government to appoint Dyson as an official war artist. The second was to secure the Australian government to intervene on his behalf when the British army moved to conscript him. That would require the Australian government to pressure the local tribunal to exempt Dyson on the ground that it was 'expedient in the public interests' for him to serve in a non-military capacity – as an Australian war artist.

The immediate problem was that Australia had no official war artists' scheme. From his remote posting as High Commissioner in London, Fisher had first to persuade Canberra to create the position, and then to secure Dyson's appointment to it. It was an exercise in bureaucratic manipulation to test the skills of an old hand. Moreover, Fisher had to be careful. The Australian High Commissioner could not be seen hatching a plot to thwart the British draft just when Prime Minister Hughes was moving to introduce a draft in Australia.

Fisher was up to the challenge. Two documents were prepared. The first was a letter from Dyson addressed to the Commonwealth of Australia, and dated 23 August 1916:

Sir:

I am an Australian artist resident at present in England and am engaged as a black-and-white cartoonist.

I write to suggest that it would be of interest to the people of Australia of today and in the future to see sketches illustrating the relationship of the Australians to the war and interpreting the feelings and character of the Australian troops in France and the feelings of the French towards them.

As this could only be fittingly done by an Australian artist I wish to express my willingness to accept a commission to go to France with this end in view, my work while there to be the property of the Australian Government.

I am
Yours faithfully
William H Dyson[30]

The second was a cable from Fisher to Defence Minister Pearce, dated 24 August 1916:

Strongly recommend Dyson, Cartoonist, be given authority to visit France to gather impressions of Australians at war from an Australian point of view to be afterwards embodied in sketches illustrating relationship of the Australians to the war and interpreting character of Australian troops which would be valuable record. All work done by him to be property of Commonwealth Government. Question of remuneration, if any, he leaves entirely to Commonwealth Government.[31]

Although Dyson's letter masqueraded as a spontaneous approach, the letter and the cable used the same stilted language. They shared many identical phrases. Either the same person drafted them both, or the author of the cable copied the wording of the letter. Fisher took no advice on the letter, and no time to consider its contents.[32] That was highly unusual – Fisher was a public servant, after all.

On 31 August 1916, Pearce replied, approving Fisher's recommendation, provided that the War Office agreed. The next day, the responsible officer in Australia House in London, Captain Collins, wrote to Dyson:

With reference to the cablegram sent to the Commonwealth Government by the High Commissioner on the 24th ultimo recommending that you be given authority to proceed to France to gather impressions of Australians at war from an Australian point of view, to be afterwards embodied in sketches, I desire to inform you that we have received a reply stating that the suggestion is approved if the War Office agrees.[33]

This letter indicates that Dyson was privy to the terms of Fisher's cable and recommendation – further evidence of a scheme. Taking the next step in the scheme, High Commissioner Fisher spoke personally with General Birdwood, commander of the Australian forces, to clear the proposal. Birdwood agreed. He was 'glad to treat Mr Dyson exactly in the same way as we do Bean, ie he will be provided with rations, quarters, etc'.[34]

But the War Office did not agree. On 24 October 1916, it replied that, 'for the present no permanent artist can be appointed in addition to the official artist now serving with the British Armies in France'.[35] The official artist referred to was Muirhead Bone! As had happened with reporting of the Gallipoli landing, the War Office saw painting the war as purely a British prerogative. The prerogative was, however, under attack from quarters other than Australia. The Canadians were also seeking to establish a war artists' scheme. On 9 October 1916, Dyson wrote to Collins that the Canadians had appointed the artist Richard Jack 'to do some Canadian picture or pictures at the front and [he] has been made a major in the Canadian army for this purpose'.[36] This was true, but the Canadians had run into the same roadblock as the Australians.

Lord Beaverbrook was a young Canadian entrepreneur who had built a business empire in London that included substantial newspaper interests. Supremely energetic, he won election to the House of Commons in 1910. He later became an influential figure in the government of David Lloyd George, who raised him to the peerage in 1917. As Lord Beaverbrook, he served as Minister of Information in Lloyd George's government throughout most of 1918, but his position in the Cabinet did not prevent him from pushing Canadian interests where they conflicted with British ones.[37] In 1916, he was promoting the Canadian war artists' scheme, and complaining that, because 'an English artist has been in France for some time, our man is held up'. Not one to accept British obfuscation, he cleared the way. The Canadian scheme was up and running by the end of November 1916.[38]

The stakes were raised for Dyson when the local tribunal came knocking on his door early in November 1916. Fisher and Dyson had anticipated this. Colonel RMM Anderson, an Australian businessman who had been appointed commandant of the Administrative Headquarters of the AIF in London, was ready to intercede with the tribunal on Dyson's behalf.[39] On 9 November 1916, Dyson wrote to Anderson that, 'The Tribunal people were not slow in sending me the enclosed notice which I send to you in accordance with your promise to deal with it'. On 10 November 1916, Anderson wrote to the tribunal, on AIF letterhead, advising that Dyson was engaged in work for the 'Military Branch of the Australian Government … of a much more important nature than he would [do] as a private in the ranks'. Anderson asked the tribunal to grant Dyson an exemption for three months, making the schoolboy error of adding: 'I take it you will see fit to grant what I suggest and ask herein'.[40]

Anderson copied his letter to the Dysons. Ruby Dyson loved it and wrote to thank him, saying: 'It is too splendid for words, and seems more like a thing of magic than anything else I can think of'. But Dyson, as a prominent anti-conscription campaigner, could expect no favours from a conscription tribunal. Moreover, it was not the place of colonials to tell a British tribunal how to do its job. On 21 November 1916, the tribunal wrote that:

after careful consideration of the whole case on its merits [the tribunal members] decided that they had no option but to disallow Mr Dyson's claim for postponement from Military Service.

Perhaps the best course to pursue under the circumstances would be for Mr Dyson to lodge an appeal to the Appeal Tribunal when it may be possible to make some arrangements such as you desire for the retention of Mr Dyson's services with the Australian Imperial Force.[41]

There were no surprises here. Faced with an intransigent tribunal, Fisher decided to follow more closely the path that had worked for Muirhead Bone. He instructed Colonel Anderson to write to the Headquarters of I Anzac Corps as follows:

During Mr Fisher's recent visit to your Headquarters, he discussed with General Birdwood the employment of Mr Will Dyson, the Australian artist, to do certain work in connection with our troops, which has been approved by the Commonwealth Government and endorsed by General Birdwood …

The idea is that he should provide us with a permanent pictorial record of Australia at war, and give us, through the medium of his pen and brush, the peculiar individuality of the Australian soldier. The War Office have been asked to sanction his visit to France, but his civilian status is against him, and the most they will do is to give permission for him to join one of the weekly parties of journalists which go across. His work, if it is to constitute the record we desire, must be the result of close and intimate acquaintance with the life and doings of our men in the field, and weekly visits, irregularly made, would not enable him to portray his subject really faithfully.

Mr Fisher urges that he be granted an honorary commission in the AIF. He desires no pay – simply payment of his carriage and keep. We, of course, would have to invite the consent of the War Office to utilise his services in this special way, but if we were to indicate our willingness to grant him an honorary commission their scruples would probably be overcome, and they would grant us the permission we seek … If you approve, will you please instruct me?[42]

The only way the local tribunal would let Dyson escape the clutches of the British army was if he joined the Australian army. If Dyson were a member of the Australian army, the War Office could hardly object if he were sent to the front. This approach mirrored the approach that the British had taken with Bone. On 10 December 1916, I Anzac Corps gave its approval, provided only that Dyson's commission was 'honorary and temporary, and that he [would] not be entitled to any payment, allowances or other expenses against the Commonwealth'.

Dyson was commissioned as an honorary lieutenant in the AIF. In December 1916, Lieutenant Will Dyson embarked for military service in France. He was Australia's first official war artist.

High Commissioner Fisher went to extraordinary lengths to save Dyson from the British draft. He strongly recommended the initial proposal to Minister Pearce. He took the unusual step of personally approaching General Birdwood to secure his cooperation. More unusual still was Colonel Anderson's ham-fisted attempt to tell a British tribunal how to exercise a statutory discretion. Fisher urged the AIF to grant Dyson an honorary commission. In all of this, Fisher went out on a limb for Dyson.

In many other respects, too, the treatment of Dyson was different from that of other official war artists. Every other official war artist was required to sign a formal, written agreement with the Commonwealth. Dyson was not required to sign any contract.[45] Every other official war artist was appointed for a limited tenure – usually, three months. Dyson was appointed indefinitely. His appointment continued until the end of the war. Every other official war artist signed the standard attestation form that all members of the AIF signed on enlistment. It confirmed that they had taken the enlistment oath. Dyson did not complete or sign the form. Where the attestation form called for the soldier's particulars to be entered, Dyson's form stated: 'No Particulars Available'.[46] Some of these differences may have been due to the fact that Dyson was the first artist appointed but, overall, the situation is clear. The absence of any form of selection process, and the choice of Dyson from a field of one, complete the picture of a government appointment made to subvert the British draft.

On 14 December 1916, Dyson joined Bean at I Anzac Corps Headquarters in the Somme Valley. Bean and Dyson made a fortunate combination. They were using different approaches towards the common goal of recording Australia's involvement in the war.

Bean threw Dyson straight in at the deep end, taking him 20 kilometres forward to the village of Montauban, near the front line.[47] Dyson was well up for the challenge. His aim was to sketch men coming out of the line. The appearance of men after a spell in the trenches shocked everyone. Lieutenant EJ Rule described the 1st Division coming out of its first battle on the Somme:

They came out one morning fairly early, having spent the night around Albert and Senlis. Although we knew it was stiff fighting, we had our eyes opened when we saw these men march by. Those who watched them will never forget it as long as they live. They looked like men who had been in hell. Almost without exception each man looked drawn and haggard, and so dazed that they appeared to be walking in a dream, and their eyes looked glassy and starey. Quite a few were silly, and these were the only noisy ones in the crowd. Their appearance before they had a night's sleep and clean-up must have been twice as ill as when we saw them.[48]

Bean's description was similar: 'a line of men, all going slowly along – no step more than about three inches – every man utterly detached as if they were living in a world by themselves'.[49] Dyson drew what Rule and Bean described.

Dyson made the sketch near Montauban in December 1916. As a

Will Dyson
Coming Out on the Somme AWM

war artist, he promised: 'I'll never draw a line to show war except as the filthy business it is'.[50] *Coming Out on the Somme* is an example, par excellence, of that approach. The men he drew had suffered no physical injury, but they had surely been damaged. Dyson did not disguise the damage; nor did Rule or Bean. Rule's description of some of the men as 'silly' was a reference to men who were suffering psychiatric harm that would today be treated as post-traumatic stress disorder. This first drawing by an Australian war artist demonstrated that, although censorship was rife, Dyson was free to draw the war as he saw it – 'as the filthy business it is'.[51]

Two of Ruby Dyson's younger brothers, Daryl and Reg Lindsay, were serving with the AIF in France. Daryl, aged twenty-seven, was a driver with the 3rd Division supply train, working to support the troops in the front line, near Ypres.[52] Reg, aged twenty-nine, was a gunner in the 22nd Field Artillery Brigade in the Somme Valley, not far from where Will Dyson was stationed.[53] On 31 December 1916, Reg was killed in action. The filthy business had struck at the heart of Ruby's family. Would Daryl be next? Or Will?

A month after Reg was killed, Daryl was called before his commanding officer in circumstances which he described in his memoir:

Will Dyson had come across from London as the first official war artist to the AIF and was working with Captain Charles Bean, war correspondent and official historian. They were attached to AIF Headquarters. Major 'Digger' Dewson of our unit, an Englishman and one of the finest soldiers I ever knew, sent for me to come to his dugout. Pushing a bottle of whisky across the box he used for a table, he said: 'Have a drink. We got a signal from Headquarters to get you transferred to join Bean and Dyson's outfit on the Somme. You'd better take it as you'll never get anywhere in this show.' A week later with another drink and 'Good luck' from Dewson, I was sent south in a staff car to join Dyson – someone unbeknown to me had been pulling strings.[54]

Daryl Lindsay was safer with Dyson at AIF Headquarters than he was at the divisional train. As an honorary lieutenant, Dyson was entitled to a batman. Dyson had friends in high places – the manner of his appointment as official war artist proved that. If he could pull strings to keep his brother-in-law safe, why not pull them? Moreover, Daryl could draw. His talents might advance Dyson's enterprise.

Bean thought it was Lindsay who had pulled strings, as he wrote in an affectionate piece, shortly after Dyson's death in 1938:

One can see him now with his batman (and brother-in-law) Daryl Lindsay, who, in order to keep his sister's husband from harm and incidentally to get an occasional chance of using his own paint box, managed to get transferred from a company of the transport to that congenial service. As they were starting off, loaded with drawing board, sketchbooks, rations, blanket, and other equipment for a week up the line, Daryl would protest that some blanky thing was or was not included.

'Now my good man, no mutiny!' Dyson would exclaim, striking the pose of an officer of the guards. 'Remember whom you are speaking to! I won't tolerate insubordination!' And off the two mates would trudge with their paraphernalia into the mud of the shelled area.[55]

The Somme battlefield had been devastated by the fighting it had seen over the past eight months. Daryl Lindsay wrote that the countryside:

was a shambles – a vast sea of shell holes, mud, the remnants of blasted tree trunks and the rubble of villages razed to the ground … Dyson like Bean was not one to stay in a comfortable billet and we moved about from one Battalion Headquarters to another, to the batteries and occasionally up to the line. [Dyson] had an unbounded respect for the men living up at the front and preferred to be with them rather than with the brass hats and, with his ready wit, was always a welcome guest in a dug-out or gun-pit.[56]

Dyson drew what he and Daryl Lindsay saw on their travels. Mouquet Farm was the scene of some of the toughest fighting that the Australians encountered on the Somme. Dyson's drawing of a dugout gave a sense of the chaotic conditions in which the men had to fight.

Dyson's drawing, on page 112, of a laconic digger smoking a pipe makes a striking contrast with his drawings of the chaos of the front, and the trauma on the faces of the men as they came out of the line.

Dyson was an accomplished cartoonist. His black and white work displayed cutting wit, incisive intelligence and a ready capacity to convey a sharp message. His drawings did not aspire to technical perfection, nor,

Will Dyson
Entrance to Mouquet Farm Dugouts
AWM

Will Dyson
*Signaller, 2nd Main Line Gun
Battalion* AWM

in most cases, to the sensitivity and subtlety seen in the drawings of a Coates or a Lambert. Dyson undertook to make sketches illustrating the relationship of the Australians to the war and interpreting the feelings and character of the Australian troops in France. Many of his sketches achieved those goals.

Bean thought that the men of the AIF would remember Dyson as the most intimate portrayer of the Australian soldier, adding that 'no other official artist, British or Australian, saw a tenth part as much of the real Western Front as did Will Dyson'.[57] Thanks to his insistence on living at the front, Dyson was wounded twice – once, lightly, at Messines and later by a shell burst at Ypres.[58] Taking shrapnel was not part of the war artist's job description.

Dyson's story pulls in contradictory directions. An ardent socialist, he used his contacts in high places to secure appointment to a government position that saved him from the draft. He was reluctant to serve in the ranks, yet he took risks when working as a war artist that he could have avoided. The scheme that Dyson and Fisher cooked up may have been unworthy, yet it blossomed into the official war artists' scheme – a scheme that boasts a long and proud history. Many fine things come from humble beginnings.

10 THE WESTERN FRONT, 1917

IN WHICH FRED LEIST AND SEPTIMUS POWER ARE
APPOINTED AS OFFICIAL WAR ARTISTS, ARTISTS IN
THE RANKS CONTINUE TO WORK FROM THEIR DUGOUTS,
AND ARTHUR STREETON MAKES TROUBLE.

*F*or the first two years of the war, painting was discouraged as a frivolous activity that could not be supported in times of total war. Artists were left to find 'proper' work that contributed to the war effort. In 1916, all that changed. Painting was no longer thought frivolous. It was an activity that could support the war effort. It was now acceptable – indeed, necessary – for the artists to give up their other work and return to the easel. There were not one, but three war artists' schemes. The British, Canadians and Australians might vie with one another for the services of the best artists. So, the Canadian scheme, which was well funded, might out-bid the British and Australian schemes in auctions for the services of British and Australian artists. In a period of just six months, the artists witnessed a remarkable turnaround. At the outset, there was no market for their services, and they were left to eke out a living as common orderlies in the military hospitals. Six months later, three governments were lining up to bid for their services as artists.

Paintings were one thing. Histories would also need to be written. The histories in contemplation were not simply British histories. The colonies would write their own histories, free from British interference. The days of deferring to British censorship were passing.

Neither Fisher nor Pearce needed to be persuaded of the need to act independently of the British, but Lord Beaverbrook made them a fine example. In 1916, acting on his own initiative, he established the Canadian War Records Office in London. It was a curious hybrid. Owned and funded by Beaverbrook, it acted as an arm of the Canadian government to collect records and trophies and disseminate news of the war. It also managed the Canadian war art scheme. Beaverbrook boasted that the Canadian War Records Office was collecting everything of interest to future historians.[1] By this, he meant Canadian historians.

The Australians had not exactly neglected the Australian history of the war, but they had taken a more leisurely approach than the Canadians. It was assumed that Charles Bean would write the history. As early as September 1914, Pearce told Bean that he expected him to 'write a book on the experiences of the force'. In Egypt, Bean learned that General Bridges and his staff expected him to write the history of the AIF.[2]

As the war dragged on, the task of writing its history grew more daunting. It was rapidly becoming too much for just one man. Bean continued to nurture the dream of writing the history of the war, but he saw that his role as a war correspondent might be both a help and a hindrance. On one view of it, proximity to events was an advantage. Bean was in the unique position 'of a man who will write about a war which he has seen all through, in which he has been in every important trench, and seen almost every important event'.[3] On another view, proximity was a handicap. Bean might be too close to events to write history with the necessary fairness and detachment.

In his work as a war correspondent, Bean kept in mind that he would later be writing the history of the AIF. His diaries are full of accounts of old battles, jotted down months or years after the battles, as he met diggers who fought in them. He also had the historian's consciousness of the need to keep safe the things he would need to write the history. In this regard, his ambitions extended far beyond the written records. Bean wanted to preserve a full range of wartime ephemera and souvenirs, which he called 'war relics'. His dream was that these would be kept in a national memorial museum.[4]

In May 1917, Australia copied Canada, and established the Australian War Records Section. A young officer from General White's staff, Captain John Treloar, was appointed to take command. Until 1917, the British army kept all the written records of the Australian army. Treloar's first job was to take these under control, but his brief did not stop there. It also extended to photographs and to war relics.[5] Bean encouraged Treloar to cast his net widely. He also pressed upon politicians their duty to commemorate the war:

Treloar rapidly extended the collection of Australian records and relics throughout France, Egypt and Palestine ... As advice concerning historical records was regarded as being within my province, I finally with the approval of our leaders, urged upon the Minister for Defence, Senator GF Pearce, that our forces should be commemorated in Australia by their own collection of records and relics worthily installed in the then unbuilt federal capital at Canberra. This was approved and the Government's decision was announced to the troops at the front.[6]

Bean, who moved easily in high circles, was positioning himself to write the history of the war. Not only was he setting himself up for the appointment, but he was making sure the he would have to hand everything he needed to do the job. The records had been secured. A museum was planned, and Treloar's men were collecting photographs and war relics to stock it. That left war art. It was another factor in the commemorative equation.

Dyson had been appointed hurriedly as an official war artist, without the luxury of time to work out the terms of his engagement. The formalities had been ignored in his case, but public accountability demanded that the terms on which artists were employed in future should be recorded formally and the expenditure of public money controlled. If there was going to be an official war artists' scheme, Fisher needed to work out the terms on which the artists would be retained before he appointed any more.

Fisher detailed Captain Henry Smart to manage the scheme. It was Smart who had finalised the publication of *The Anzac Book*. Smart asked IH Galbraith, the solicitor for the High Commissioner, to draft a standard-form agreement under which the Commonwealth would retain the war artists.[7] Drafting the agreement was a task of some subtlety. It needed to give the government bureaucratic control over the artists, without stifling their creativity.

Galbraith struck a good balance.[8] The artist would be appointed for three months. He would make at least twenty-five studies, drawings and sketches of 'events occurring in the present war and battles now pending'. The sketches would be the property of the Commonwealth, but the artist could inspect them if the Commonwealth agreed. The artist would receive food, board and an allowance of £1 a day (later increased to £2) to cover expenses away from London. The Commonwealth agreed to provide painting materials to the value of £30.

This first part of the agreement gave the artist a firm deal – twenty-five sketches in three months at an agreed fee. The deal was perfectly adequate to protect the Commonwealth. Fisher and Smart chose the artists.

They knew what sort of sketches they might attempt. If the Commonwealth did not like what an artist produced, it could let the artist go after three months, and no hard feelings. If there was a problem with any of the work, the Commonwealth owned it, and could prevent its display, or even destroy it, if it felt strongly enough.

There was a coda to the agreement that was not a firm deal. The final clause allowed the Commonwealth to 'require' the artist to paint a composition of a battle scene involving the AIF 'at a price to be named by the Commonwealth'. This clause was a gesture only. As a matter of law, it was unenforceable – the size of the composition and its subject remained to be agreed, not to mention that the price-fixing mechanism was an instrument of slavery.[9] The later works, if they were commissioned at all, would be the subject of a separate agreement to be negotiated later.

Galbraith's agreement worked particularly well for landscape artists because it reflected the way many of them worked – making sketches and drawings in the field, then using the sketches to make major works in the studio. It was not so apt for portraitists, many of whom preferred to work in sittings with the subject, making few or no preparatory sketches.

Captain Smart proved an excellent choice for the management role. He was a flexible and patient administrator. If the portraitists produced good portraits, he did not chase them for the contractual quota of sketches. If a black and white artist produced a lot of drawings, Smart was relaxed if he produced few, if any, paintings. After all, he was administering an art scheme, not a charter of rights.[10]

Fisher's next appointments were Fred Leist and Septimus Power.

Leist was a black and white artist. He came from Sydney, where he had been a student at Julian Ashton's school. His standing in the art world of Sydney was that of an aspirant, knocking on the door of acclaim, repeatedly listed as an also-ran, but never breaking through to the top rank.[11] He enjoyed greater success in London, however, exhibiting at the Royal Academy in 1911 and 1914. He also exhibited in the French Salon in 1912.[12] He was a member of the Chelsea Arts Club, where he was friendly with George Bell.[13] Aged forty-one when the war broke out, he was too old to serve in the ranks, so he found work in the War Office, designing recruiting posters.[14]

On 3 July 1917, Smart notified Leist that the Commonwealth government had approved of his proceeding to France for three months. Leist signed the new agreement. He eagerly provided a list of the materials he required: a full set of oil paints; 54 canvas panels; 54 oil brushes; a full set of watercolours; 14 watercolour brushes. The total cost was just short of £30.[15] Leist was going to be busy indeed if he was to use all this gear in just three months of painting.

On 3 September 1917, Leist joined the AIF as an honorary lieutenant.[16] He served in France from September until December 1917. He returned for a second spell in June and July 1918, and for a third time in June and July 1919.

Septimus Power occupied a more elevated position in the art world than Leist. He was not a black and white man and he did not come from the world of newspapers. Rather, he had established a lucrative niche in London, painting animals and celebrities. His work was exhibited regularly at the Royal Academy. Power was thirty-six when war broke out – young enough to serve in the ranks. He volunteered, but was rejected because he was deaf. Deafness was permissible in a war artist. Power enlisted on the same day as Leist. He was appointed as an honorary lieutenant on the terms of the standard agreement.[17] He served in France from September until December 1917. He returned for a second spell in August 1918. Like Leist, Power took advantage of the standard-form agreement to stock up on painting materials.[18]

Once again, Bean played nursemaid to the artist new chums. Bean found Leist to be a man of the world. Power, by contrast, was shy, gauche and nervous, which Bean attributed to his deafness. He found Power 'a lovable man'. Leist's best quality, according to Bean, was his anxiety that Power should be well looked after and 'not left to himself amongst strange scenes and people'. Bean took his charges to Hazebrouck, near Ypres, where the battle for Passchendaele was unfolding. That night, a German plane came over. It was caught in the spotlights. Bean described the scene in the cellar to which the trio retreated:

The old owner of the house was there – next to him his old wife with her long, strong off-white face and blue almost unseeing eyes and the family fox terrier curled up on her lap. The girl – the servant – a plucky little round-faced beggar that on previous occasions had refused to come down stairs until everyone else was down there – sat next; and by their side and opposite sat a dozen jolly Australian clerks in khaki on benches and barrels round the wall. The solitary candle threw a bold bright light on the old people's faces, and the glinting black

Septimus Power
War AWM

Septimus Power
In the Horse Lines AWM

bottle ends under the low arched recesses behind them, and the white-washed cellar wall – all in brilliant light and shade like a picture by Rembrandt.[19]

In the field, Power worked to his strengths, making wonderful sketches of horses in action. Horses were the mainstay of the artillery. Most of the guns were mobile, and horses were used to haul them. In works such as *War*, Power captured the urgency as the teams of horses rushed guns and ammunition into battle through mud and desolate terrain.

The soft blue palette of *In the Horse Lines* conveyed a different feeling altogether, as the men tended the horses. Power's love of the horses came through in all of his work.

Leist paid a price for being fitter than Power. One of the Australian triumphs at Passchendaele was the victory at Polygon Wood. In the lead-up to the battle, on 23 September 1917, Bean took Leist with him on a reconnaissance trip to explore the area where the battle was about to take place.

It was a fine, hot day. The party was Bean, Leist, Henry Gullett, a young official Australian correspondent who later worked with Bean on the *Official History*, and GL Gilmour, a journalist representing the Australian Press Association. They left their car beyond the Menin Gate, outside Ypres, and walked several kilometres towards Polygon Wood. The Germans were shelling. Shells were landing quite close to the party. At the front line, Bean led the group along the Polygon Wood plateau. As they neared Polygon Wood, they came to 'a length of trench which was occupied only with [German] dead. It had been lashed with shells that morning'. Bean led the party along the trench, through country that was 'merely a stubble of thin sapling-stumps projecting between shell-holes'. The dusty track was barely visible. Bean and Gullett went ahead, leaving Leist and Gilmour 50 metres or so behind. It was a risky excursion. 'There was no sign of a soul either in front or behind us.' As Bean and Gullet made their way along the northern edge of the ridge, 4.2 'universal' shells were bursting every few minutes, so Bean moved off the path. Another shell burst, but the fragments passed safely over Bean and Gullett. Leist and Gilmour, by now 100 metres in the rear, had to run the same gauntlet. Bean signed to Leist and Gilmour to hurry, 'but it was pretty rough on them'.[20]

Leist might have been killed, but Bean was unapologetic:

they got through and the thing that pleased me was that Leist had now been round this battlefield within a day or two of the actual attack which he might have to paint. He had seen a more active battlefield than any of our artists except Will Dyson, and the knowledge he gained would be very valuable to him and to the Australian records.

It was afterwards arranged that one of the pictures he was commissioned to paint should be that of an incident on this plateau in this battle (the death of Lieutenant Turnour, of the 59th Battalion).[21]

Leist's description of this episode in the *Sydney Morning Herald* was no less dramatic.

[Leist] was introduced to the front by Mr Bean, the official war correspondent [who] seems not to have any nerves at all, walks the most precarious regions of the front trenches with incredible confidence, and appears to take his best delight in investigating unpleasant corners of the field. For the newcomer, he is a positively terrifying companion … Leist's first experience of the front line was a walk of what he believes to have been many miles, in the course of which he lived a lifetime and expected to die at any moment, a walk which consisted very largely of near shell-bursts, deafening explosions, constant duckings and dodgings in the hope of avoiding the same, frequent plunges at full length into the mud of the gutter-trench, and then a sudden dreadful sight of a strew of dead German soldiers heaped upon the field with all the devastating effect of that battle-ground spectacle.[22]

As Leist looked back at the front, the bombardment was lifting the ground 'in great puffs … as though a giant syringe was at work beneath the surface'.

The battle for Polygon Wood took place on 26 September 1917, only two days after this frightening initiation ceremony. Leist recovered sufficiently to exceed his quota of sketches by a good margin. At the end of his tour in France, he handed over twenty-seven oil paintings, twenty watercolours and four black and white drawings.[23]

Leist's work included a watercolour of Gibraltar, the famous German observation post at Pozières, near the trenches where Major Nicholas won his DSO.

Leist captured a good pictorial likeness in his sketches. He had an eye for unusual scenes of day-to-day life at the front. One of the quainter aspects of life in the battle zone was the use of carrier pigeons. Although carrier pigeons were old technology, even in 1917, that did not stop the British army using them, often alongside newer technology. The juxtaposition is seen in the photograph opposite of a motorcycle despatch rider setting out on his bike, carrying a basket full of carrier pigeons.

The carrier pigeons had to be kept somewhere while they waited to

Fred Leist
Gibraltar, Pozières AWM

Motorcycle despatch rider with
pigeon basket AWM

Fred Leist
The Pigeon Loft AGNSW

Charles Gould
*Extract from Intelligence Report:
'Yesterday two of our pigeons
failed to return'* AWM

fly their missions. For this, the carrier pigeon corps had purpose-built pigeon lofts. These were built on wheels in case mobile warfare should ever resume. Leist painted one of these lofts, complete with its own motorcycle despatch rider.

The carrier pigeons were reluctant participants in the war. When their handlers wanted them to fly home with a message through the chaos and noise of a battle, they sometimes refused to leave the safety of the basket. In this, they were well advised. Not only was shrapnel a hazard for birds, just as it was for men, but the sneaky Germans had brought in hawks to intercept the pigeons on the flight home. Many pigeons were lost.[24] Sometimes, the unfortunate birds could not even trust their own handlers.

The cartoon opposite of two pigeon handlers roasting their pigeons was drawn by CH Gould and published in *From the Australian Front Xmas 1917*, the sequel to *The Anzac Book*.[25] Like so many sequels, it was a disappointment. In the introduction, General Birdwood explained:

At Christmas two years ago, as a result of the hard work of its Editors and other members of the AIF, we were presented with an excellent production in the form of the 'Anzac Book'. That was our second Christmas at war. We are now approaching our fourth, and let us hope it may be the last one during which we find ourselves fighting. Our kind friends have again come forward and presented us with a book, not quite so ambitious as the 'Anzac Book' was, but one which we hope will convey to those whom we left behind in Australia, and who we know are thinking of us, some idea of the surroundings on the battle fronts of the Australians, and which carries with it our whole-hearted hopes and good wishes for those at home.[26]

A major point of difference between *From the Australian Front* and *The Anzac Book* was the generous use of photographs in the second book. With the ban on photography lifted, *From the Australian Front* reproduced photographs taken by the official photographers – Captain F Hurley, Lieutenant E Brooks, Lieutenant HF Baldwin and Lieutenant GH Wilkins AFC.[27] The use of the photographs showed how official attitudes had changed since Gallipoli.[28]

In addition to Gould's pigeon cartoon, *From the Australian Front* included cartoons and black and white drawings by a number of artists who were serving in the ranks, among them: Bernie Bragg, Frank Crozier, John

Cecil Hartt
Sub[altern]: 'Don't you know what to do when you pass an officer? You're a soldier are you not?'
Private Anzac: 'No – I'm a farmer!'

P Davis, LH Howie, P Huthnance, WL King, Allen M Lewi, Vernon Lorimer, S Perks, AH Picking, Alf Saville and Stuart Shaw.[29] Will Dyson contributed one drawing and Daryl Lindsay three.

In 1917, Cecil L Hartt, a black and white artist serving in the ranks, who had drawn cartoons for the *Clarion* and the *Bulletin* before the war, published a book of cartoons called *Humorosities*. It was a runaway success, selling more than 60,000 copies at 1s a pop. For Hartt, it was a better business model than giving his cartoons to the AIF to publish.[30]

Hartt's cartoon, 'Officer Saluting', went to the character of the digger. British soldiers were conscripts who were bound to strict disciplinary traditions. Australian soldiers were volunteers who agreed to suspend their normal lives and occupations for as long as it took to finish the job of fighting the Germans. They were disciplined when discipline would help defeat the Germans, but they would not submit to discipline for discipline's sake.

Bean made the character of the digger a central theme of the *Official History*. He devoted pages to describing, always in heroic terms, the 'great-hearted men' of the AIF. For him, the diggers displayed 'qualities of independence, originality, the faculty of rising to an occasion, and loyalty to a "mate", [that] became recognizable as parts of the national character'.[31] The Australian in Hartt's cartoon was a farmer. It was a deliberate choice. Bean also put the Australian bushman on a pedestal: 'The bush still sets the standard of personal efficiency even in the Australian cities. The bushman is the hero of the Australian boy; the arts of the bush life are his ambition'.[32] In different ways, Bean and Hartt both told how Australians were different from the British. While they acknowledged the mother country, they also felt and expressed the sense of an independent Australia.

Like Cecil Hartt, another serving soldier, Penleigh Boyd, published a book of sketches. Boyd explained that the sketches in *Salvage*, mostly made in 1917, were:

done under circumstances scarcely calculated to induce the atmosphere of tranquil detachment from external and material things … necessary for the production of great art. A dugout has generally been my studio and I drew chiefly to occupy my time and thoughts during the long hours of rumbling bombardment overhead.[33]

From his studio in the trenches, Boyd succeeded in capturing the essence of the digger.

Boyd was a member of the Boyd family of artists. His older brother, Merric, was a potter. Another brother, Martin, was a novelist. Penleigh Boyd survived the war, only to be killed in a car accident in 1923, when he was thirty-three.[34]

Artists serving in the ranks envied those in the official scheme. As a wartime job, that of war artist had many advantages – the privileges of rank, a batman and a daily fee that was generous compared to the 6s per day paid to private soldiers in the AIF, and generous to a fault compared to the 1s per day paid to medical orderlies at Wandsworth Hospital.[35] Since the AIF provided board and lodging, the daily fee – £1 in 1917, doubled to £2 in 1918 – could be devoted to the bar bill.

The selection process for the official scheme was opaque, to say the least. Fisher and Smart did not spell out the qualifications required to be appointed as an official war artist. They did not advertise the positions and did not engage experts to suggest who might be suitable for appointment. They kept the selection process very much to themselves. They seem to have identified the artists between themselves, leaving Smart to approach the artists behind closed doors.

Some of the artists who had given hard service in the ranks believed they had earned the privilege of appointment under the scheme, but were not invited to apply. They were disgruntled, and with good reason. On 4 December 1916, two weeks before Dyson arrived in France, Bean met with Smart. At the meeting, Smart told Bean of the proposal for Leist to paint in France in 1917. Bean wrote in his diary that:

I must say I feel a little jealous for the Anzac Book artists. They have been through the turmoil – they began at the beginning – old Crozier enlisted as a private in the infantry; here is this bumptious chap [Leist] coming straight into a job which they have asked for for ages … He may turn out a great picture, but it is the others who have seen the events – Pozières and Anzac.[36]

Streeton, in particular, had given hard service. The work at Wandsworth had affected his health so badly that he had been hospitalised twice, and invalided out of the Royal Army Medical Corps.[37] On 10 July 1917, he wrote to Fisher, asking for information about the plan for sending Australian artists to France. Smart replied on 20 July 1917, explaining how the scheme would work in future: five or six Australian artists would be sent to France, each for periods of three months, on the terms of the standard-form agreement.[38]

Penleigh Boyd
Digger

On 21 September 1917, a fortnight after Leist and Power left for France, Streeton wrote a curt note to Fisher: 'I wish to notify that I have no further interest in the plan of sending Australian artists to work in France'. Ignoring Streeton's letter, Smart wrote back on 27 September 1917: would Streeton be able to go France in about eight weeks? On 4 October 1917, Streeton replied: 'I can only repeat that my interest in the plan ceased a month ago. I might add that the interest and enthusiasm of other representative Australian artists has dropped also'.[39]

This letter caught Smart's attention. On 11 October 1917, he wrote to Streeton that 'naturally we are very concerned to learn a statement of this sort', and asked: why the change of heart?[40] Streeton took full advantage of the invitation to speak his mind. He wrote to Smart the next day:

Regarding your letter of 11 October, it may assist explanation if I inform you that, in April 1915, several of us, Australian, British and all over military age, enlisted as privates in the Army (3 London General Hospital) when there was an urgent demand for men to live in barracks, draw ½d [halfpenny] pay per day, and help the wounded soldiers, working 10, 12 and 14 hours a day and performing hard duty and dangerous work.

Some may regard this as stupid, others as patriotic, *but we did our duty*, after months of drill beforehand to prepare ourselves for such work.[41]

If you refer to the enclosed list, you will find our artists of all ages have engaged in war work of one kind or another with about the sole exception of the three chosen to represent Australian Art in France.

We are of the opinion that the three artists chosen (our juniors by 10 years) do not fairly represent the best of Australian Fine Art. These roughly are the reasons why your choice has been unpopular with some of our foremost artists.

In my own case, I was most keen to go 8 or 9 months ago when two competent authorities Mr Mackennal ARA MVD and Professor Spencer FRS CMG etc asked Mr Fisher to send me to France. That was my offer of service to Australia.

He, after pressure, so Prof Spencer tells me, promised to refer the matter to Australia, having already sent over Mr Dyson, the fine weather of spring and summer passes and no further word on the matter, save rumours through Mr Dyson who advised us not to rely on anything he [Fisher] told us and he is not a recognised authority on Australian Art.

And so I withdrew my offer of service and notified you that my interest ceased in the matter, and made fresh plans for work which I am now engaged upon.

Next comes your offer to me to go over for 3 months of winter, an impossible time for such work. No Sir: I'm clean off it.

Yours faithfully
Arthur Streeton[42]

The enclosed list was as follows:

War Work by Australian Artists in London				
Coates	Over Age	Enlisted	RAMC	April 1915
Roberts (1 son in war)	Over Age	Enlisted	RAMC	April 1915
Fullwood	Over Age	Enlisted	RAMC	April 1915
Streeton	Over Age	Enlisted	RAMC	April 1915
Blashki	Over Age	Enlisted	RAMC	April 1915
Burgess	Military Age	Enlisted	Navy	April 1915
Mrs Coates	–	Enlisted	Munitions	April 1915
Mackennal	Over Age	Enlisted	Police Duty	April 1915
Longstaff (3 sons in war)	Over Age	Enlisted	Police Duty	April 1915
Bell	Military Age	Enlisted	Munitions	1916
Lambert (1 son in war)	Over Age	Enlisted	Horse breaking & timber getting	1916
Daplyn[43]	Over Age	Enlisted	Splint making	1917

Commissioned by Hon Andrew Fisher to go to France and draw and paint records of the War for 3 months. Allowance for expenses £30. Pay £1 per day. All work to be the property of the Commonwealth Government:-

Dyson	Understood to be of military age	Commissioned	July 1917
Leist	Understood to be of military age	Commissioned	September 1917
Power	Understood to be of military age	Commissioned	September 1917

P.S. It might interest you to have an individual expression of opinion in the matter from the Australian Artists themselves – Mr Mackennal, our chairman, would no doubt be glad to give you any assistance.[44]

Streeton made three big points: the artists left behind had done their patriotic duty – this gave them a higher claim to be appointed to paint the war than the artists already sent to France; the artists left behind were better artists than those sent to France; and Fisher had botched the administration of the scheme by failing to select the best and most deserving artists.

In his letter, Streeton claimed to speak on behalf of the other artists, using the words 'we', 'us' and 'our' to refer to unnamed complainants. He singled out Mackennal as one who would support his claims. It was a measure of Streeton's anger that he sent a copy of his letter to the *Argus* newspaper in Melbourne, although he later claimed to have done this at the request of Coates, Fullwood and Quinn.[45]

Streeton was invited to Australia House to discuss the matter. It was a willing and unhappy discussion, during which Streeton repeated to Smart that he would not go to France.[46]

On 28 November 1917, Streeton wrote the first part of a long letter to Sir Baldwin Spencer. Spencer was an English-born biologist who held the chair of biology at the University of Melbourne. In addition to his academic interests, Spencer was a patron of the arts and a major collector. He was friendly with the Lindsay bothers, Hans Heysen, Streeton, Roberts and Lambert. In his capacity as a trustee of the National Gallery of Victoria, he had travelled to England in 1916 to select advisers for that gallery's Felton Bequest trustees.[47]

Streeton's letter not only gave an account of the meeting at Australia House, it ranged widely over the arts scene in wartime England. The big story was the Canadian war art scheme. The Canadians had put together a major exhibition of Canadian war photographs which started at the Grafton Gallery, in London, and then toured America and the Canadian provinces. They were using the proceeds of the exhibition to commission the finest English and Canadian artists to make works that would hang in the Canadian Parliament. John, Nevinson, Jack, Orpen and Wood were among the artists participating. The scale and ambition of the Canadian scheme contrasted with the poverty of the Australian scheme:

The Commonwealth Govt. (Fisher) have had 10 months to do something, and they have sent as representing Australia Dyson, Power & Leist (who is son of a German) but is very thick with Mr Smart, a young man who apparently has control of War Records under Fisher – When I refused his offer to go over three months (Dec. Jan. Feb.) the other boys having the Summer & Autumn I told [him] that the interest of the foremost Australians had fallen away – & he was astonished that Leist & Power were not considered superior artists to Longstaff, Lambert, Coates, Quinn & myself – he made me angry and I told him he has chosen the Shirkers, & missed his chance of getting the best men.[48]

Streeton called a meeting of the Australian artists, with a view to boycotting Fisher's scheme and establishing a non-government program similar to the Canadian scheme. He told Spencer that 'The boys backed me up when I proposed this at once', but their enthusiasm soon waned. By the time Streeton finished his letter to Spencer on 15 December 1917, he had to report:

Since writing the foregoing my backing has fallen away, & there seems not sufficient Public spirit to carry out a scheme like Canada's. We in Australia take a back seat after Canada. So I've given up my single handed (almost) agitation, & I suppose I am now very unpopular at Australia House.[49]

This moment of insight – perhaps rare for Streeton – signified that he would have to work on his 'other plans', which were to 'work for Canada … & afterwards [I] *may* do one or two *small* ones for Australia'.[50]

The *Argus* published Streeton's letter to Smart on 17 December 1917, under cover of a note from Streeton saying that his letter would 'explain the resentment of some foremost Australian painters at the choice of artists to go to France and produce artistic records of the war for the Commonwealth government'.[51] In truth, the resentment towards Dyson needed no explanation. Streeton's letter effectively accused Dyson of being a slacker and slackers were universally condemned.

Will Dyson's brother sent him a copy of the letter in the *Argus*. Dyson, in London, and angry at being singled out as a slacker, called a meeting at the Chelsea Arts Club.[52] He, Leist and Power demanded retractions. Streeton refused. He was on strong ground in his argument with Dyson, but he had been wrong to attack Leist and Power. Aged forty-one in 1914, Leist was over military age. Power had volunteered, but had been rejected on account of his deafness. Whatever Dyson may have been, Streeton had no case that Leist and Power were slackers.

In the result, Streeton published a retraction in the *Argus*. He acknowledged that Leist was over military age, and that he had done war work, designing recruiting posters. He also acknowledged that Power had

THE SLACKERS ON THE BEACH.
FIRST: *Ullo! There's a chap out there in difficulties!"*
SECOND: *"By Jove, so there is. Oh, well, I 'ope 'e pulls through all right!"*

Norman Lindsay
The Slackers on the Beach
First: 'Ullo! There's a chap out there in difficulties!'
Second: 'By Jove, so there is. Oh, well, I 'ope 'e pulls through all right!'

volunteered for enlistment in the British army, but had been rejected. As to Dyson, Streeton said: 'Mr Dyson went to France December 1916 as war artist for Australia when refused as private. Engaged in propaganda war work since the outbreak of war; twice wounded'.[53]

Dyson's zeal to set the record straight did not extend to telling Streeton that he had refused to be drafted, or that he had asked the local tribunal to excuse him from serving as a private in the ranks. It did not extend to telling Streeton that he had fixed it for Colonel Anderson to write to the local tribunal on his behalf, or that the tribunal had disallowed his claim for exemption. If Dyson had disclosed these facts, Streeton would never have retracted, and with good reason. No retraction was required or deserved. Was Dyson refused as private? Not by the British army.

Was Dyson a slacker? He fought hard to avoid serving as a private in the ranks of the British army and the life in the trenches that may have followed. Enlisting as an honorary lieutenant in the war artists' program of the Australian army, Dyson did not go so far as to join the slackers on the beach in Norman Lindsay's cartoon, but he did engineer a much softer posting for himself than he would have had as a private in the British army. By contrast with Dyson, the artists serving as medical orderlies at Wandsworth were under no obligation to enlist, but they volunteered for hard service as private soldiers in the hospital wards. It is difficult to imagine Dyson swapping places with them, much as they wanted to swap places with Dyson.

Dyson touted patriotic views in support of the war and the men who fought it, yet went to great lengths to avoid joining them in the ranks. It was a curious working out of his socialist ideology that he should privilege himself to draw the war, but not to fight in it.[54]

As 1917 drew to an end, hostilities on the Western Front wound down. The weather in Europe made it impossible to fight over the winter months.

Hostilities on the artists' front came to an end at much the same time. Streeton's agitation had run its course. A boycott of Fisher's scheme was no longer on the cards, but none of the artists was prepared to go to France just yet – all insisted on waiting for some better weather. On

28 December 1917, Smart reported to Bean that:

They have all been invited to go, including Streeton, Longstaff, Spence, Full-wood and Bell. None of them will go in the winter. As soon as the weather im-proves, I suggest we invite Streeton, Fullwood and Longstaff to go over. Indeed, I have already asked them to do so. Streeton has been very troublesome. I am told he has attempted to induce the other artists not to accept our offer from the start, but we have broken the combination down.[55]

11 THE MIDDLE EAST

IN WHICH GEORGE LAMBERT EMERGES FROM THE FORESTS
OF WALES TO WORK AS A WAR ARTIST IN THE MIDDLE EAST.

*L*ate in 1917, Smart wrote once more to Bean, saying: 'It has occurred to me that it will be a good thing to send an artist to Palestine to paint AIF stuff. There is not likely to be much work for our artists in France during the winter. Perhaps it would do if we sent one artist to France and one or two to Egypt'.[1] Bean agreed. He asked Smart to find an artist willing to go.

George Lambert had been working as a divisional works officer in a timber-getting operation in Wales. The timber was used to produce pit props, picket stakes and wire entanglement poles with pointed ends. The off-cuts were used to make ash, which in turn was used in the manufacture of aeroplanes. Lambert had once worked in the Australian bush. He drew on that experience, 'making roads practicable, throwing rough but serviceable bridges over awkward passages where hauling heavy loads would have been difficult or impossible, inspecting the working facilities of water or steam sawmills, arranging for water transport wherever possible'.[2] It was tough, physical work and Lambert, ever the man's man, did not hesitate to do his share. In time, his health suffered.

Lambert had received an offer from the Canadians to paint a 'battle-picture' for their scheme. The offer was attractive: a major's commission; £40 per month, plus allowances; £50 for expenses and, as the Canadians boasted in their letter of offer, their scheme was 'going to be the biggest thing in Art that has ever been done and you really cannot afford to be out of it'.[3] It was a better deal than Smart offered when he wrote to Lambert on 23 November 1917 asking him to go to France with a lieutenant's commission on the modest terms of the Australian scheme. On 4 December 1917, however, Smart changed his offer. He asked Lambert if he would go to Palestine to make sketches of the operations of the AIF there. Lambert agreed.

Lambert was presented with two agreements. The first was the standard-form agreement, adapted for Palestine. The second was for a commission painting of the cavalry charge that the men of the Australian Light Horse made when they took Beersheba as recently as 31 October 1917. The price for this painting would be £500 – a figure that did rival the offer from the Canadians.[4]

Lambert left London on Christmas Day 1917. He travelled by train to Southampton for the crossing to Cherbourg, then by train to Taranto in southern Italy. From there, he went by boat to Alexandria, making the final stage of his journey to Cairo by train. Thanks to a lively imagination, Lambert derived more enjoyment from exotic locations than the average traveller. It was a release beyond dreams to be liberated from the forests of Wales and the miseries of the British winter and delivered into the bazaars of Cairo, and Lambert was soon working his way down a list of Australian 'must-do' activities in Cairo: a room at Shepheard's Hotel, the best hotel in Cairo; 'a bottle of the best by way of cleaning the palate from the after-taste of ship's cabin and train compartment'; and a visit to the Wazza.[5] The Wazza's real name was 'Haret el Wasser'. It was a street of brothels 'in a low quarter of Cairo', not far from Shepheard's Hotel.[6]

It was at the Wazza, on Good Friday in 1915, that an Anzac force first saw action. It was also the occasion of Bean's first battlefield report. Bean reported that, on the day they received their orders to leave for the front, 'a few Australian and New Zealand soldiers determined to exact some sort of punishment for certain injuries which they believed themselves to have incurred at some of the brothels'. Alcohol may conceivably have played a part, but Bean absolved the drinkers and instead blamed the 'bad drink sold in the neighbourhood [which] led this demonstration to greater lengths than were intended – beds, mattresses and clothing from several houses were thrown out of the windows and piled in a bonfire in the street'. The Anzacs found the bonfire a pleasing spectacle, so much so that 'The native Egyptian fire brigade which was rather pluckily trying to put out the bonfire was … roughly handled'. British military police were called – 'always a red rag to the Australian soldier'. The police fired their revolvers, intending to disperse the crowd, but the shooting had the opposite effect, attracting a bigger and rowdier crowd, who came to watch and join the fun.[7] Outnumbered, the hated police withdrew, leaving the Anzacs to celebrate their first victory.

The battle went into Anzac legend as '1st Wazza'. A follow-up battle, '2nd Wazza', similar in scale and nature to 1st Wazza, came some months later.[8]

Lambert saw himself as an artist-historian charged with recording the truth about the Anzacs.[9] True to his brief, he had to paint the place where the diggers first saw action.

What was remarkable about Lambert's Wazza painting was his use of pastel shades, more reminiscent of a French village than the seamy side of Cairo. Bean compared the Wazza battles to university 'rags'.[10] Lambert's painting conveyed a similar light-hearted sense. The Wazza battle was nothing to be proud of, but the score line – Colonials 1 : British MPs 0 – was.[11]

The AIF was a small world.[12] It was difficult to go far without bumping into old friends. On 15 January 1918, Lambert met up with a mate: 'I am sitting in Banjo Paterson's tent! … I am ridiculously happy. Already I have done three pieces of work and everywhere I look there are glorious pictures, magnificent men and real top-hole Australian horses'.[13]

Lambert and Paterson were kindred spirits. Lambert had earlier illustrated Paterson's ballad, *Clancy of the Overflow*, as well as an essay Paterson had written on buffalo shooting.[14] He also painted a portrait of Paterson's wife, in return for which the Banjo wrote:

An Essay on Australian Art and Literature.
In recognition of Lambert's really excellent portrait of Mrs Paterson

Come all ye men of paint and pen.
Who toil with hand and brain.
Forsake the town and take the brown
And dusty roads again.
The tracks that we old-timers know,
Who showed you all the way to go
With Clancy of the Overflow
Across the Black Soil Plain.[15]

Lambert painted the AIF base at Moascar. The camp was a few minutes' walk from Ismalia, on the Suez Canal. Fresh from the English winter, Lambert found 'miles of tents and desert, thousands of sweating sun-bronzed men and beautiful horses. The miles of tents out there give the artist a continuous but ever-changing problem in colour, line and form'. He marvelled at the colours, noting in his diary: 'the gorgeous colour of the Orient'; the 'gay colour of the native costume'; the 'oriental

George Lambert
Major Andrew Barton (Banjo)
Paterson AWM

George Lambert
The Wassah, Cairo AWM

grandeur of Egypt, past and present, stimulating in its kaleidoscopic colour-pattern'; and 'fruits and vegetables, colourful and refreshing'. Ismalia boasted a salt lake and green, tropical gardens. Lambert found it a 'delightful place for an artist who likes typical Egyptian colour and peoples'.[16]

Lambert painted the camp, with a horse in the foreground, as seen from Banjo Paterson's tent. It was a sketch made in oil on the lid of a

Walter Di Qual
The Sinai Peninsula

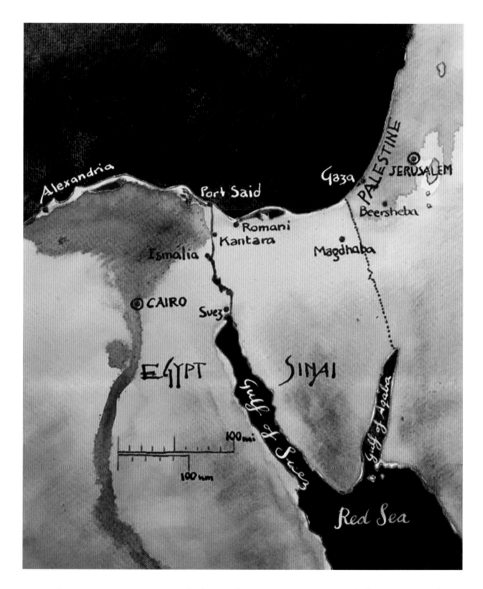

cigar box – reminiscent of the *9 by 5 Impression Exhibition*. Lambert wrote that he was painting 'with a speed never before achieved by me'.[17] The sketch, on the opposite page, suggests that speed brought clarity.

From Ismalia, Lambert headed north to another camp at Kantara. Here he encountered camels: 'beautiful to draw and paint, but ... an animal one cannot love', adding, in case anyone was tempted, 'never attempt to caress a camel'.[18] In Kantara, Lambert came across the re-doubtable Mrs Chisholm. She was the centre of an inspiring group of women, as the *Official History* later acknowledged:

Mrs Alice Chisholm's work was a very bright example of the devotion of Australia's womanhood to the distant troops. Early in the war, this Sydney lady, on her own initiative and mainly with her own money, established a canteen at Heliopolis [in Cairo]. Soon after the mounted troops moved into Sinai, Miss Rout, a New Zealander, opened an advanced canteen at Kantara, practically in defiance of the army leaders; but, falling ill, she handed it over to Mrs Chisholm, who meanwhile had shifted her canteen to Port Said, where many Australians and New Zealanders spent their brief periods of leave. The venture at Kantara was joined by Miss Rania McPhillamy, the daughter of a well-known pastoralist in the Forbes district of New South Wales, and was so welcomed by the lonely troops that its expansion was of a remarkable character. Soon these two noble Australian women were at the head of a large establishment which, employing a great staff, made up mainly of Egyptians, was able to supply meals and refreshments to thousands of troops daily. British and Australians were treated alike; and at one time, when an infantry division was in camp on the Canal, the canteen was cooking upwards of sixty thousand eggs a day.[19]

How resourceful were these three women? Not only did they find their way from Australia to the heart of the Egyptian desert; they also found 60,000 eggs to sell – per day – in the canteen they established there.

Lambert stayed in the Officers' Rest at Kantara. It was part of Mrs Chisholm's canteen: 'Here,' said Lambert:

one could halt and have a bath and good food. It had a touch of home, so pleasant, so grateful. When I asked her for a sitting, she modestly protested that she was not important enough. I got her to sit in a strong light; she had an interest-

George Lambert
Moascar, from Major 'Banjo'
Paterson's Tent AWM

George Lambert
Mrs Chisholm of Kantara AWM

George Lambert
*Romani, Mount Royston in
Background* AWM

ing care-worn face, and a very charming personality, and her portrait was one of the best of my carefully-made drawings.[20]

Lambert's sketch not only brought out the character of the sitter; it was a showpiece of his skill at drawing.

All of the ladies in the desert went on to bigger and better things. Mrs Chisholm became Dame Alice Chisholm;[21] Miss McPhillamy opened a branch of the canteen in Jerusalem – this time, 'with General Allenby's cordial approval and assistance';[22] and the eponymous Miss Rout became famous as a campaigner against sexually transmitted diseases. She moved to Paris where she met the leave trains to give the men free condoms before they headed off for a week's leave in Paris.[23]

From Kantara, Lambert crossed the Suez Canal and moved east across the northern part of the Sinai Peninsula. He went first to Romani, where the Light Horse had fought the Turks in August 1916. He made a rough sketch in oil on a wood panel.

Lambert found painting at Romani hard going.

A word to those who would paint this country. Leave your gay pigments at home. Approach Nature with a simple palette but an extravagant love of form.

The sand-hills take on shapes and curves, cuts concave and convex, interwoven in an entrancing pattern, here rhythmical, there jagged and eccentrically opposed. With all the knowledge the artist may, nay must, bring to bear, he need only copy and he achieves art; but it takes doing.[24]

The journey continued by camel to Magdhaba. On a halt to water the camels, Lambert painted another oil, this time on a maple board. He held it to be his 'sincerest and most successful effort'.

The painting is tiny, only 19 × 24 centimetres, and unfinished. According to Lambert:

It was painted in the heat of the day, a breathless heat that made the camels

George Lambert
*Wadi Bed between El Arish and
Magdhaba* AWM

lie down and look more sorry for themselves than usual. Myriads of flies, seeing both my hands busily engaged, settled down and enjoyed an almost uninterrupted feast on the perspiration that literally saturated every stitch of my uniform, including leggings and boots. Despite these difficulties and that curse of the official artist, the sense of hurry caused by having to work to military schedule, I accomplished my six by four masterpiece.[26]

Why did Lambert regard this as a masterpiece? It had none of the polish of his studio paintings. Yet, in its brevity, it captured the moment when it was made. It was an impression in the sense in which Roberts used the word – momentary, faithful and fleeting.[27] Critics would never pick it as a masterpiece, but artists judge their work differently than critics. They compare what was achieved with what was possible. By Lambert's standard, *Wadi Bed* was a masterpiece – in the circumstances of its making, it achieved all that was possible.

The main purpose of Lambert's trip was to gather material to use in making his commissioned painting of the charge at Beersheba. The Beersheba battle was the culmination of a long campaign against the Turks. The crisis of the battle was the charge of the Australian Light Horse, in which the light-horsemen took their horses at full gallop straight at the machine guns and artillery protecting the Turkish trenches. Trooper Ion Idriess was an eyewitness to the charge. No one dreamed, he wrote:

that mounted troops would be madmen enough to attempt rushing infantry redoubts protected by machine-guns and artillery. At a mile distant their thousand hooves were stuttering thunder, coming at a rate that frightened a man – they were an awe-inspiring sight, galloping through the red haze – knee to knee and horse to horse – the dying sun glinting on bayonet points. Machine-guns and rifle fire just roared but the 4th Brigade galloped on.

The Turks did their best to withstand the charge, but their gunners lost the range of the advancing horsemen, and fired high, over the heads of the men and their horses. When the light-horsemen cleared the trenches, the game was up. The victory at Beersheba was everything the Western Front had not been. It was open warfare trumping the trenches. It was the Australian Light Horse bidding defiance to the guns and cannons of modern warfare. It was the Australian bushman showing his true colours.

Lambert's challenge was to capture in his painting the energy that Idriess conveyed so strongly. Lambert worked hard to gain an understanding of the battlefield, making pencil surveys and sketching the landscape. The Turkish trenches were still visible. Lambert rode over them, imagining them filled with Turks, their bayonets fixed. From his own experience as a horseman, he could gauge the force with which the charge was carried through. The conclusions he drew from his observations were reinforced by the fact that, against all the odds, the casualties were very few.[29] While he sketched and painted the trenches at Beersheba, for the most part he drew the horses that would be the painting's main focus.

Lambert's tour of the Middle East ended in May 1918. As he left Cairo, he deposited 117 pieces with the Australian Depot Stores.

Lambert was the only Australian official war artist who was invited to paint in the Middle East during the war. In that situation, as art critic Bernard Smith had said of Roberts, Lambert was painting 'important historical records [that showed] an important aspect of Australian life during a significant phase of its development'.[30] Lambert went to great pains to ensure the accuracy of his drawings. His sketches gave him a record of the countryside and the topography. The subjects of his sketches – the desert, the horses, and the men of the Light Horse – were reminiscent of his youth. According to JS MacDonald, Lambert found his work in the Middle East entirely congenial:

Among his beloved horses, he was in his element, and once more he moved in light, and an atmosphere such as he had known and loved in his station days. The horsemen, too, absorbingly interested him; the inimitable 'mounted Diggers'; and Lambert sketched them from every angle, in oil and pencil.[31]

When Fisher suggested the appointment of Dyson as the first Australian official war artist, he told Pearce that the artist would 'gather impressions of Australians at war from an Australian point of view ... in sketches illustrating [the] relationship of the Australians to the war and interpreting character of Australian troops which would be [a] valuable record'.[32] He did not attempt to weigh the artists down with the burden of historical accuracy. They were free to create an artist's record – interpretative and impressionistic. Lambert, more than most, aimed to create a faithful record, striving, at once, to achieve accuracy and a worthwhile painting.

12 FACE WOUNDS

IN WHICH THE ARTISTS MAKE AN UNEXPECTED
CONTRIBUTION – TO THE DEVELOPMENT
OF PLASTIC SURGERY.

Cecil Hartt

'We find the shrapnel helmets very useful'

"We find the shrapnel helmets very useful"

One alarming feature of *The Anzac Book* was that none of the men in it were wearing steel helmets. By turning a blind eye to the casualty counts of the American Civil War and the Russo-Japanese War, the military geniuses on both sides of the Great War sent men to fight wearing cloth or felt hats. It was not until 1916 that steel helmets were issued to the Allied troops. It took two years for the planners to realise that trench warfare and head wounds went hand in glove.

The diggers joked about the shrapnel helmets, but they served a grim, if limited, purpose – they shielded the wearer from shrapnel falling from above. They did not help men who looked above the parapet and were shot in the face. Bullets that travelled through the head from front to back were mostly fatal. Nor did the helmets protect against shrapnel bursting from the side. Shrapnel 'pursued a side to side course', so that 'the mutilation [caused to the face], though frequently great, was not nearly so apt to be fatal'.[1]

Those who survived such injuries confronted a life of shocking disfigurement. Treating men with face wounds was one of the greatest challenges of working in a military hospital. Forms of plastic surgery had been around since antiquity, but the war forced surgeons to come to grips with challenges and complications never before contemplated, and with a volume of cases never before experienced.[2] The institutional response began in January 1916, when surgeons working under Colonel Sir Arbuthnot Lane established wards dedicated to the treatment of wounds of the face and jaw at the Cambridge Hospital at Aldershot in England. The leading light of the medical show was Major Sir Harold Gillies, a New Zealander, who wrote up his wartime experiences in a medical textbook, *Plastic Surgery of the Face*, published in 1920. In it, he described how demand soon overran the facilities at Aldershot. The response was to establish a centre of excellence at Queen Mary's Hospital at Sidcup:

A rapid increase in the scope of the work led to the removal of the hospital to Sidcup, where ... it was placed on an Imperial basis. The collection of the cases of facial injuries from the British, Canadian, Australian and New Zealand forces in one hospital under their own medical officers ... proved a factor of prime importance in the improvement of methods of treatment.[3]

Doctors from all parts of the Empire, wrote Gillies, 'joined heartily in friendly rivalry and healthy competition, to the great benefit of these poor *mutilées*'. Gillies himself invented new methods and treatments. It 'was largely due to him that such rapid progress was effected in this special and difficult form of surgery, of which little or nothing was known before the war. Methods were employed and scrapped with great rapidity as improvements were devised'.[4] In 1917, an Australian facio-maxillary unit was formed at Sidcup under Lieutenant Colonel Sir Henry Newland.[5]

As the surgeons developed new operating techniques, they needed to record what they had done for medical posterity. Photography could not always deliver the clarity required, so the surgeons turned to artists to draw their operations. The first artist chosen was Henry Tonks, who was uniquely qualified for the job. In addition to being Professor of Fine Art at the Slade School and a member of the Chelsea Arts Club, Tonks had studied medicine as a young man, becoming a Fellow of the Royal College of Surgeons in 1888. He taught anatomy at the London Hospital Medical School. His knowledge of anatomy was one of his strengths as a drawing master. Working for Gillies, he was able to combine his skills as artist and anatomist.[6] As Gillies wrote in his textbook:

Not a small feature in the development of [the work at Sidcup] is the compilation of case records. The foundation of the graphic method of recording these cases lies to the credit of Professor H Tonks (Slade Professor), many of whose diagrams and photographs of his remarkable pastel drawings adorn these pages.[7]

Newland and the Australian facio-maxillary unit followed a similar approach in recording their work. As Newland wrote: 'The work carried out was carefully recorded, and was illustrated by the photographic department of the hospital and by the Australian section's own artist'. The artist was Daryl Lindsay.[8]

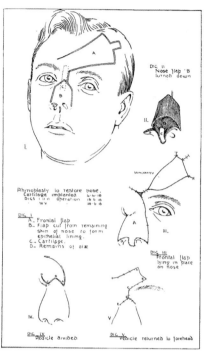

DIAGRAM 3
RHINOPLASTY AFTER LOW NASAL LOSS

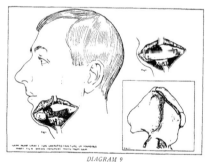

DIAGRAM 9
Graft from the iliac crest (the fragment taken is outlined).

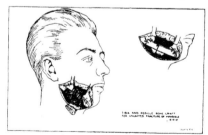

DIAGRAM 10
Graft from tibia with pedicle.
FRACTURES OF THE MANDIBLE

To face p. 321

On leave in London in 1918, Lindsay ran into Colonel Jock Anderson at AIF Headquarters in Horseferry Road.[9] Anderson asked: 'You can draw, can't you?' When Lindsay agreed, Anderson took him to see General Sir Neville Howse VC, the director of medical services of the AIF.[10] Howse told Lindsay that Newland 'wanted someone urgently who could do medical diagrams'. He asked Lindsay to go to Sidcup to meet Newland. At their meeting, Lindsay told Newland that he knew little of anatomy and doubted he could do the job, but Newland asked him to give it a go.[11]

'Smothered in gown and cap', Lindsay spent his first day on the job with Newland in the operating theatre. Newland told him:

that he was going to do the second stage of a rhinoplasty for the restoration of the nose; he said I could leave if it upset me. I had seen a good deal of blood one way and another, and it did not worry me. He got to work explaining a point here and there, but mainly he was absorbed in the job. I became fascinated by his dexterity, but I was really more concerned with my own thoughts: how was I going to translate what looked like a mess of flesh and blood into a diagram that a student could understand?[12]

Lindsay became deeply interested in the work. He and Newland would 'stay up half the night trying to reduce a complicated plastic operation to diagrammatical terms that could be understood by other surgeons and students'.[13] Lindsay's diagrams appeared in the section Newland later wrote of the *Official Australian Medical History of the Great War*.[14]

Sidcup brought together a rare array of talent. For Lindsay, Gillies was the brightest star. He was 'not only the greatest plastic surgeon of his day but a versatile artist in more ways than one: a landscape painter of no mean ability who exhibited at the Royal Academy, a golfer and skater with an international reputation, an excellent actor and a born mimic'. Henry Tonks, too, had an enviable list of achievements as surgeon, teacher, and artist. Tonks did not spare Lindsay's feelings when he gave opinions of his drawing. One day, when Lindsay was drawing, he:

became aware of being overlooked by a tall, hatchet-faced man, who looked like a cross between a Roman emperor and a wedge-tailed eagle. He asked me what I was doing and I said: 'Trying to draw.' He said, 'I'm glad you say "trying" which is the best that can be said of it; but I think I may be able to help you.'[15]

Newland gave Lindsay leave to go to the Slade once a week to study with Tonks. When Tonks criticised one of Lindsay's attempts, Lindsay replied: 'I'm sorry, but I don't know what you are talking about. I know the meaning of the words, but not their application to art'. His fellow students thought that this would be the end of Lindsay as a student, but it led to his being invited to dinner at Tonks' house – a rare privilege for a mere student. Lindsay found Tonks:

without exception the most interesting and remarkable man I ever met. He was a great student, widely read in the classics and the best modern writers. He had no time for half-baked intellectuals. He was a magnificent draughtsman, and possibly the finest teacher that England has produced in the last hundred years.

Lindsay and Tonks became lifelong friends.[16]

Whilst the pioneering work was done at Sidcup, the surgeons at Wandsworth put the innovations into daily practice. Tom Roberts saw some of that work in the dental surgery. In an article for the *Gazette*, Roberts described the work of the dental surgeons. On a single Sunday, they dealt with twenty cases. One man had been shot through the lower jaw, so that the two sides of his jaw worked independently. The surgeons built a splint to hold the jaw together and built up the jaw so that it looked almost normal. The lower jaw of a second man had been shot away. The surgeons brought the jaw into position and built it up to preserve the bite, in spite of the loss of bone. A third man had injuries that were worse still:

the whole upper jaw and left eye [had been] carried away, leaving only one thing human-looking, on a strange front to the man's head, an eye – an eye that, through the pain, the operations, stayed bright. Now a Palate has been introduced, a nose made up, the cheek built up by plastic operation by the surgeon in charge, and there will be a presentable face. The clear eye – the very expression of patience and cheeriness – twinkles, as the dental surgeon says, he will make a good-looking chap yet, and a queer voice comes out: *It'll be all right. I never was a Don Juan.*[17]

Simply looking at the faces of the damaged men involved a risk of betraying, by an expression of horror, how awful their appearance was. Ward Muir, editor of the *Gazette*, wrote that 'Hideous is the only word for the smashed faces' – a small slit where an eye once was, a skewed mouth or, 'worse, far the worst, the brutalising effects which are the consequences of wounds of the nose … which reach a climax of mournful grotesquerie when the nose is missing altogether'.[18]

The damage to some men was so great that, even with the best the

Daryl Lindsay
Diagram 3 Rhinoplasty after Low Nasal Loss AWM

Daryl Lindsay
Diagram 9 Fracture of the Mandible AWM

Daryl Lindsay
Diagram 10 Fracture of the Mandible AWM

Derwent Wood at Wandsworth
AWM

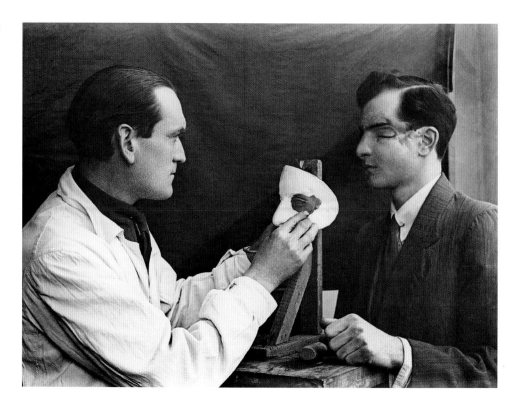

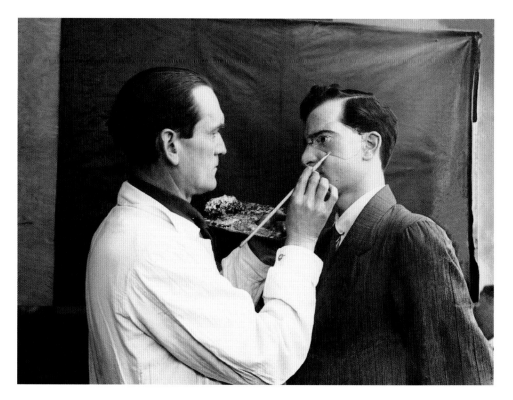

surgeons could offer, they dared not go into society for fear that their faces would frighten the citizens. What could the hospital do for them?

Derwent Wood was using his skills a sculptor to make splints for broken bones, working as a sergeant in the hospital's splint room. He realised that he could help the men with face wounds by making face masks, not dissimilar to those made famous in *The Phantom of the Opera*. Bruce-Porter saw the potential and exploited it. With funding from the Benevolent Fund, Bruce-Porter formed a new department, under Derwent Wood, to make the masks. Overnight, Sergeant Derwent Wood became Captain Derwent Wood, officer in charge of the Masks for Facial Disfigurement Department. The men disliked the title of the new clinic. They renamed it the 'Tin Noses Shop'.[19] Ward Muir devoted a chapter of the *Happy Hospital* to describing the new shop:

In the workshop we encounter a Lance-Corporal who, as a civilian, was a sculptor's moulder by trade – not a job learnt in a day. He presides over a bench, a litter of esoteric implements, a bag of plaster of Paris, some plasticine, a sink and a geyser for hot water. In the studio we find the sculptor (but a sculptor attired as a Captain of the British Army); and likewise, some of his odd sculptures, frail little painted bits of human visages, some with neat moustaches and pairs of spectacles attached to them; and on the walls a frieze of souvenirs in the shape of casts of those visages, with photographs of the owners in the flesh – the 'before' and 'after' records which so promptly demolish the criticisms of the theorising objector.[20]

Wood's technique was so well received in medical circles that the editors of the *Lancet*, the leading medical journal, invited him to write it up in one of its 1917 issues:

I endeavour by means of the skill I happen to possess as a sculptor to make a man's face as near as possible to what it looked like before he was wounded. My cases are generally extreme cases that plastic surgery has, perforce, had to abandon; but, as in plastic surgery, the psychological effect is the same. The patient acquires his old self-respect, self-assurance, self-reliance, and, discarding his induced despondency, takes once more to a pride in his personal appearance. His presence is no longer a source of melancholy to himself nor of sadness to his relatives and friends.[21]

The technique involved making a mask of the patient's face in plaster of Paris. Using pre-wound photographs of the patient, the mask was built up to resemble his old face. The model was used to create a copper electrotype plate, to which the fittings for a glass eye were added before the whole model was silver-plated. The mask was attached to the face, generally using spectacles to secure it in place. Finally, it was painted with the features matching those of the patient.[22]

Bruce-Porter described two of Derwent Wood's cases:

Tpr E had a severe injury to his face, which resulted in the loss of his nose and the opening up of the nasal cavity from the side. After the surgeons had done their best for him by plastic operation, the patient was still in such a condition that it was not possible for him to follow his former occupation of cab driver. Derwent Wood has fitted him with an artificial nose and moustache so successfully that he has resumed his old job, and at a very short distance it is impossible to notice the injury. Sgt F had a more extensive injury, resulting in the loss of one eye and cheek. The process of repair has been more complicated in this case, and called for the sculptor's art in building up in plasticine the side of the face so as to get the plate to match the other side of the face. An artificial eye is carried in the mask, and this man will be able to walk about the world without calling for comment.[23]

Derwent Wood was undertaking groundbreaking work. Bruce-Porter, a man of vision and a true leader, was optimistic about its prospects:

The soldier is by nature independent, and the men who had the pluck to throw up their jobs and go to the help of the country are not the men who will wish to exist on pensions granted by the Government; they will prefer to resume their former tasks when possible. The formation of this new department will, I am sure, make this possible for many. In addition to the practical side is the aesthetic side, and a properly modelled portion of face carrying an artificial eye to match the remaining eye will be a great advance on the old-fashioned vulcanite shield.[24]

Bruce-Porter gave the doctor's viewpoint. Technically, no doubt, he was correct. But the gift that Wood was able to give these men – the confidence to walk down the street again – was deeply human. According to Muir, 'the doctor, the surgeon, the masseur, the dentist – all our specialists' came to watch and admire Derwent Wood at work. It was a curious crossing over. Wood was outside the domain of the medical men and they were outside his – 'For they are scientists and he is – simply – an artist'.[25]

13   AWAY FROM THE FRONT

IN WHICH THE SEARCH FOR PAINTINGS
OF THE HOME FRONT REVEALS A
SURPRISINGLY BARE CUPBOARD.

*T*he war closed down large parts of the art market. Many Australian artists stopped painting for the duration of the war. Many were in the AIF. Artists who could not join the AIF because they were too old, unfit or not men did war work, often in hospitals, in munitions, or in civil defence. A few artists continued to paint – John Longstaff and Norman Lindsay were two of them.

One barometer of the Australian art world was the magazine, *Art in Australia*, first published in 1916.[1] It made no mention of the war until its fifth number, which was published in 1918. It contained a short article complaining that the Australian official war artists' scheme was not up to the standard of the Canadian scheme. It was not until the sixth number, published in 1919, that there was comprehensive coverage of war art. Until then, the magazine served up a safe diet of landscapes, portraits and etchings that artists working in Australia were producing. Judging by the contents of *Art in Australia*, the war was not a subject that Australian artists were happy to paint. Perhaps they found it too confronting.

Some artists took advantage of the brisk trade in portraits of young men in uniform. Dora Coates' *Leaving for the Front* gave a sentimental treatment to the theme of a man leaving his family to go to the front. Hilda Rix Nicholas tried to catch the sense of bereavement in her work following the death of her husband. George Coates and Rupert Bunny painted wounded men in the course of medical treatment. Henry Fullwood painted or drew scenes that emphasised the industrial nature of the systems developed to handle the streams of wounded men.

The effects of the war were not limited to the front line. They reached throughout society. It is odd, therefore, that few artists painted what was happening behind the scenes, away from the front.

Iso Rae
Rue de la Gare (Station Street) AWM

Iso Rae
Étaples, 1915 NGA

The war changed Étaples from a sleepy seaside town to a busy military base. Situated on the north-western coast of France, about 125 kilometres from the Somme Valley front, it became the site of a major British base that served as a railhead and supply depot for the entire Western Front. The base included a hospital and a camp, where men returning to the front underwent final conditioning training before they joined their units. 'The Bullring' was the name given to the area where the most rigorous training took place. It was especially unpopular.

Most of the British artists who painted in Étaples before the war had fled to England when the war broke out, but Australian painter, Iso Rae, continued to live there throughout the war. She sketched the British camp. Her sketch of the *Rue de la Gare* under wartime conditions showed soldiers of many nationalities, including a group of diggers lounging outside the Terminus Café. It was an interesting composition, with the traditional French town buildings in the foreground and the tent city of the base in the background.

Another work by Rae, *Étaples*, is a sketch of tents at the base at night, introducing blue and orange lights into a drab military scene.

Hilda Rix Nicholas made a series of paintings and drawings of French women during her time in Étaples.[2] One of them was a wonderful painting called *A Mother of France 1914*. The painting dates from 1914. Recalling that Rix Nicholas fled Étaples on 2 August 1914, it is a challenge to work out exactly when she painted it.

The Australian War Memorial has the painting. In 1941, the Memorial described it as a painting of 'an old French woman, resigned in her existence but not broken by it [who] had twice seen the invader desecrate her native soil. In 1914 war laid claim to her sons just as in 1870 it called her husband'.[3] On that view of it, Hilda must have made the painting in England between August and December 1914, amid the turmoil of her sister's death, which is possible, but seems unlikely. The Memorial has changed the wording in its current catalogue, describing the painting as 'a comment on the grief of mothers whose sons are killed in war'.[4] It seems more likely that Hilda made the painting in Étaples before the war broke out, in which case it was not painted as a comment on wartime grief, leastwise not about grief caused by the Great War, nor on the death of the poor lady's sons.

Hilda Rix Nicholas
A Mother of France 1914 AWM

Thea Proctor
Stunting NGA

Grace Cossington Smith
The Sock Knitter AGNSW

Grace Cossington Smith
Reinforcements: Troops Marching
AGNSW

The emergence of the aeroplane as a weapon of war led to air raids on London. By 1917, air raids were common, and they did considerable damage. As the war progressed, night raids became increasingly common, and searchlights were used to defend against them. On leave in London in September 1917, Gunner Arthur Howell complained that 'the only thing which seems to concern the Londoner is the likelihood of an air raid, but still there are some who regard an air raid as some special form of excitement arranged for their special benefit'.[5] He might have been talking about Thea Proctor, whose 1918 lithograph, *Stunting*, on page 151, shows fashionable women pointing out a plane trapped in spotlights in the night sky.

The lithograph and its racy title downplay the fact that the spotlight operators were trying to shoot the plane out of the sky. WH Downing's dictionary of Great War slang, *Digger Dialects*, offers a definition of 'stunting' and an example of its usage: 'Aerial bombing by night is a "stunt" liberally indulged in by both sides; and to anyone who has once experienced the joke, a second helping is not appreciated'.[6]

Although Thea Proctor was in London throughout most of the war, this lithograph appears to be her only work with a wartime subject.

Grace Cossington Smith, painting in Turramurra on Sydney's North Shore, could not have been much further away from the front line. In 1915, she painted *The Sock Knitter*.

It may not be immediately apparent that *The Sock Knitter* is a war painting. These days, it is probably necessary to point out that it was common in the Great War to knit socks for soldiers at the front, which is what the subject of this painting – Grace's sister, Madge – was doing.[7]

Grace Cossington Smith
The Refugees AGNSW

Grace Cossington Smith's father was once Crown Solicitor of the Colony of New South Wales. He sent Grace to Abbotsleigh, a private school for girls in Sydney's Wahroonga. In 1912, Grace and her sister Mabel travelled to England, returning in April 1914. By 1915, when Grace painted *The Sock Knitter*, the family was living at 43 Kuringai Avenue, Turramurra, which was her home for the rest of her life. Grace was taking classes with Antonio Dattilo-Rubbo. Fortunate to have such a talented student, Rubbo called his prodigy 'Mrs van Gogh', although 'Mrs Cézanne' may have been closer to the mark.[8]

Cossington Smith chose a rather more obviously war-like subject when she painted *Reinforcements: Troops Marching* in 1917.

Both *The Sock Knitter* and *Reinforcements: Troops Marching* are terrific paintings, showing a command of colour and composition. It reflects no credit on the art cognoscenti of Sydney that they allowed such a wonderful artist to fly below the radar for most of her long life.[9]

Striking quite a different note than her paintings, Cossington Smith's 1918 pencil drawing, *The Refugees*, shows a sensitivity for the suffering of the displaced people it portrays.

It is this type of drawing that is largely missing from the output of artists working in Australia during the Great War. Grace Cossington Smith showed that it was perfectly possible to draw and paint wartime subjects from the comfort of a studio in Australia, but her countrymen and women did not rise to the challenge. It was a response of surprising timidity.

14 THE WESTERN FRONT, 1918

IN WHICH THE WAR ARTISTS CAPITALISE ON THE
CHANCE TO SKETCH THE BATTLES THAT ENDED THE WAR.

*T*he trouble with Streeton blew over almost as quickly as it had begun. The final resolution came when Australia House announced that 'every Australian artist with any reputation as an artist' would be invited 'to paint pictures of the operations of the AIF'.[1] With the threat of a boycott withdrawn, Smart invited Charles Bryant, Arthur Streeton and John Longstaff to go to France.

Charles Bryant was the first to go. Fisher and Smart categorised Bryant as a marine artist. They asked him to work on three subjects: the embarkation of Australian wounded on hospital ships in French ports; the disembarkation of AIF men returning from leave; and 'any similar subject of Australian interest', which might include hospital barges. Bryant signed the standard-form agreement on 11 December 1917 and left for the port of Boulogne the next day. He was delayed in starting work while sketching permits were obtained.[2] This was a sensible precaution – artists found sketching French ports without a permit were liable to be arrested as spies.

Bryant handed over twenty-two oil paintings, six watercolours and three sketches when he returned from France three months later, on 15 March 1918.

The oil painting opposite of the funnels of the leave ships showed the bright camouflage colours that the Royal Navy used to paint ships that crossed the Channel.[3] The camouflage paint stood out against the background. Rain lay in puddles on the wharf. The diggers were huddled in greatcoats against the cold. Leave was over. The front was beckoning. Welcome back to France, boys! Bryant's painting not only conveyed

the grim greyness of the French winter, it underlined the good sense of Streeton's refusal to paint in winter.

On 18 January 1918, while Bryant was in France, Fisher cabled the Prime Minister's Department in Canberra with an update on the progress of his war artists' scheme. He was able to report that Leist and Power had provided excellent sketches from their tours in France, Lambert was in Palestine with the Light Horse, Bryant was in France, and Streeton and Longstaff were due to go to France when the weather improved.

Fisher sought approval to add the names of Quinn, Coates, Fullwood and Bell to his list. He told Prime Minister Hughes that each artist would produce twenty-five drawings for inclusion in the 'National Collection [of] War Pictures'. In addition, each artist would be commissioned to paint 'large compositions from [their] sketches' at prices that would be set by a committee in England, but ultimately approved by the Prime Minister's Department.[4] Hughes approved this proposal on 28 March 1918.[5]

Will Dyson returned from France in November 1917 to prepare an exhibition of his Western Front drawings that opened at the Leicester Galleries in London on 5 January 1918.[6] He followed the exhibition with a book of drawings called *Australia at War*, published in May 1918. Also in May 1918, the Grafton Gallery, also in London, held an exhibition called *Australian Official Photographs* and *Pictures* that included many photographs by the Australian war photographer, Frank Hurley.

The fighting on the Western Front in 1918 can be divided into three phases.

In the first phase, from 21 March 1918 until 24 April 1918, the Germans launched a massive offensive aimed at winning the war before the men arriving from the United States tipped the scales in favour of the Allies. They very nearly succeeded. In the Somme Valley, their principal target was the cathedral town of Amiens. Both rail lines linking the Channel ports with Paris passed through Amiens. If the Germans could take Amiens, they would split the British and French armies, and prevent the flow of supplies between them. The village of Villers-Bretonneux was the key to the battle for Amiens. It was on high ground 25 kilometres east of Amiens. With artillery near Villers-Bretonneux, the Germans would be in excellent position for a final assault on Amiens.

The Germans came very close to taking Villers-Bretonneux on 4 April 1918, but Australian troops drove them back, and held the village. However, on 24 April 1918, the Germans succeeded in taking Villers-Bretonneux after two tired British divisions took over its defence from the Australians. Two Australian brigades re-took Villers-Bretonneux on the evening of 24 April 1918 and in the early morning of Anzac Day 1918. In a violent and bloody battle, the 13th and 15th brigades surrounded the village in a pincer movement. They then turned back through the village, killing or driving out any Germans still in the ruins. With the battle won:

there was a weird silence. An extraordinary scene then took place. 'Markers' were set out as if it were an ordinary parade ground, and a thousand men fell in in two ranks, in close order, dressed by the right, and were numbered and checked by platoon commanders. The lurid glare of the burning houses in the town shone fitfully on the quiet ranks, where each man stood erect and steady with his rifle at the order, bloody, shining bayonet fixed, the flames reflected at intervals on all our faces.[8]

General Birdwood thought that this action was 'the great turning point of the war'. After it, he wrote, 'the Germans never advanced a foot. For them it was the beginning of the end'.[9] No one foresaw the end of the war on the morning of 25 April 1918, but there was a great sense of relief that Villers-Bretonneux had been re-taken and the pressure on Amiens relieved.

The second phase of the 1918 battles ran from 25 April until 7 August 1918. During this phase, the Allies consolidated their position in front of Amiens. Although Villers-Bretonneux had been re-taken, it remained within range of the German guns and was constantly shelled. The Germans continued to bombard Villers-Bretonneux until 4 July 1918, when the Australians attacked the Germans at Hamel, another small village, east of Villers-Bretonneux. In a battle lasting only 93 minutes, the diggers recorded a famous victory, driving the Germans back down the Somme Valley. As the Germans retreated from Hamel, they withdrew the guns that had been shelling Villers-Bretonneux and it finally became safe to re-enter the village.

The third phase of the 1918 battles, from 8 August until the Armistice on 11 November, was famous as the hundred days of battles that ended the war. Starting with an attack near Corbie on 8 August 1918, the Allies drove the Germans back up the Somme Valley as far as Péronne and Mont St Quentin. The Armistice came almost as a surprise. The Germans had been on the cusp of winning the war in April. Just six months later, they were beaten.

Portrait painters were not affected by the weather, or by the battles at the front. They worked in the safety and comfort of the Australian Headquarters. The next men sent by Fisher and Smart to France – James Quinn and John Longstaff – both painted portraits.

Quinn's agreement took effect from 15 February 1918. He left for France the next day. He was posted to the Headquarters of the newly formed Australian Corps. By 12 March 1918, he had completed portraits of Generals Birdwood, Monash, Walker and Hobbs and had started on a portrait of General White.[10]

Thus, in the space of only a month, Quinn painted portraits of the two most distinguished generals in the AIF. The diggers loved Birdwood and Birdwood loved the diggers. He displayed an understanding of the diggers rare among British officers. Quinn gave Birdwood, an Englishman, an Australian flag and a Rising Sun badge in the background as emblems of his status as an adopted Australian. Birdwood later served as Governor-General of Australia. His warm and open portrait contrasted with that of General Monash, to whom Quinn gave a rather guarded appearance.

James Quinn
General Sir William Birdwood AWM

James Quinn
Lieutenant General Sir John Monash AWM

John Longstaff
Lieutenant General Sir John Monash
AWM

John Longstaff went to France on 3 May 1918. In a month of painting, he completed portraits of General McNicoll, Lieutenant Colonel Jess and Lieutenant Colonel Jackson, but he did not quite finish a portrait of General Monash.[11]

Over the years to come, Longstaff painted several studies and finished portraits of Sir John Monash. This one, completed in 1919, is more finished than Quinn's sketch. Monash's reputation as a general was second to none. Field Marshal Bernard Montgomery regarded him as the best general on the Western Front, and made the call, unprecedented for a British general, that Monash 'possessed real creative originality, and the war might well have been over sooner, and certainly with fewer casualties, had Haig been relieved of his command and Monash appointed to command the British Armies in his place'.[12] But Monash polarised opinion. Although his work on the Western Front was regarded as outstanding, he had been seen as an average commander at Gallipoli.[13] Bean so disliked Monash that he opposed his appointment to command the Australian Corps, when it was formed in 1918.[14] Longstaff liked Monash.[15] Did that explain the difference between Longstaff's portrait and Quinn's?

Streeton and Fullwood were the next artists to be sent to France.

Streeton had been threatening to paint for the Canadians. When Smart approached him, early in 1918, he gradually allowed himself to be persuaded to paint for Australia. Smart was diplomat enough to accept his change of heart without comment. Streeton signed his agreement on 3 May 1918 and left for France on 14 May 1918.[16] He had two stints in France: the first from May until August 1918; the second from October until the end of November 1918, three weeks after the war ended. Fullwood was in France from May until August 1918. He, too, returned to France for a second tour. It ran from December 1918 until January 1919.

Bryant, Quinn and Longstaff had been able to paint in safe locations, well behind the front line. Streeton and Fullwood, as landscape artists, had the job of painting the front line, as Dyson, Leist and Power had done before them. Fisher and Smart told Streeton that the Commonwealth government wanted his work to be 'descriptive'.[17] Fullwood was probably given a similar instruction – certainly, his work was highly descriptive.

Fullwood and Streeton arrived in the Somme Valley early in the

Arthur Streeton
Staff Clerks at Work, Headquarters,
St Gratien AWM

Arthur Streeton
St Gratien: General Birdwood Bidding
Farewell to Headquarters Staff AWM

Henry Fullwood
Villers-Bretonneux from Bussy AWM

Arthur Streeton
Amiens Cathedral AWM

second phase of the 1918 battles, when it was still uncertain that the Allies had halted the German advance. They were billeted at General Birdwood's headquarters. Birdwood had chosen a suitably comfortable chateau at St Gratien for his headquarters. Twelve kilometres north-east of Amiens and a similar distance north of Villers-Bretonneux, the chateau was close enough to the front that Streeton was worried about enemy shelling. Streeton described it as a mixture of battle-zone and oasis:

with a delightful old garden & serenity everywhere. [The] sense of comfort comes almost as a shock – the tune of guns & machines [aeroplanes] goes on all round ... The HQ staff are most kind to me ... The air is hot & bright & all I need is one good long sleep. I've slept in my boots for the last 2 nights.[18]

The chateau was not Birdwood's headquarters for much longer. In May 1918, he said farewell to the staff at St Gratien and handed over command of the Australian Corps to General Monash.

While Villers-Bretonneux was still being shelled, it was not safe for artists to go there to draw. Fullwood made a watercolour sketch of Villers-Bretonneux being shelled in May 1918. The painting showed the dominant position of Villers-Bretonneux on its hill.

Avoiding Villers-Bretonneux, Streeton worked further west, in the area of Amiens. Even there, occasional shells still fell. Streeton wrote to Roberts that Amiens, 'the dear old Cathedral town ... is an awful mess now – I got a few drawings & a water colour there under shellfire'.[19]

If Streeton's painting since he left Australia had languished because he was missing the sweep and scale of the Australian bush, in northern France, he found himself once again in a landscape that suited his way

of painting. Near Amiens, the Somme Valley is broad, open and inviting – reminiscent of Australian wheat country. Streeton saw the similarity. He wrote to Roberts, describing a green and gold landscape: 'below me the steep little gully, all green with upright trees, & the last afternoon light all golden like Australia catches the stems in patches & is diffused among the foliage in most beautiful fashion'.[20]

Streeton made a watercolour sketch, *Souvenir, Amiens*. In the finest traditions of the *9 by 5 Impression Exhibition, Souvenir, Amiens* had 'a certain want as of finish or arrangement'.[21] Turned out quickly, it was a classic impression. The sky was dominant, like an Australian sky; the fields were parched, like Australian paddocks; the cathedral was hardly Australian, but it was painted in the far and hazy distance, on an Australian horizon. Key to the sketch was the general impression of colour – the yellow/grey of an Australian paddock in summer.

Fullwood also chose yellows and greys when he painted a distant view of Amiens with a windmill in the foreground. The consistency of the colour in the works of Streeton and Fullwood is striking.

Fullwood sketched the attack on Hamel on 4 July 1918 from an elevated observation point across the river.

On 6 July 1918, only two days after the Hamel battle, Streeton spent the day drawing in Villers-Bretonneux. He drew the ruins of the town. Made three months after the battle, his drawing of a street in ruins captures the brooding mood of the rollcall that marked the end of the battle.

At the more prosperous end of the housing scale, he drew *Chateau, Villers-Bretonneux*, showing the Red Chateau.

A month later, the Red Chateau played host to a group of elderly,

Arthur Streeton
Souvenir, Amiens AWM

Henry Fullwood
Distant View of Amiens AWM

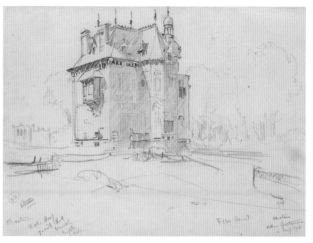

Henry Fullwood
Attack on Hamel-Vaire AWM

Arthur Streeton
Chateau, Villers-Bretonneux AWM

Arthur Streeton
Street in Ruins, Villers-Bretonneux, France
AWM

Arthur Streeton
The Somme from Above Corbie AWM

Henry Fullwood
Valley of the Somme AWM

white-haired, gentlemen. They sat in chairs on the grass of the chateau, enjoying the warm afternoon weather in the shade of a beech tree. Maps were strewn carelessly around them. The men represented the 'top brass' of the Allied forces: French Premier Clemenceau; French Finance Minister Klotz; Field Marshal Haig; Generals Rawlinson, Currie, Kavanagh, Godley, Monash, Montgomery, Budworth, Wilson, Blamey, Glasgow, Rosenthal, Gellibrand, Sinclair-MacLagan and Hobbs. It was 11 August 1918. They were taking the time to celebrate the success of the battle of 8 August 1918.[22]

Streeton told Roberts:

I've done a lot of work, turned out at a great pace, but it is all that we can do here rapid studies, it's all too restless & exciting for the repose necessary for fine art – &

Henry Fullwood
Courtyard at Bertangles AWM

Henry Fullwood
AIF Aerodrome Near Bertangles AWM

I can't tell how my efforts will look till I return and see them in a quiet room. [I hope] to reflect some of it all, in a few canvases I want to paint on my return.[23]

Streeton hunted for elevated vantage points that would best suit the paintings he had in mind. He wrote to Roberts that he went in an ambulance north from Corbie:

up a steep hill where I had a fine view of the valley with a flat covered with lovely trees & the Somme winding through & the towers of the old church of [Corbie] – & other villages & V–B on the distant skyline – a grand spread, & the area of battle, shell bursts, & shrapnel occasionally spotting a fine sky – But everything must be done rapidly or left alone.[24]

This was the sketch *The Somme from Above Corbie*. Streeton made the most of the opportunities that Fisher's scheme provided. He was sketching and drawing impressions, not caring if they were not finished perfectly, but knowing that they would be the basis for grander paintings to be done in the future. It was the genius of Fisher's scheme that it accommodated this style of painting so well.

Fullwood, too, painted the Somme winding through its valley, on page 163, again in similar colours to those chosen by Streeton.

Making descriptive paintings came easily to Fullwood. What his sketches lacked in panache, they made up for in historical detail. Two paintings of Monash's headquarters at Bertangles were good examples of his eye for detail: one showed the *pigeonnier* at the back of the chateau; the other the nearby AIF airfield. The airfield sketch gave details of a subject rarely painted in the Great War.

Fisher's war artists' scheme was limited to civilians. It did nothing for the artists serving in the AIF. Bean felt badly for them. He made the same point about the artists in the ranks that Streeton had made about the artists at Wandsworth – artists who had given hard service had earned the right to be appointed as war artists. In March 1918, the Australian army finally recognised the claims of the artists in the ranks. It established an artists' scheme of its own, open to men serving in the AIF. The men chosen would serve under Treloar in the Australian War Records Section.

When the army invited applications, 114 men applied.[26] A committee was appointed to vet the applications. Its members were Lieutenants Dyson, Leist, John Longstaff and Power. They were asked to select seven artists. 'After careful consideration', the committee selected Daryl Lindsay for medical work and six other artists for general work.[27] The committee ranked the six generalists in order of merit. First came Frank Crozier. The committee had a high opinion of his work and placed him easily first on their list.[28] He was a protégé of Bean's. Since October 1917, he had been working with the Australian War Records Section. He was serving there when the committee endorsed his appointment.[29] Second came George Benson. Another veteran of Gallipoli, he had been promoted through the ranks, eventually becoming a lieutenant in the artillery in March 1918.[30] Third was Staff Sergeant JS MacDonald – the same JS MacDonald whose opinions have already been repeated many times in this book. Fourth was Louis McCubbin, the son of Frederick

Frank Crozier
The Beach at Anzac AWM

Frank Crozier
Bombardment of Pozières,
July 1916 AWM

James Scott
Loft at Saint-Sylvestre-Cappel
AWM

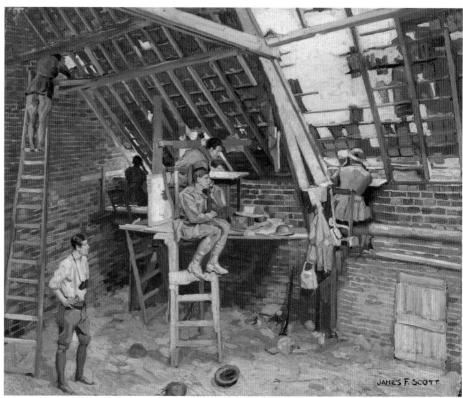

Will Longstaff
*Australians Advancing from
Villers-Bretonneux, August 8th 1918*
AWM

Will Longstaff
Mont St Quentin AWM

McCubbin.[31] Fifth was James Scott. He had been in England since suffering a gunshot wound in France in September 1917.[32] Sixth, and last, came Will Longstaff. He was a cousin of John Longstaff. Will Longstaff was a captain serving on Salisbury Plain in England.[33]

The committee made its choices with a fine disregard for the risk of being accused of parochialism. It was pure coincidence that the finest artists in the AIF just happened to include Dyson's brother-in-law, John Longstaff's cousin, Bean's protégé and Frederick McCubbin's son.

In May 1918, orders were issued posting the artists. Lindsay was to continue his medical work. Most of the other artists were sent to France: Scott to the 1st Australian Division; Will Longstaff to the 2nd; McCubbin to the 3rd; Benson to the 4th; and MacDonald to the 5th. Longstaff, MacDonald and Scott left for France on 6 June 1918. One justification for recruiting the artists was that they would help with camouflage. To that end, Benson and McCubbin were sent to a camouflage school in England before they went to France.[34] In August, after serving a probationary term of three months, all of the new artists, except MacDonald, were confirmed in their new positions, and those not already holding commissions were commissioned as honorary lieutenants. MacDonald was unwell. He returned to Australia in October 1918.[35] Crozier, who was already engaged on large-scale oil paintings of Gallipoli and Pozières, was to stay in London to complete them. The Gallipoli and Pozières battles had so far gone without a serious painted record. Crozier had fought in both battles. His paintings were eyewitness accounts, even if they were made two and three years after the events they recorded.

His painting, *The Beach at Anzac*, on page 165, creates a distinctly Australian paradox, portraying the battlefield as a day at the beach.

The dominant feature of the Pozières battlefield was the ridge separating Albert from Mouquet Farm and Thiepval. Crozier showed the

ridge under shellfire in the background. Bean wrote that 'the whole surface of the ground [at Pozières] was like that of a choppy sea'.[36] Crozier
captured this in the craters in the mid-ground of his painting, on page
166. He chose pinks and greys for the sea-like soil of the Somme Valley.

Scott's sketch of an observation post, *Loft at Saint-Sylvestre-Cappel*,
on page 166, attracted Bean's approval. It was a simple enough painting, but Bean wrote in his diary that it was 'excellently typical, with a
number of observers in a loft looking out through holes in the broken
tile roof'.[37]

Will Longstaff made sketches of scenes, on page 167, from the hundred days of battles that ended the war.

The sketch of the 8 August 1918 battle was in the nature of an aide
mémoire, showing different facets of the advance, whereas his watercolour of Mont St Quentin, showing the start line and the line of approach
to the hill, seems more in preparation for a large-scale landscape painting.

Louis McCubbin avoided the standard Somme Valley subjects. Instead, he painted a distant view of the front line across a cemetery.

By cable dated 24 June 1918, Fisher asked Prime Minister Hughes to approve the commissioning of four composition paintings, each 8 × 6 feet.
The paintings were: Fred Leist, the Battle of Polygon Wood, £400; Septimus Power, the 1st Australian Divisional Artillery going into action,
£400; Charles Bryant, the sinking of the *Southland*, £250; and Arthur

Burgess (a marine painter, whose name came from nowhere to find its way into Fisher's cable), the fight between the *Sydney* and the *Emden*, £300. On 28 June 1918, Fisher sent a second cable, adding Lambert's name to the list, and recommending that he paint an 8 × 6 foot composition of the Australian Light Horse in action for £500.

The prices – £1850 in total – were high enough to frighten the horses in Canberra. Asked his opinion, Pearce doubted that the expenditure was justified. He thought it was a needless extravagance coming at the end of four years of wartime expenditure. He added that his department (Defence) lacked the expertise to assess whether the prices were reasonable. Pearce suggested that the Prime Minister's Department take the matter in hand and formulate a whole-of-government policy.[38]

Back in Chelsea, Lambert was anxious to start work on his picture of the charge at Beersheba. It was the real earner in his Middle Eastern adventure. Fisher and Smart agreed. Concerned at the delay, Fisher cabled Canberra on 31 August 1918: 'Artist now waiting [to] paint composition pictures as outlined [in] my cables [of] January 18th, 24th. Would be glad to have urgent reply'.[39]

Sensing that price was the stumbling block, Bean cabled Pearce on 14 September 1918, proposing the establishment of a Corps of Artists. Instead of paying artists £300 to £500 for each picture, they should be commissioned as captains in the AIF, paid as majors (£1 10s 0d per day), and 'work thereafter entirely for [the] Commonwealth'.

Bean told Pearce that the war had laid a foundation to transform Australia from a colony into a nation in her own right: 'Most important result for Australia from war is the great unifying tradition as basis for future nationality and it is logically right that [a] small corps [of] artists should be formed to consolidate tradition'.[40] He proposed a standard socialist solution. If market forces made the paintings too expensive, nationalise the artists. Let them work on wages, and tell the world it is for the greater glory of the nation.

Lambert did not share Bean's socialist viewpoint. He was pinning his faith on free enterprise – and a £500 commission. By 26 September 1918, he could wait no longer. He wrote to Fisher, complaining that Smart had told him to look for private work because the government could not make up its mind. Lambert told Fisher he was keen to paint, but the government was stringing him along. As an artist, he needed to keep painting Palestine subjects because they were 'fixed in my brain by the impressions received out there. These impressions should belong to Australia'.[41]

Fisher passed Lambert's letter on to Smart with a note: 'Looks like a matter that needs early attention,' as, indeed, it was. With Canberra's knowledge and approval, Fisher had led the artists to believe that they would be commissioned to paint composition paintings. He had agreed the details of the compositions and the prices to be paid. Now Canberra was dragging the chain. While Canberra dithered, the second part of Fisher's scheme – the creation of the great composition paintings – hung in limbo.

On 20 September 1918, Fisher cabled the Prime Minister's Department to raise the stakes. In addition to the paintings recommended in his earlier cables, he recommended commissioning works by Streeton, for £400; Fullwood, for £300; Quinn, two portraits at £100 each; and John Longstaff, two portraits at £100 each. The new proposals brought the total value of the paintings on Fisher's wish list to £2950.[43] Fisher certainly had the courage of his convictions.

Fisher had the good sense to keep his scheme outside the military hierarchy. As High Commissioner, he appointed the artists. The army's involvement was limited to appointing the men to honorary commissions, providing them with materials, and accommodating them at the front. Not only did this allow Fisher and Smart to deal with the foibles of the artists in ways that might have been difficult within the military hierarchy, it also meant that Defence bureaucrats had no say in funding the scheme. In the debate about the funding of the composition paintings, Fisher was able to avoid tiresome arguments from Defence that £2950 would buy a lot of bombs. Even so, he was meeting resistance to the prices from Canberra.

The last of Fisher's appointees to go to France was George Bell. He was not appointed until 5 October 1918, and arrived too late to see the diggers in action. The Australian divisions fought their last battles late in September. In any event, Fisher regarded Bell primarily as a portraitist. Bell's sketches of a downed German plane and of the town of Le Cateau both depict events in November 1918, in the last days of the war.

Streeton returned to France in October 1918, as the action was coming to an end. Fullwood returned in December 1918, after the Armistice. Streeton made a number of sketches of the fighting around Péronne, where the Australians fought their last battles. One was a sketch of the entrance to the St Quentin tunnel at Bellicourt, where the Canal du Nord runs underground. As the Australians and the Americans attacked

George Bell
German Plane Brought Down Near Ors, France AWM

George Bell
Le Cateau AWM

HINDENBURG LINE
TUNNEL AT BELLICOURT

across the land above the tunnel, the Germans hid below, emerging to cause trouble in the rear as the main attack swept forward.

Streeton also made a notebook sketch of Péronne, looking towards Mont St Quentin.

❧

The year 1918 had been a productive one for Fisher's scheme. Having left the turmoil of 1917 behind, a number of Australian artists had made sketches of the operations of the AIF. They had worked with great application, and produced a satisfying crop of sketches and drawings. With the sketches finished, the artists were ready to move on to their major works. But Canberra had dropped the ball, baulking at the prices that Fisher suggested.

Although it began late in the war, the army artists' scheme also made good progress. Most of the artists worked on sketches and drawings, with pleasing results. One artist, Crozier, had started on composition paintings of Gallipoli and Pozières. The artists in the army scheme were working on wages, and glad of it. For Bean, this was the way of the future. It was cheaper than Fisher's scheme, but questions of quality intruded. If the civilian artists were better than the artists drawn from the ranks, maybe price was not everything.

The Australian government had come a long way since it meekly accepted British censorship of the exploits of the diggers at Gallipoli. It was a mark of emerging Australian nationalism that the Australian government had sent the best Australian artists to paint the deeds of the diggers in France.

Arthur Streeton
Péronne, Looking Towards Mont St Quentin AWM

Arthur Streeton
Bellicourt, Entrance to St Quentin Tunnel AWM

15 PEACE, MEMORY AND COMMEMORATION

IN WHICH THE ARTISTS COMPLETE AND PERFECT THEIR PAINTINGS OF THE WAR.

Armistice Day brought celebrations, but, for those many who had suffered loss, it was also an occasion for reflection and sadness.

Vida Lahey's charcoal and watercolour, *Rejoicing and Remembrance*, made in 1924, conveyed that sense. The drawing showed the portico of St Martin in the Fields, a church on the edge of Trafalgar Square. In the Square, to the right, a crowd was celebrating the Armistice, while to the left sombre women entered the church to take part in a remembrance service.[1]

Lahey was a Queensland artist who had studied at the National Gallery School in Melbourne under Bernard Hall and Frederick McCubbin, before returning to paint in Brisbane. In 1915 or 1916, she travelled to London to establish a base for her three brothers, who were serving with the AIF. In London, she involved herself in war work and the care of her brothers, to the exclusion of her painting. Of her brothers, Noel died of wounds after the Battle of Messines, Jack was invalided back to Australia after he was wounded later in 1917, and Romeo survived the war to join Vida in London.[2] The Lahey family knew well the ambivalent feelings that came with peace.

When Will Longstaff's painting, *Menin Gate at Midnight*, on page 176, was first displayed in 1927, it attracted huge crowds. It was a sentimental painting of the memorial erected to commemorate the men killed in the Ypres salient who have no known grave. The painting struck a chord with those who saw spiritualism as a means of contacting men lost in the war.[3] There was a brisk trade in reproductions of the painting. In 1928, the Scotch whisky magnate, Lord Woolavington, paid £2000 for the original and donated it to the Australian government.[4] Today, the painting is in the Australian War Memorial, where it remains as

Vida Lahey
Rejoicing and Remembrance,
Armistice Day, London, 1918 AWM

popular as ever. According to the Memorial, it 'has achieved the status of a national icon. The painting retains its ability to provoke an emotional response and to communicate the scale of the loss of life and the devastation of war'.[5] Recognising he was onto a good thing, Will Longstaff painted other paintings in the same vein.[6]

Will Longstaff
Menin Gate at Midnight AWM

Arthur Streeton
*Australians Burning Effigy of Kaiser
in Square, Armistice Day* AWM

Evelyn Chapman
Ruined Church, Villers-Bretonneux
AGNSW

When the Germans capitulated, Streeton was on the front line at Péronne in northern France. He sketched diggers marking the ceasefire by burning the Kaiser in effigy on a bonfire made from wood gathered from the ruined buildings of the town.[7]

The Armistice freed many artists from their wartime occupations. Evelyn Chapman, a Sydney-born artist who, like Grace Cossington Smith, trained with Antonio Dattilo-Rubbo, had spent the war years in London. When the war ended, she travelled with her father, a member of the New Zealand War Graves Commission, to France, where she resumed painting, making several colourful works in the former battlefields.[8]

Other artists freed from wartime occupations were Jessie Traill, a friend of Tom Roberts, who served in the Voluntary Aid Detachment, nursing in hospitals near Rouen;[9] Margaret Preston, who taught ceramics to shell-shocked soldiers at a military hospital in Devon;[10] and Bessie Davidson, who lived in France during the war and served as a nurse in a hospital in Auteuil in Paris.[11] Like Roberts, Traill and Davidson had painted little during the war.[12]

Hilda Rix Nicholas had returned to Australia in 1918, and then, in October 1919, left Melbourne for Sydney to settle in Mosman.[13] In 1921, she painted *A Man*. One the finest paintings of the Great War, it was the distillation of the grief that the war inflicted on this gallant and talented artist. In the war cemetery at Villers-Bretonneux, lies a digger whose gravestone carries the inscription: 'Think what a man should be. He was all that'. That inscription could have been written for Hilda's *Man*.

Hilda Rix Nicholas
A Man AWM

The Armistice meant that those whose role it was to create a record of the war could switch from eyewitness mode to recording, documenting and interpreting the war. Bean had long anticipated the change from war correspondent to historian. He had used his influence with government to ensure that all the material he would need to write the history was in place.

The Australian War Records Section was collecting records, photographs and relics to display in the war memorial museum to be built in Canberra.[14] Captain Treloar was also in charge of the army's war artists' scheme. He was planning to use its soldier-artists to work on displays for the new museum.

News that Canberra had approved the acquisition of all the composition pictures on Fisher's list came early in November 1918.[15] Fisher's civilian artists could now turn their attention to their great composition paintings. With peace came the chance to take their studies into a quiet room and see how they looked. It was the occasion for the 'repose necessary for fine art'.[16]

Although Bean's scheme to nationalise the artists had been knocked back, he was pleased with the results of Fisher's scheme. On 19 January 1919, he wrote:

The Canadians have spent I suppose … twenty times as much as we – and yet they have been on the wrong lines. They have got English artists of the fashionable sort to paint their national pictures – we have employed Australian artists only. Their artists had no real feeling for their work – each wanted to make a hit *for himself*. Ours were mostly enthusiastic men doing their best to help their country's record. The result is that while the Canadian pictures fill the Royal Academy with a very interesting exhibit of curious styles of contemporary art, the Australian pictures are a far more interesting set, and a suitable memorial – about 1,000 sketches and small pictures of what the artists actually saw at the front.[17]

The artists may have been alarmed to learn what Bean thought of them: that compared to the artists painting for Canada, they were enthusiastic toilers, who had painted what they actually saw at the front, and none of the fashionable rubbish that filled the Royal Academy. Bean's comments were a catalogue of the reasons why state-sponsored art schemes often produce awful art. Thankfully, the Australian government ignored most of his gratuitous advice on what made good art.

The meagre deal that Bean proposed for the artists may be contrasted with the deal he made for himself when he secured appointment as official historian on 19 February 1919. Not for him the pay of a major – his salary was £1200 per annum, the salary of a major general.[18] Bean was living the socialist dream.

In fairness to Bean, however, in addition to securing an excellent deal for himself, he also worked wonders in securing the memory and commemoration of the sacrifices of those who had fought in the war. There remained one point of weakness – Gallipoli. It was impossible to turn back the clock on the failure to keep a contemporary record of events there, but Bean was determined to do what he could to supply the missing record after the event. He persuaded the Commonwealth government to let him return to Australia by way of Gallipoli. It looked like a paid stopover in the Greek islands, but Bean portrayed it as a 'Mission' (always with a capital 'M'), of which he would be Mission leader. In 1948, Bean wrote *Gallipoli Mission*, a book glorifying the Mission and his central role in it. It was Bean at his grandstanding best:

I obtained General Birdwood's authority to visit London and arrange for my return to Australia by way of Gallipoli, taking with me such officers and others as I considered necessary for securing the required records on the old battle-grounds. From Gallipoli I would return with most of the party via Egypt to Australia where the Australian Government wished me to complete arrangements for the history and initiate those [arrangements] for the eventual establishment of the nation's memorial to those who fell in the war … I told General Dodds that we would call ourselves the 'Australian Historical Mission'. He spoke of us as such … and from that time the Australian Historical Mission we became.[19]

The first objective of the Mission was to find answers to 'riddles about Gallipoli' that still puzzled Bean and the men who had fought there. Bean wanted to answer questions such as: How far had the initial advance penetrated? Where had the Turkish guns been hidden? What could be seen from the Turkish positions? The second objective was to collect relics of the occupation of Gallipoli. The third was to report on the condition of the Australian cemeteries on the Peninsula. And the fourth was for an artist 'to obtain sketches and notes for a picture of the Gallipoli Landing for the memorial'.[20]

Bean had all the qualities of the digger, except modesty. He wrote that:

The Mission assembled for the first time at the boat train – six officers and two sergeants. Needless to say, being Australians, we travelled together, lodged together, and ate together on our journey; and from first to last we had no batmen. I myself (then thirty-nine years of age, lean, active, and with an accurate memory) represented 'war records' – fortunately we did not have to carry many books as my memory covered most of the history we would need to know.[21]

The other members of the Mission were Lieutenant John Balfour and Staff Sergeant Arthur Bazley, both with the Australian War Records Section, who 'were to be my main assistants in the compilation of the Official History'; Lieutenant HS Buchanan and Sergeant G Hunter Rogers, in charge of maps and mapping; Brigadier General EA Drake-Brockman and Lieutenant Hedley Vickers Howe, West Australians chosen for their knowledge of the campaign; Captain Hubert Wilkins, the photographer; and an artist, Captain George Lambert.[22]

Promoted to captain, Lambert bought into the whole expeditionary package: 'the golden beard, the hat, the cloak, the spurs, the gait, the laugh and the conviviality of a cavalier'. Bean described how Lambert:

rolled out one after another of his store of good yarns from a mental cellar stocked by experiences of dukes and Diggers and broached with rich appreciation of their humour; as his teeth gleamed, and his nostrils expanded, and his cavalier's beard was thrust out in each quivering prelude to his 'robustious' laughter – one could not help wondering whether he did not consciously mould himself on the contemporaries of Van Dyck and Velasquez whose art so evidently influenced his own.

Best of all, Lambert teased Bean, insisting on calling him 'Skipper'.[23]

The Mission had about it an overriding feeling of release of tension. The shooting was over. There were no battles left to fight. After five years of war, it was time to go home. Nine men, friends mostly, were lucky enough to find themselves on a paid trip to research a history book, take photographs, collect souvenirs and paint. Dressing it up as a military operation, wearing uniforms and spurs, and calling it a Mission did not change the fact that it was a junket.

The Mission arrived at Gallipoli on 16 February 1919. Lambert looked around, familiarising himself with the features of the battlefield. On 27 February 1919, he visited Gaba Tepe, 'whence Jacko [the Turks] used to pound Anzac Beach'. He painted a small oil on a wood panel, showing 'the stuff one sees of Anzac from Gaba Tepe'.[24] In 1915, William Eltham's drawing of Gaba Tepe from Anzac had been included in *The Anzac Book*. This was the reverse view.

Skipper Bean discussed with Lambert:

the big pictures which he would be commissioned to paint for the future memorial – one of the Landing of the Australians on April 25th; one of the heroic charge of the Light Horse (dismounted, of course – they could not bring their horses to Gallipoli) at the Nek on August 7th, at the climax of the second offensive of the Allies; and possibly a third of the advance of the 2nd Australian Infantry Brigade, sent to help the British at Cape Helles, on May 8th.[25]

Lambert walked over Lone Pine and Anzac Beach. He made a sketch of the Sphinx, but his mind was on the 'Neck' – this was how Lambert spelled it – 'where three lines of gallant Australians went down, to a man, and a fourth line was about to go over but was stopped by command of some sensible person on our side'.[26] The scene Lambert described will be familiar to many – the Battle of the Nek was the climax of Peter Weir's 1981 film, *Gallipoli*.[27]

On 17 February 1919, Lambert wrote that:

I was conducted by the Mission from the point on the beach where part of the Australians landed, right up to the Neck, which is the ground whereon the terrific sacrifice … took place. Descriptions are all too true; evidence grins coldly at us non-combatants and I feel thankful that I have been trained by circumstances of the past to stop my emotions at the borderline. From the point of view of the artist-historian the Neck is a wonderful setting for the tragedy and I could not wait for the proper time, which was just before sunrise, but abandoned the Mission and did a sketch which is buckshee souvenir.[28]

George Lambert
Anzac, from Gaba Tepe AWM

Lambert had stumbled on a truly awful sight. The battlefield was strewn with bodies. Shortly afterwards, men of the Commonwealth Graves Commission 'found and buried more than three hundred Australians in that strip the size of three tennis courts'.[29]

As artist-historian, Lambert not only sketched at Gallipoli, he made detailed inquiries about the men, their equipment and their dress. He learned that the men were wearing more or less standard issue when they landed in April, but that, by August when the Nek battle took place, their clothing had taken on a much more raffish appearance. In the heat of summer, shirt sleeves had been cut off, long trousers had been turned into shorts and hats had been modified against the sun. These changes featured in many of the drawings in *The Anzac Book*. In discussions with Bean, Lambert took careful note of them.[30] He asked Bean how he thought 'a man would fall if hit on one side and spun round; Lambert used to jerk himself forward as he imagined this charging man would'.[31] Lambert shook himself out of bed:

at twenty minutes to sunrise to get the effect of light for the charge at the neck [sic]. Very cold, bleak and lonely. The jackals, damn them, were chorusing their hate, the bones showed up white even in the faint dawn and I felt rotten; but as soon as I got to my spot the colour of the dawn on this scrubby, scrubby hill-land was very beautiful and I did my little sketch quite well before breakfast.[32]

It was all part of the care that Lambert put into preparing to paint the big canvases on his return to London.

George Lambert
*Lone Pine, Looking Towards the Nek,
Walker's Ridge* AWM

George Lambert
*Study for Dead Trooper and Detail
of Turkish Trench, Gallipoli* AWM

Trooper William Henry Spruce of the 7th Light Horse was assigned to help Lambert transport his painting gear.[33] Spruce was in charge of a female pack-mule named Jinny. Spruce entertained Lambert with the acrobatics he performed in the course of tending the mule. He was also pleased to advise Lambert about art, which advice Lambert recorded as follows:

Spruce says he has always had a leaning towards Art and beauty and he thinks Port Stephens is the most beautiful place in the world. When I told him he would never be as good a painter as a mule-catcher, he replied that a man doesn't value the gifts that are handed to him at birth.[34]

Lambert sketched while Spruce argued with Jinny, three happy souls making the most of the Mediterranean sunshine. On 23 February 1919, Lambert found:

a very interesting Turkish trench on a hill called 'Johnson's Jolly,' and there did a good correct study of Spruce, the Light Horseman, as a 'stiff'. It was quite exciting in that I had the right kind of man in right clothes and right ground. In addition to correct surroundings and light I may mention the webbing equipment; in fact, everything right. A four hours' stretch and worth it![35]

Lambert left Anzac on 7 March 1919, pleased with the work he had done: 'I can safely say now that I know Anzac, its gullies, bushes, flowers, trenches and bones. My small collection of paintings, amounting to twenty pieces, are fair souvenirs and most useful reference notes'.[36]

Having separated from his comrades on the Mission, Lambert headed to Palestine via Constantinople. After a long trip by train from Constantinople, he fell ill with a bout of dysentery that left him a patient in the 14th Australian General Hospital at Abbassia, on the outskirts of Cairo from mid-March until late May 1919. The illness was so serious that Lambert confessed to Amy that he thought his 'number was up for the Eternity Stakes'.[37] He pulled through, albeit with health problems that plagued the rest of his life.

During his convalescence, he became well enough to paint again. He produced a painting which, in contrast to the paintings he had made at Gallipoli, was remarkable for its use of light and colour.

The trooper is wearing the blue uniform of the convalescent soldier. The nurse is coy. There is palpable electricity between the two. After decades in England, after years of drab wartime colours, after kicking over the bones of dead diggers at Gallipoli, and after a near-death experience in the Egyptian hospital, Lambert made a painting of quintessential Australianness. It showed an outbreak of love across the hospital

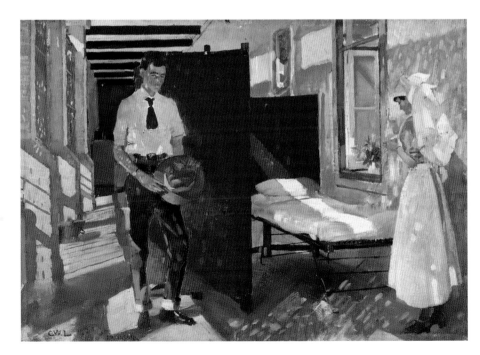

George Lambert
Balcony of Troopers' Ward,
14th Australian General Hospital,
Abbassia AWM

ward, and the patient and nurse were as unmistakeably Australian as the brightness and the sunshine.

When Lambert was well enough to travel again, he took the train to Galilee, where he made more sketches. In Damascus, he met Sergeant Harry Ivers, an artist enlisted in the Light Horse, who was working as a map maker with the Australian War Records Section.[38] The two struck up a friendship which continued after they returned to London.

Lambert headed home through Kantara. At Moascar on 1 July 1919, he wrote to Amy: 'I am in the first possie when I joined up about eighteen months or more back. Remounts are still here and many of my old pals, but a lot of desert has come back, and a lot of tents have been folded and a lot of good and tried men have left for their homes in Australia'.[39]

Lambert painted the last tents at Moascar as he, too, folded his tent to return to London. It was among the last of his sketches as a war artist, and a fine example of what he had achieved as artist-historian.

Peace allowed the artists to work on their commission paintings. Those whose work was well received found a willing buyer in the Commonwealth government. The composition paintings commissioned at the end of 1918 were only the start. The artists were able to continue painting the war well into the 1920s. There were commissions for landscapes and for portraits. The Commonwealth was not the only buyer. There was a good market for war-related art works in the state and regional galleries, and among private collectors.

Fred Leist was commissioned to paint the *Sinking of the 'Southland'*. *Southland* and *Ballarat* were torpedoed by submarines when transporting men from Egypt to the Dardanelles in September 1915. The men on board were rescued as the ship sank, but the episode passed into digger legend because the men sang 'Australia's battle song – *Australia will be there* – ... when they stood in the sea-water that covered the decks of these torpedoed troop-ships'.[40]

Bean made sure that Leist painted the battle for Polygon Wood as one of his commission paintings. Leist had endured a terrifying initiation to the front line only two days before that battle. During the battle, Lieutenant John Turnour, a divinity student from Cohuna in northern Victoria, received a shrapnel wound to the abdomen. He was taken to the 17th Casualty Clearing Station, where he died of his wounds two days later.[41] Leist's painting was of Turnour being wounded.

George Lambert
The Last Tents at Moascar AWM

Fred Leist
Sinking of the 'Southland' AWM

Fred Leist
*Australian Infantry Attack in
Polygon Wood* AWM

Grave of Lieutenant JEG Turnour
AWM

Leist showed Lieutenant Turnour on a ridge in a dusty field with a stubble of thin sapling stumps projecting between shell-holes leading the attack on the German concrete pillbox. Shells were bursting nearby. The painting was the expression of the knowledge that Leist gained so painfully by tagging along behind Bean and Gullett on that frightening reconnaissance.

Bean not only took credit for showing Leist the scene of the painting, he was happy to criticise it. On 22 August 1920, he wrote to Leist:

I have seen the Polygon Wood picture which I like very well with the exception of one figure only – that of the man who is lying dead, rather foreshortened, on the parapet of the trench in the centre of the picture. His figure seemed to me, if I remember right, rather small and somewhat wooden. Except for that, it is an excellent picture in my opinion.[42]

Leist included in the picture a German gun lying on its side in the trench to the right of the dead man whose appearance upset Bean. The gun was almost certainly a Krupp 15 centimetre sFH13-L17 model heavy field howitzer.[43] It was painted in the camouflage colours that the Germans used on the Western Front in the last two years of the war. If the gun was not noticeable on first glance at the painting, the camouflage paint did its work. It would be more common to find the camouflage colours –

field grey, light olive, pale peach and deep green – in a decorator's colour scheme than on a battlefield, yet Leist's painting showed how well they disguised the gun.[44]

The inclusion of the gun in the painting was an artist's flourish. According to the *Official History*, Lieutenant Turnour was killed leading an attack on a pillbox before he and his men reached their first objective – that is, he was still in no man's land when he was wounded.[45] The painting is correctly situated in no man's land. It shows the pillbox, but there would have been no German guns in that part of the battlefield. They would all have been firing from positions well behind the lines.

There is no record of the Australians capturing such a gun at Polygon Wood – the Germans lost very few guns before 1918. This inaccuracy may not have happened but for the delay in commissioning the paintings. Leist was commissioned to paint the Polygon Wood painting in 1919, by which time many German trophy guns – fully camouflaged – were available for him to copy.

The Passchendaele battles that Leist and Power witnessed were notorious for the muddy conditions. Power's paintings, *Bringing up the Guns* and *Bringing up the Ammunition*, showed brilliantly the muddy conditions and their impact on the men and horses. Here was a skilled oil painter, making wonderful paintings of men in action. Power combined the British tradition of painting the cavalry with an Australian flavour, giving the men in the paintings the strength of the Australian horseman.

Charles Bryant completed his composite painting of the harbour at Boulogne in 1923. With Boulogne in the background, and ambulances in the foreground, Bryant showed hospital ships in their camouflage colours. For the sake of completeness, he added a French seaplane making a splash at the right of the bay. The painting is on page 188.

Septimus Powers
Bringing up the Ammunition,
Flanders, Autumn 1917 AWM

Septimus Powers
Bringing up the Guns AWM

Charles Bryant
Boulogne in Wartime, January 1918
AWM

Henry Fullwood
Attack on Péronne AWM

Will Dyson
The Amateur ('Who's cutting this hair, you or me?') AWM

Also in 1923, Bryant was commissioned to create, after the event, a record of another 'forgotten' campaign – that in which the Australian Naval and Military Expeditionary Force overcame the small German force holding German New Guinea in August 1914. Bryant spent three months in 1923 sketching in Rabaul, before completing a series of not very distinguished paintings of the campaign in the studio.[46]

Henry Fullwood was one artist whose composition work was not well received. He was commissioned to paint the attack of the 53rd Battalion on Péronne on 1 September 1918. Fullwood was not in France when the attack took place, although he may have visited Péronne when he was in France after the Armistice.

His painting was considered a disappointment. Murky and dull, it had little to recommend it as a painting. Moreover, it bore little resemblance to Péronne. Fullwood received no further commissions from the government.[47]

Will Dyson was another artist whose postwar paintings were disappointing. His success as a cartoonist was due more to his sharp wit than to the finesse of his black and white work. In France, he was at his best in his pencil drawings, but his oil paintings were undistinguished. They were fine as caricature and cartoon, but lacked basic qualities that might be expected of oil paintings to be included in a national commemorative collection.[48] *The Amateur* captured the humour of the digger as would-be hairdresser, but was little more than a sketch. It lacked the finesse seen, for example, in the commissioned oil paintings that Streeton produced. This, of course, imposes an exacting standard. Of the Australian artists who painted the Western Front, Streeton was the most polished, and the best equipped to carry off grand landscapes. He made the most of the opportunity.

When Streeton was in the Somme Valley, he wrote three letters to Roberts. In all of them, he commented on the trees.[49] What is striking in Streeton's large-scale paintings of the Somme Valley is that he painted the trees as eucalypts. Australian art critic, Robert Hughes, wrote that when French artist Louis Buvelot came to Australia, he attempted 'to adapt the vocabulary of middle nineteenth-century French landscape to unfamiliar scenery and light'.[50] Streeton did the reverse – adapting Australian techniques for painting trees to the French landscape.

The Somme Valley Near Corbie showed the view from the high ground north of Corbie, where Streeton had sketched. On the right, in the distance, the painting showed Villers-Bretonneux on its hilltop. Upriver, in the left and centre background, the German lines were visible where there was gunfire on the far horizon. This painting was of the battle on 8 August 1918.[51]

Streeton's commission painting, *Bellicourt Tunnel*, also showed gunfire.

Arthur Streeton
The Somme Valley Near Corbie AWM

Arthur Streeton
Bellicourt Tunnel AWM

Arthur Streeton
Amiens, the Key of the West
AWM

It recorded the battle which took place in the fields over the tunnel at the end of September 1918. It was one of the last actions in which the diggers fought. The composition of the painting, looking down on the dark entrance of the tunnel, was similar to that of Streeton's *Fire's On! Lapstone Tunnel*.

Amiens, the Key of the West was another large canvas, almost 1.5 × 2 metres. Streeton began working on it in September 1918, as soon as he returned from France, and before he had official approval to paint it. As he was working on the canvas, he wrote to Smart:

I've got quite a big canvas on here, of 'Amiens, the Key of the West' which I hope you can spare time to come & see one day.

It's a view from Blangy Tronville & Glissy [sic] down the valley of the Somme, with Amiens in the distance, & a 15mm French Gun on left of picture firing on Chaulnes 18 miles away.[53]

Amiens is west of Blangy, Tronville and Glisy which, in turn, are west of Chaulnes. Streeton's painting was looking west, towards Amiens, from the Glisy area. The Germans, the front line and Chaulnes were, therefore, behind the artist's back. According to Streeton's letter, the only gunfire in the painting was from a French gun in the left of the painting firing over the artist's head towards the Germans at Chaulnes. This level of detail is significant because the Australian War Memorial, which has this painting, claims in its catalogue that there is 'gunfire at the horizon', that is, west of Amiens.[54] When this picture was made (and, indeed, throughout the war), there was no gunfire west of Amiens – the Germans never penetrated that far.

Streeton painted other works at the same time as he painted his commission works for the Commonwealth. In another letter to Smart in September 1918, he reported that he had painted 'an oil memory study of the 4 balloons afire which the Melb. Gallery have acquired'.[55] It was another panoramic painting of the Somme Valley, on page 192, albeit smaller than the commission paintings. These paintings demonstrated a skill shared by the best landscape artists – virtuosity in painting sky and clouds.

The portrait painters found a steady trade painting soldiers. In addition to his portrait of Monash, John Longstaff painted Generals Brudenell White, Robertson, Herring, Cox, Rosenthal, Wisdom, McNicoll, Mackay and a range of others, many of whom had been decorated for bravery.[56] General Sir Cyril Brudenell White, Birdwood's chief of staff,

Arthur Streeton
Balloons on Fire NGV

was a contender with Monash for the mantle of Australia's finest general of the Great War. John Longstaff painted his portrait in 1921.

In addition to portraits of Birdwood and Monash, James Quinn painted Generals Walker, Chauvel, Glasgow, Howse and Gellibrand and Admiral Glossop.[57] George Bell painted twelve portraits, including portraits of Generals Herring, Glasgow and Leane, and of men decorated for bravery, among them, Lieutenant Colonel 'Mad Harry' Murray VC, CMG, DSO and Bar, DCM and Sergeant William 'Rusty' Ruthven VC.[58]

Portraits of high-ranking officers are a mainstay of war art. The compulsion to paint generals and admirals cannot be explained by the quality of the paintings. The Australian War Memorial has a huge collection of paintings of middle-aged men in military uniform, many of whom look the same.[59] Most of the paintings never make it out of the vaults. The portraits are made to complete the national record – to make sure that there is on file a good likeness of men who have served their country in trying roles and tough times. That is a matter of respect and commemoration. It does not seem to have been a matter of vanity. In the case of Fisher's artists' scheme, at least, the soldiers had no say over whose portrait was painted and whose was not. Many of those who were painted, far from welcoming the chance, in fact begrudged the artists time for the sittings.

John Longstaff painted one wartime portrait that did not fit the standard mould. It was a portrait of his son, Ralph, who, as Captain Longstaff MC, served in the British army. Lionel Lindsay thought that 'the whole of his art [was] compassed in the remarkable portrait of his soldier son'.[60] It was odd that, in November 1921, Longstaff senior agreed to accept 300 guineas to sell the painting to the New South Wales art gallery. In the circumstances, the comment of Longstaff's biographer – 'Ralph was very hostile towards his father' – seems understandable.[61]

The enlisted men in the army artists' scheme also worked on their major works. John Longstaff's cousin, Will Longstaff, made a brilliant painting of an Australian howitzer crew in action.

James Scott drew on his own experience to make the highly pictorial *4th Division Artillery and Infantry Moving into Battle*, on page 194. Painting with an eye to the historical record, he paid great attention to the detail of the men's kit and uniforms.

John Longstaff
General Sir Cyril Brudenell White AWM

Will Longstaff
Australian 9.2 Howitzer AWM

James Scott
4th Division Artillery and
Infantry Moving into Battle
AWM

George Benson
The Drover AWM

Longstaff's howitzer and Scott's painting of the 4th Division showed the value of employing artists who had served in the ranks to create an accurate historical record. George Benson took Bean's reverence for the digger as bushman to its logical conclusion. Using the classic theme of the 'drover', he cast the digger as drover and German prisoners as cattle in a Western Front version of Banjo Paterson's *Clancy of the Overflow*.

As the stock are slowly stringing, Clancy rides behind them singing,
For the drover's life has pleasures that the townsfolk never know.[62]

In April 1918, George Coates was invited to join the official war artists but, as Dora Coates explained:

For some unexplained reason the War Office, while yet giving approval for his services being made available for duty as an official artist, refused to grant the honorary commission and to release him from the English army, and he was therefore kept to his duties as orderly, while other artists, Australian and English, went as commissioned officers to paint in France.[63]

It was only after Dora called on Captain Smart and 'pointed it out', that George was commissioned 'to paint one or two portraits of generals'.[64] He eventually painted portraits of General Smyth, Brigadier Griffiths, Brigadier Foott and Captain Albert Jacka VC.[65] George stood at his orderly's post at Wandsworth until he was discharged in April 1919. By then, he was suffering from neurasthenia, no longer fit for service, 'a mere scarecrow of a man and a mass of nerves'.[66]

Shortly after his discharge, Coates painted *Casualty Clearing Station*. The painting showed stretcher-bearers bringing a wounded man into a clearing station, but owed a lot to artist's licence.

Casualty clearing stations were large hospitals situated as close as possible to the front, while remaining out of range of enemy artillery.[67] They had four functions: triage of casualties, including the clearance of those who could be moved to the ambulance trains; for the seriously wounded – resuscitation, effective operation, and adequate after-treatment; interim treatment of slightly wounded and 'gassed' men, and of the sick; and the effective treatment and return to duty of minor forms of injury and disease.[68] Although casualty clearing stations were supposed to be in safe locations, in practice, they could be much closer to the action. Sister Ida O'Dwyer worked at the Australian casualty clearing station at Gezaincourt in the Somme. She described how, in times of

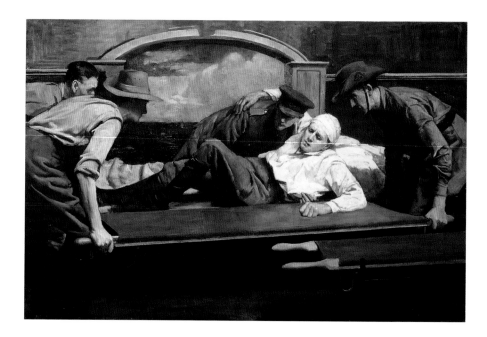

crisis, 'Every man [was] just as he was carried out of the trenches in his wet khaki and stone cold'. The patient with a broken thigh arrived with his 'leg clothed in khaki boot and mud of the trench with a splint over all that was supplied at the dressing station', and 'You [could] see death written in most of their faces'.[69]

Coates was stationed at Wandsworth in London throughout the war, so it is unlikely that he ever visited a casualty clearing station. Elements of *Casualty Clearing Station* were plainly based on his own experience – indeed, Dora wrote that it represented 'a scene in which he had often actively taken part'.[70] Yet the painting is at odds with Sister O'Dwyer's eyewitness description of a casualty clearing station.

Coates portrayed a calmer scene than Sister O'Dwyer described. The stretcher-bearers were Australian – both were wearing slouch hats. That, in itself, was significant. The fact that they were not wearing shrapnel helmets suggested that they were under no threat from enemy artillery. The man wearing the cap and cradling the patient was in the uniform of a Royal Army Medical Corps orderly – the same uniform that Coates wore at Wandsworth. The wounded man was a mystery. His boots were spotlessly clean, with not the slightest trace of mud. Odder still, he was wearing a pristine white shirt, its whiteness matched only by the whiteness of the bandage on his head. Where on the battlefield did he find a clean white shirt? And yet, death was written in his face – the white shirt and bandage emphasised his pallor.

George Coates
*First Australian Wounded to Arrive
in England from Gallipoli* AWM

Shortly after painting *Casualty Clearing Station*, Coates made a finished version of the painting he had sketched earlier, in 1915, at Wandsworth.

The fair copy, entitled *First Australian Wounded to Arrive in England from Gallipoli*, followed closely the sketch made in 1915, but there were a couple of differences. The sister on the left of the painting lost her severe appearance. In the fair copy, Coates painted her looking almost placid. The patient, who looked so terribly ill as a result of his wound and the depredations of the sea voyage, still looked ill, but now had his slouch hat with him. After the long sea voyage, there it was, sitting on his bedside table.

Of the two paintings, *First Australian Wounded* takes its force from its factual accuracy, while *Casualty Clearing Station* takes its force from the connection between the wounded man and those caring for him. The *Casualty Clearing Station* would have been in France, yet Coates framed the subjects in an archway reminiscent of the archway in the receiving ward at Wandsworth, and used the archway as a painterly device to highlight the connection between the men in the painting. *Casualty Clearing Station* is the better painting – but *First Australian Wounded* is the more accurate historical record.

In 1920, Coates painted *Australian Official War Artists*, on page iii, a composition including the portraits of all the other official war artists.

Dora wrote that, far from making things easy for Coates, the war artists behaved badly when they had to sit for their own portraits:

It was difficult to get any of them to sit decently for him. He only had Lambert to pose for a few minutes; for Streeton he had to go up to his studio in St John's Wood to do his head; Longstaff also could only give two short afternoon sittings, and Quinn less. Perhaps the most satisfactory as portraits are those of W. Dyson and George Bell in the foreground. He usually did a life-size head and copied it into the group in proportion. As he had none of them to pose together, it is astonishing he was able to make such a harmonious and well-proportioned group of the whole.[71]

In 1921, the Coates made a visit to Australia.

Treloar, now in charge of the Australian War Museum (the original name of the Australia War Memorial), approached Coates to paint a composed picture, a group of generals at the foot of the pyramids. The painting was pure make-believe, commissioned as part of the effort to create a record of the campaign at Gallipoli. George was reluctant to accept the commission. His nerves were still troubling him, and he was cautious about undertaking a painting of this sort, not least because most of the subjects would have to be painted from photographs. Bean lent his encouragement, but the project was left in abeyance until November, when George and Dora bought a canvas and, together, set about the painting outdoors at a holiday house by the sea at Brighton, in Melbourne. Dora wrote:

we had a thoroughly happy fortnight together – lovely sea, space, air; sunshine and showers; bathes; freedom from care – sheer animal enjoyment, with good food, in a pleasant, simple little, old-fashioned wooden bungalow, with a long front garden, where the hens clucked under our window … At times the heat was tropical, but in the afternoons George did some good painting with his models in khaki on the sand, and the evenings were delicious, when we walked on the little wooden pier … George could go up to General Foott's house in a neighbouring suburb to carry on his portrait, while I worked on the 'Pyramid picture' in the boat shed, which we had as a studio and where we could paint in bad weather.[72]

Bean became increasingly involved in details of the composition of the painting:

Also the matter of the position of the group in relation to the Pyramids was gone into very carefully and minutely by Mr Bean, the Australian official historian. And then the *time of day* had to be settled, and whether the generals would seated on the ground or standing, George thinking it would be more dignified if they were sitting at a camp table.[73]

Bean's interference was not calculated to calm Coates' nerves. It was finally settled that George and Dora would stop off in Egypt on their journey back to London 'so as to better understand the *mise en scène* of the group'.[74]

The Coates spent twelve days in Cairo, without finishing the painting.

George Coates and Dora Meeson
*General William Bridges and His
Staff Watching the Manoeuvres of the
1st Australian Division in the Desert
in Egypt, March 1915* AWM

George worked on it again in London, 'but messed up the composition so badly it was distressing'. To calm his nerves, he took up golf, in the hope that the exercise would relax him. The exercise was fine, but the sport was a poor choice for someone suffering anxiety: 'he was too nervous at the time to make a good player, for the knowledge that others were coming on behind put him off his game'.[75] Throughout 1923, the pyramid picture languished: 'some officer friends on coming into the studio had said that the staff chiefs would not be *seated* while looking on at manoeuvres, but would all be *standing*. So a standing group was designed'.[76]

In April 1924, Treloar wrote to reject the new layout. He asked the Coates to return to that which had been approved. On 13 September 1924, George started the pyramid picture over again, on a fresh canvas. Work went well initially, but by December, George was stale, and Dora took over. Bean and his wife visited to see the new version and – unsurprisingly – 'gave many valuable hints'.[77] By 1925, Dora wrote, 'At last, the "Pyramid picture" was well under way', but it was not until 1927 that George and Dora finally delivered the finished work to Australia House and collected the £400 fee. It was the largest sum George ever received for one picture, but the return, calculated on an hourly rate cannot have been much at all.[78]

The Pyramid picture was a disappointment. The pyramid in the background told where the action was taking place, but added nothing to the narrative. The composition lacked coherence. The grouping was a cut and paste exercise. Many of the subjects were looking into the distance, but no two of them were looking at the same thing. The idea of taking a card table into the desert was a failure. It made Generals White and Bridges – men whom Bean revered as 'two great Australians, the founders of the AIF'[79] – look like grandfathers on a primary school visiting day, sitting perched on the children's chairs.[80] Great art is seldom created by committee.

In London once again, Lambert had plenty of work. His priority from his trip to the Sinai was *The Charge of the Australian Light Horse at Beersheba, 1917*, but he also wanted to paint *The Battle of Romani, 4 August 1916*. His priority from his trip to Gallipoli was *Anzac, the Landing 1915*, but he also wanted to paint *The Charge of the 3rd Light Horse Brigade at the Nek, 7 August 1915*.

He started on the *Landing* and *Beersheba* paintings. At 2 × 3.7 metres,

George Lambert

The Charge of the Australian Light Horse at Beersheba, 1917 AWM

the *Landing* was a huge canvas. *Beersheba* was smaller (1.4 × 2.6 metres), but still large. Working on both together demanded a big space. To add to the space needed, Lambert was working with Luigi di Luca, an artist's model with whom he had worked before the war. Sergeant Ivers (whom Lambert had met in Damascus) also lent a hand.[81] Lambert also pressed his artist-son, Maurice, into service. Maurice acted as a model and transferred Lambert's sketches onto the canvases. Beersheba also needed horses as models.[82]

After struggling with makeshift studios in London, Lambert borrowed a country house in Cornwall from a friendly artist. There was a chance there would be sun in Cornwall, which would help with the *plein air* effects that both paintings demanded. The country house had a generous studio, but it remained impossible to find models – human or equine – in the labour shortages that followed the war. When Lambert needed sun to help him finish the *Beersheba* painting, Cornwall turned on rain. He wrote to Amy: 'I try to preserve a philosophic calm about *Beersheba*, and this damnable lack of sunlight. Tonight it howls and rains forty cats to the dozen; there can't be much more left above'. He eventually finished *Beersheba* in London towards the end of 1920.[83]

Beersheba included reminders of Lambert's small 'masterpiece' painting, both in the colour of the desert and in the scratchy foliage it

George Lambert
A Sergeant of the Light Horse NGV

George Lambert
The Official Artist NGV

depicted. For the most part, however, the painting was the culmination of the work Lambert had put into sketching the light-horsemen and their horses during his time in Palestine in late 1917. The painting gave further evidence of the serendipity of Fisher's scheme. Time spent in sketching on location was not wasted. It paid handsome dividends when Lambert came to paint the grand painting. As Lambert said, 'Painting cannot exist without drawing'.[84]

At this time, Lambert also painted two portraits that make an interesting comparison.

A Sergeant of the Light Horse was a beautiful portrait of Sergeant Ivers, set against a background of Palestine hills. Ivers' jacket, with its sergeant's stripes, hangs on the back of the chair he sits on. Jackets of that type buttoned up to the neck. Under it, the men wore soft, grey, collarless flannel shirts. Lambert painted Ivers wearing his collarless shirt, with the sleeves rolled up. He holds the felt hat of the digger with the emu plume that was distinctive of the Light Horse. Lambert believed that, although Australians were commonly painted as tall, wiry men, 'the average Australian – if there is one – is short and stout'.[85] Nevertheless, Lambert followed the painterly fashion, giving Ivers the appearance of a tall, rangy man. In fact, Ivers was only 1.7 metres tall.[86]

The Official Artist was a whimsical self-portrait, showing Lambert as a soldier, but a very casual soldier. The painting made a pigeon pair with that of Sergeant Ivers. Lambert painted himself wearing uniform trousers and the collarless flannel shirt with sleeves pushed up. In one hand, he held a few of his Light Horse painting props and the plumed hat of the Light Horse. In the other, he lifted a glass, as if to make a toast. The label completed the package. It read: 'Dedicated to the Aust. Light Horse Palestine', perhaps reflecting how Lambert felt after spending two years painting little else than the Light Horse.

The end of the war triggered a migration. Bean returned to Australia at the end of the Mission. Treloar, Ivers and the other men of the Australian War Records Section had already returned. Daryl Lindsay returned to Australia in June 1919.[87] Roberts and his family were in Melbourne for Christmas 1919.[88] Streeton took his family to Melbourne, arriving there in February 1920.[89] George and Dora Coates had already returned; so had George Bell.[90] Longstaff left England in July 1920.[91]

The pull of the herd combined with the dismal weather to sharpen Lambert's yearning for Australia. According to Amy, his thoughts turned to 'a country where he knew that sunlight, horses and sympathetic assistance and whole-hearted appreciation awaited him'.[92] He arrived in Melbourne in May 1921. He found the welcome he had hoped for: 'Streeton and Sir Baldwin [Spencer], George Coates and George Bell have come along and made me welcome; Major Treloar most obliging and courteous'. Lambert began by holding a short, but successful, one-man show at the Fine Art Society, at which the National Gallery of Victoria bought both *A Sergeant of the Light Horse* and *The Official Artist*. But the respite was brief. Lambert wrote to Amy: 'Next week I go into harness again for the Government'.[93]

The distractions were considerable, not only in the form of friends keen to party, but also in the form of opportunities to paint new and interesting subjects. It did not take long for the attractions of rural Australia to turn Lambert's head. He wrote to Amy that he was planning 'a very important picture indeed, to be called "Weighing the Fleece"'. He also had in mind a 'cattle picture' – a young man, positioned amongst trees, undulating plains, mountains, cockatoos, galahs, shadows, camp-fire and sunlight.[94]

Lambert was tiring quickly of the war paintings: 'I feel I shall be alright when I get Gallipoli off the stocks and can get away to the Monaro'. He spent Christmas painting on a friend's property in the Monaro.[95] Finishing the *Landing* was a battle against loneliness:

But the war stuff must be finished … It is not uninteresting and the heroism of the artist marches with the people in the picture; the difference that hurts is that I do it on my own. But even this is a test of staying power and in my most miserable moments I apply the spur.

Lambert's stomach began to give him trouble. He wrote to Amy: 'The whole beastly business of this Australian trip amounts to this: my working power is not what it was, but I hasten to add that my keenness has increased and my desire to do the three or four big subjects which I have for so many years longed to do stronger than ever'.[97] Eventually Treloar intervened. He closeted Lambert in the disused ward of a military hospital in Sydney's Randwick, insisting that he use it as a studio until his work for the Commonwealth was finished. Treloar set Lambert up with the uniforms and other equipment he used as props and with the unfinished works that weighed so heavily on his conscience, and locked

George Lambert
The Charge of the 3rd Light Horse Brigade at the Nek, 7 August 1915
AWM

George Lambert
Anzac, the Landing, 1915 AWM

him away to finish his assignments. The Randwick studio became a little factory. Lambert gathered a small staff around him and, with their companionship to ward off his loneliness, the *Landing* was finally completed.

It was another two years before the *Nek* was finished, and three years more until the *Romani* painting surfaced.[98]

Lambert claimed to be an artist-historian, which might suggest that he intended his work to be historically accurate. His two great paintings of Gallipoli provide commentary on that notion. During their Mission at Gallipoli, Lambert asked Bean and Balfour about the dress of the men who took part in the landing. Balfour told him that, at the landing, the men had been ordered to roll up their sleeves to distinguish them from the Turks in the half-light of dawn. Moreover, none of the men who landed at Anzac on 25 April 1915 was wearing an Australian slouch hat. Bean wrote that:

In his great picture [the *Landing*], of all the scores of climbing men who, in the flat morning light, almost blend into the colour of the scrub, every one has his sleeves down to his wrist, and everyone wears an Australian hat, though Lambert knew that they landed in the little round peaked caps which were the general wear of Australian infantry in that great battle.[99]

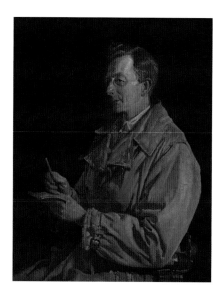

George Lambert
Charles EW Bean AWM

By contrast, in the *Nek*, on page 204, Lambert painted the clothing accurately. The men in that painting were wearing 'Anzac uniform' – shorts, sleeveless shirts, slouch hats, no leggings. Lambert showed all the variations and modifications that they had made to their uniforms to accommodate the Mediterranean summer.[100]

In his letters written when he was at Gallipoli, Lambert described the soil as 'sandy clay with stones or gravel' and the scrub as 'greenish with nice dead stuff showing grey-purple here and there'. He later wrote that 'the whole landscape is a dull mauvey grey with a sage green admixture and very delicate if sombre in tone'.[101] When he came to finish the paintings, Lambert used a distinctly purple palette for the distant mountains. The terrain, the scrub and their colouring as Lambert painted them, especially in the *Nek*, were reminiscent of the Flinders Ranges, in South Australia. By contrast, the foreground in the *Landing* was orange, interspersed with the green of the stunted vegetation. It is tempting to suggest that the paintings evoked the Australian bush, but Lambert was not thinking of remote Australia when he made the paintings. He wrote that 'the country resembles moorland in Yorkshire or South England, not unlike the bare stuff around Frensham Ponds'.[102] They are bleak and beautiful places, where heather is queen and the scrub is grey, purple and sombre green.

In 1924, Lambert painted CEW Bean. The painting showed Bean, pencil and notebook at the ready, in the finest Jimmy Olsen, cub reporter, mould.[103]

Bean could not bring himself to let Lambert's joke go through to the keeper. Instead, he took time in his book, *Gallipoli Mission*, to set the record straight:

Needless to say I did not begin my interrogations with pencil and notebook in hand (as in a portrait which George Lambert some years later did me the honour of painting) ... Never since my earliest days as a reporter have I produced a notebook or pencil at the beginning of such an interview. One must, of course, let one's subject know that he is speaking for publication, but if one also starts by bringing out this apparatus any but the most hardened public person is immediately scared.[104]

Apparatus? It was pencil and paper. Was there ever a man who took himself more seriously than Bean?

EPILOGUE

Many artists lost family and friends in the war. Hilda Rix Nicholas lost her mother, her sister, her husband and her brother-in-law. The Lindsays lost their brother. On one day in July 1916, Reginald Longstaff was wounded and John Longstaff junior was killed. John Longstaff's third son, Ralph, had been wounded earlier in 1916.[1] Other artists suffered ill-health – George Lambert and George Coates both suffered illnesses that shortened their lives.

With the Armistice, came the prospect of a return to normal life. The artists were free to resume their work. More than that, they had a role to play in the healing process, whether in commemorating the war, or in demonstrating that mankind was as capable of creating things of beauty as things of horror. It would take time, but normality would return, and wounds would heal.

On 12 March 1919, Ruby Lindsay, Will Dyson's wife, died.[2] It seemed impossible that the gods could be so malign.

At the end of the Great War, Australians were still British, but they were proud to be different from the British, and they celebrated the differences. They were still British subjects, but they had marked out an identity as citizens of a new nation. They were still members of the British Empire, but they were ready to redefine their ties with the mother country in terms of equality, not subservience.

In 1926, Great Britain joined with the Dominions – Australia, Canada, the Irish Free State, New Zealand and South Africa – in declaring that the Dominions were:

Will Dyson
Peace and Future Cannon Fodder
The Tiger is saying: 'Curious, I seem
to hear a child weeping!'
Dyson's drawing shows the weeping
baby as one of the conscription class
of 1940

autonomous Communities within the British Empire, equal in status, in no way subordinate to one another in any aspect of their domestic or external affairs, though united by a common allegiance to the Crown, and freely associated as members of the British Commonwealth of Nations.[3]

In 1914, it had been unthinkable that the Dominions were equal with Great Britain.

The Prime Minister of France, 'Tiger' Georges Clemenceau, presided over the peace conference that produced the Treaty of Versailles. It was a bad peace. It did not so much end the war, as postpone its resumption.

Will Dyson understood. His cartoon of the peace conference showed Tiger Clemenceau leading (left to right) British Prime Minister Lloyd George, Italian Prime Minister Orlando and US President Wilson past a weeping child with the misfortune to reach the age of conscription into a European army in 1940.

When the artists returned to Australia, were they also retreating to safety?

They had set out for Europe in search of success and acclaim on the world stage. Cynics would argue that they returned in rather more chastened circumstances. They would point out that, in 1920, Roberts was sixty-four, John Longstaff was fifty-nine, Streeton was fifty-three, George and Dora Coates were fifty-one, Lambert was forty-seven, and Rix Nicholas was thirty-six. Roberts was no longer the charismatic fundamentalist who had converted Streeton and Conder to painting impressions. Longstaff was living on his reputation. Streeton was a touchy old stager, jealous of his status and anxious to maximise his legacy. George Coates and Lambert were not well.

It is true that the artists had lost some of the ardour of their youth. After what they had endured, who could blame them? They measured success differently than they had when they set out. The French Salon and the British Academy no longer loomed so large in their eyes. They saw that their art owed debts to Australia and to Europe. These had to be set in balance.

When Tom Roberts returned to Australia in 1923, he was a father figure of Australian art. He said: 'Australia has just found her nationhood, and that is bound to be reflected in her art'.[4] Roberts had a foot in two camps. Australia was 'a place of sunshine and good health; a place that is always so inspiriting to me and so full of suggestion; one reaches out instinctively for the palette'. But, he added, 'don't run away with the idea that we didn't appreciate dear old England'. She had been good to Roberts, accepting him as a painter of portraits and of landscapes.[5] Coates was uncertain whether to live in Australia or England, eventually choosing England.[6] Streeton, who had fought so hard for acceptance at the Royal Academy, fretted when a critic suggested that he 'was no longer an Australian artist'.[7]

There was no retreat to safety. The New World offered benefits; so did the Old. There was no question of preferring one over the other:

For what could be more limiting for any country than only to see, with few exceptions, local works of art? What could be more limiting for the artists of that country than to be denied the opportunity of pitting their art against art of other parts of the world? The small ones amongst them may fear the competition: fear that some little pennies may go into the incomers' pockets instead of their own. But the bigger souls must want to conquer bigger worlds – for how much greater is the triumph of battles won amongst the champions of the wide world, than won just locally?[8]

This was Hilda Rix Nicholas. After all that the war had done to her, she still talked of art in terms of competition and conquest, battles and triumph. It was as if her experience had taught nothing of risk avoidance.

The artists who left Australia at the turn of the last century encountered more of life than of painting. If their lives tell us anything, it is that life lived safely is no life at all.

Bigger souls want to conquer bigger worlds. Let it always be so.

ARTISTS WHO SERVED WITH THE AIF

Source: *Art in Australia*,
Sixth number, 1919

NEW SOUTH WALES
Harwood Addison
LE Allworth
G Bailey
J Ballman
David Barker
PC Blackett
Fred Brown
George Browne
C Bostock
Harry Burne
WC Chapple
Ted Colles
LC Dalley-Cooper
Roy De Mestre
P Elmes
_ Foley
R Gates
HR Geer
Elliott Gruner
Cecil Hartt
JS Hawkes
CJ Heasely
B Johnson
HV Keane
WE Lang
Norman Lloyd
Vernon Lorimer
HG Meek
MS Mison
George Moore
H Moore-Jones
Adrian John Peachey
Cecil Percival
JF Scott
WH Sheppard
Ellis Silas DCM
Brian Simpson[†]
Fred Small
HW Smith
GK Townsend
AL Turnbridge
H Woolcott
JC Wright[†]

SOUTH AUSTRALIA
FC Britton
A Hay
LH Howie
R Waden
FA Williams
HE Winter

VICTORIA
W Wallace Anderson
G Benson
Merric Boyd
T Penleigh Boyd
CB Campbell
George G Colville
PW Corser[†]
HL Darvall
Wilson Dobbs
G Dunstan
Louis C de G Foulet
GF Garrard
F Latimer
Daryl Lindsay
Reg Lindsay[†]
Will Longstaff
JS MacDonald
Louis McCubbin
W Mont Montgomery[†]
Arthur CS Murray
Chris Murray MM
F Noonan
Hector Paterson
Jack M Paterson[†]
AH Picking
EL Robbins
Wm Russell-Coleman MC
Henry Sennett
Jack Sommers
JB Trinnick
M Napier Waller
Ralph W Waugh
Chas Wheeler DCM
Cyril L White
Nurse Louisa B Riggall

QUEENSLAND
JH Cadell
GW Caseldine
Eric H Dickenson
Haviland Durand[†]
H Justelius
Hugh McLean

WESTERN AUSTRALIA
Michael McKinley
Cyril Ross MC

[†] Killed in action
Nurse Riggall died
while serving in France.

Artists in addition to
those from the *Art in
Australia* list
Source: William Moore,
*The Story of Australian
Art,* vol 2, pp 149–150

N Allen
ES Bailey
PA Batham
D Barker
AC Bleach
JLC Booth
CWF Buchanan
JS Butler
A Cash
GHP Clark
HF Coates
WR Coleman
HO Coulson
T Cross
FR Crozier
B Dubois
W Farrow
A Feint
GM Fenwick
F Finley
H Gallop
J Goodchild
T Gootch
LF Gordon
CH Gould
CF Hale
CM Hallett
G Handfield
A Hay
AE Henderson
WO Hewitt
FG Hoare
P Huthnance
TH Ivers

RC Jacobs
JJ Johnson
CF Kitchin-Kerr
G Little
N Lloyd
V Loureiro
C Lowther
RH Luxmore
A McPherson
KR Macqueen
VF Marshall
L Mattinson
FH Molony
WK Moss
ACS Murray
H Newell
W Nicholl
S Perks
AG Record
GTM Roach
EL Robbins
PV Ryan
C Samuels
EG Scott
S Shaw
A Storr
RW Sturgess
W Taylor
R Trevelan
R Waden
DC Walker
R Wenban
E Wolf

Additional artists
who contributed to
*From the Australian
Front Xmas 1917*

Bernie Bragg
John P Davis
WL King
Allen M Lewi
Alf Saville

NOTES

PRINCIPAL ARTISTS

[1] RH Croll, *Tom Roberts: Father of Australian Landscape Painting* (Melbourne: Robertson & Mullens, 1935). See also Tom Roberts et al, *Tom Roberts* (Adelaide and Sydney: Art Gallery of South Australia and Art Exhibitions Australia, 1996).

[2] 'James Stuart MacDonald (1878–1952)', *Australian Dictionary of Biography*, vol 10, pp 263–64. For Roberts, see James MacDonald, *Australian Painting Desiderata [with a Portrait]* (Melbourne: Lothian Publishing, 1958), pp 33–34.

[3] MacDonald, *Australian Painting Desiderata*, p 37.

1 BEING AUSTRALIAN

[1] Helen Irving, *The Centenary Companion to Australian Federation* (Cambridge and Melbourne: Cambridge University Press, 1999), p 30. In 1887, the other self-governing colonies were Victoria, Queensland, South Australia and Tasmania. Western Australia did not gain the right of self-government until 1890.

[2] Robert Garran, *Prosper the Commonwealth* (Sydney: Angus & Robertson, 1958), p 80.

[3] Jack Pollard, *The Complete Illustrated History of Australian Cricket*, rev edn (Ringwood, Vic: Viking, 1995), p 75.

[4] Nellie Melba and John Cargher, *Melodies and Memories* (West Melbourne: Nelson, 1980), pp 1–2.

[5] Manning Clark, *Select Documents in Australian History, 1851–1900* (Sydney: Angus & Robertson, 1977), p 796. Sowden was a South Australian journalist and newspaper proprietor, and a founder of the South Australian branch of the Australian Natives' Association.

[6] Irving, *The Centenary Companion to Australian Federation*, pp 66, 199. Few Australians today regard themselves as Australian and British, but some do think of themselves as, for example, Queenslanders and Australians. There is still some way to go in establishing a coherent national identity.

[7] The Commonwealth of Australia was inaugurated on 1 January 1901.

[8] It was not until 1984 that 'Advance Australia Fair' became Australia's national anthem. Peter Dodds McCormack wrote the song in 1878, twenty-three years before the Commonwealth of Australia was inaugurated. As early as that, an Australian identity was sufficiently coherent and well developed for English settlers in the colonies to join in a song that began with the words 'Australians all let us rejoice'.

[9] Sir Charles Harington, *Plumer of Messines* (London: John Murray, 1935), pp 45–46.

2 PAINTING AUSTRALIA

[1] James MacDonald, *Australian Painting Desiderata [with a Portrait]* (Melbourne: Lothian Publishing, 1958), p 37.

[2] ibid, pp 37–38. It is ironic to quote James MacDonald in this context. Later in life, he became notorious for his caustic criticisms of new developments in the art world, taking a stand against modernism that would have brought a tear to the eye of King Canute himself. Wearing this hat, he gave evidence in the famous court case challenging the award of the Archibald Prize to William Dobell for his portrait of fellow artist Joshua Smith. MacDonald's testimony? Dobell's portrait of Smith was 'a pictorial defamation of character': Brian Adams and William Dobell, *Portrait of an Artist: A Biography of William Dobell* (Milsons Point, NSW: Vintage, 1992), p 100. For an overview of the arts scene in turn-of-the-century Melbourne, see Ann Galbally, 'Shackled & Set Free: Art, Music and Theatre in Melbourne in the 1890s' in Thérèse Radic and Suzanne Robinson (eds), *Marshall-Hall's Melbourne: Music, Art and Controversy 1891–1915* (North Melbourne: Australian Scholarly Publishing, 2012).

[3] 'John Peter Russell (1858–1930)', *Australian Dictionary of Biography*, vol 11, pp 483–84.

[4] William Moore, *The Story of Australian Art: From the Earliest Known Art of the Continent to the Art of To-Day*, 2 vols (Sydney: Angus & Robertson, 1934), vol 1, p 93. RH Croll, *Tom Roberts: Father of Australian Landscape Painting* (Melbourne: Robertson & Mullens, 1935), p 13. Croll wrote his biography of Roberts on a commission from Mrs Roberts: RH Croll and Walter Murdoch, *I Recall: Collections and Recollections*, 1st cheaper edn (Melbourne: Robertson & Mullens, 1939), p 69. It was more or less an official biography.

[5] Helen Topliss and Tom Roberts, *Tom Roberts, 1856–1931 : A Catalogue Raisonnee*, 2 vols (Melbourne: Oxford University Press, 1985), vol 1, pp 7, 68.

[6] MacDonald, *Australian Painting Desiderata*, p 39.

[7] Croll, *Tom Roberts*, p 14.

[8] The Roberts family evidently liked the painting. They kept it until 2005, when they gave it to the National Gallery of Victoria.

[9] MacDonald, *Australian Painting Desiderata*, p 33. Bitumen was sometimes used as a paint additive to enrich darker tones. It imparted a dark colouring when used for the preliminary underpainting of an oil painting. Lionel Lindsay, one of the Lindsay family of artists, described Folingsby as 'a typical schoolman out of touch with all modernity': *Art in Australia*, Fourth number, 1918, pages unnumbered.

[10] Moore, *The Story of Australian Art*, vol 1, p 93. Streeton was eighteen when he first met Roberts.

[11] John Rothenstein and Charles Edward Conder, *The Life and Death of Conder [with Plates, Including Portraits]* (London: JM Dent & Sons, 1938), pp 12–14. Conder later shared a studio in Paris with John Rothenstein's father, the English artist, Sir William Rothenstein. Conder was nineteen years old when he met Roberts in the wine shop in Mosman.

[12] ibid, p 14

[13] Mostly spelt 'Proff'! See, for example, Croll, *Tom Roberts*, pp 54, 55.

[14] James Smith, *Argus*, 11 September 1888.

[15] Bernard Smith, *Documents on Art and Taste in Australia: The Colonial Period, 1770–1914* (Melbourne: Oxford University Press, 1975), p 205.

[16] Croll, *Tom Roberts*, p 26.

[17] Bernard Smith, *Place, Taste and Tradition: A Study of Australian Art since 1788*, 2nd edn (Melbourne: Oxford University Press, 1979), p 129.

[18] Bernard Smith, *Documents on Art and Taste in Australia*, p 204.

[19] ibid, p 206.

[20] ibid, pp 206–07.

[21] In 1916, McCubbin wrote of the artists at this exhibition – he was one of them – that 'Their war cry was *relative values*, the necessity to paint everything on the spot': James MacDonald, Frederick McCubbin, and Alexander McCubbin, *The Art of F McCubbin* (Brisbane: Boolarong Publications, 1986), p 86.

[22] Bernard Smith, *Documents on Art and Taste in Australia*, p 208.

[23] ibid, pp 209–10. Of course, the notion that there was a single 'true method of interpreting' the landscape in painting was misplaced. Many forms of interpretation are possible. Many Aboriginal artists have other, quite different, ways of painting the Australian bush.

[24] 'Heidelberg School Review', *The Australian Critic*, 1 July 1891.

[25] For a description of the artists' camps, see Albie Thoms and Art Gallery of New South Wales, *Bohemians in the Bush: The Artists' Camps of Mosman* (Sydney: Art Gallery of New South Wales, 1991). The zoo did not move to Mosman until 1916. Before that, it was located in Moore Park, on the site now occupied by Sydney Boys High School and Sydney Girls High School.

[26] ibid, p 71.

[27] Arthur Streeton, Ann Galbally, and Anne Gray, *Letters from Smike: The Letters of Arthur Streeton, 1890–1943* (Melbourne: Oxford University Press, 1989), p 34.

[28] Bernard Smith, *Place, Taste and Tradition*, p 242.

[29] Streeton, Galbally, and Gray, *Letters from Smike*, pp 39–40.

[30] Review in the *Sun*, 3 June 1892, quoted in Geoffrey Smith, Arthur Streeton, and National Gallery of Victoria, *Arthur Streeton, 1867–1943* (Melbourne: National Gallery of Victoria, 1995), p 84.

[31] Who can?

[32] Moore, *The Story of Australian Art*, vol 1, p 96.

[33] Streeton, Galbally, and Gray, *Letters from Smike*, p 68.

[34] Croll, *Tom Roberts*, p 61.

[35] Geoffrey Caban, *A Fine Line: A History of Australian Commercial Art* (Sydney: Hale & Iremonger, 1983).

[36] ibid, p 27 and following.

[37] Robert Garran, *Prosper the Commonwealth* (Sydney: Angus & Robertson, 1958), p 143. An influential bureaucrat, Garran was the first secretary of the Attorney-General's Department.

[38] ibid, pp 143–44.

[39] According to Museum Victoria, the dome of the Exhibition Building was modelled on that of the Duomo in Florence: Elizabeth Wills, *The Royal Exhibition Building, Melbourne: A Guide* (Melbourne: Museum Victoria, 2004). Brunelleschi under southern stars!

[40] There had not been time since the death of Queen Victoria to promote the Duke of Cornwall and York to be Prince of Wales. This came later, in November 1901. The Duke/Prince reigned as King George V from 1910 until 1936.

[41] JA La Nauze, *Alfred Deakin: A Biography*, 2 vols (Carlton, Vic: Melbourne University Press, 1965), vol 1, p 228.

[42] 'Speech delivered by His Royal Highness the Duke of Cornwall and York at the Opening of the First Federal Parliament, 9th May 1901' (Australian Government Printer, 1901).

[43] The Duke and the King were perfectly correct. The Commonwealth of Australia was a British colony after Federation, just as the individual states had been colonies before; Australia was proudly part of the British Empire; and her inhabitants were subjects of the King. The Australian Constitution did not create or recognise Australian citizenship. At the time of Federation, all Australians were British subjects. Australian citizenship was first recognised with the enactment of the *Australian Citizenship Act 1948*.

[44] Humphrey McQueen, *Tom Roberts* (Sydney: Macmillan, 1996), p 462.

[45] Waite's portrait of gallery benefactor Alfred Felton, made in 1905, was hung in the boardroom of the National Gallery of Victoria: Alan McCulloch, *Encyclopedia of Australian Art* (New York: Frederick A Praeger, 1968), p 566.

[46] Croll, *Tom Roberts*, p 60.

[47] ibid, p 61.

[48] ibid, p 62.

3 FROM HEIDELBERG TO LONDON – OR PARIS

[1] 'Bertram Mackennal (1863–1931)', *Australian Dictionary of Biography*, vol 10, pp 301–02.

[2] 'Rupert Bunny (1864–1947)', *Australian Dictionary of Biography*, vol 7, pp 479–80.

[3] Jillian Dwyer, 'The "Work" of Art: The National Gallery of Victoria Travelling Scholarship 1887–1932', MA thesis, Monash University, 1997.

[4] Nina Murdoch, *Portrait in Youth of Sir John Longstaff (1861–1941)* (Sydney: Angus & Robertson, 1948), p 49.

[5] Prue Joske, *Debonair Jack: A Biography of Sir John Longstaff 1861–1941* (Hawthorn, Vic: Claremont, 1994), p 51 and following. According to artist and teacher, Julian Ashton, Longstaff had a 'courteous and rather diffident manner [that] endeared him to all who knew him': Julian Ashton, *Now Came Still Evening On* (Sydney: Angus & Robertson, 1941), p 100.

[6] Joske, *Debonair Jack*, p 70 and following.

[7] ibid, p 95.

[8] Aby Altson, the 1890 winner, left Australia, never to return. Art critic Bernard Smith described Altson's scholarship painting, *The Golden Age*, as 'a large, rather immature painting in which slender, lissom *art nouveau* youths and maidens disport themselves': Bernard Smith, *Australian Painting, 1788–1970*, 2nd edn (Melbourne: Oxford University Press, 1971), p 98. The description is more interesting than the painting. Max Meldrum won the scholarship in 1899. Working in Europe from 1900 until he returned to Australia in 1912, Meldrum lived in Australia during the war years.

[9] 'James Quinn (1869–1951)', *Australian Dictionary of Biography*, vol 11, pp 319–20.

[10] Dora Meeson Coates, *George Coates: His Art and His Life* (London: JM Dent, 1937), p 2.

[11] Ross McMullin, *Will Dyson: Cartoonist, Etcher and Australia's Finest War Artist* (Sydney: Angus & Robertson, 1984), p 17 and following. The Ishmael Club had similar goals and similar membership: p 19 and following. For an account of both clubs, see Stephen F Mead, 'Bohemia & Brotherhood in Late Nineteenth Century Melbourne: Marshall-Hall's Involvement with the Cannibal and Ishmael Clubs' in Thérèse Radic and Suzanne Robinson (eds), *Marshall-Hall's Melbourne: Music, Art and Controversy 1891–1915* (North Melbourne: Australian Scholarly Publishing, 2012). See also William Moore, *The Story of Australian Art: From the Earliest Known Art of the Continent to the Art of To-Day*, 2 vols (Sydney: Angus & Robertson, 1934), vol 1, p 166 and following.

[12] Lionel Lindsay, *Comedy of Life: An Autobiography* (Sydney: Angus & Robertson, 1967), p 35.

[13] McMullin, *Will Dyson* (1984), p 16 and following.

[14] Lionel Lindsay, *Comedy of Life*, pp 56–57.

[15] ibid, p 59.

[16] Coates, *George Coates*, p 9.

17 ibid, p 10.

18 ibid, p 11 and following.

19 ibid, pp 14–15.

20 ibid, pp 15–16.

21 ibid, p 16.

22 ibid, p 18.

23 Lionel Lindsay, *Comedy of Life*, pp 206–07. Joanna Mendelssohn, *Lionel Lindsay: An Artist and His Family* (London: Chatto & Windus, 1988), pp 222–23.

24 For a history of commercial art in Australia, see Geoffrey Caban, *A Fine Line: A History of Australian Commercial Art* (Sydney: Hale & Iremonger, 1983).

25 Mendelssohn, *Lionel Lindsay*, p 110 and following.

26 Norman Lindsay, *My Mask: For What Little I Know of the Man Behind It, An Autobiography* (Sydney: Angus & Robertson, 1970), p 178.

27 Ross McMullin, *Will Dyson: Australia's Radical Genius* (Carlton North, Vic: Scribe Publications, 2006), p 29.

28 For Rose's description of the Northwood house, see Rose Lindsay, *Model Wife: My Life with Norman Lindsay* (Sydney: Ure Smith, 1967), p 26 and following.

29 John Hetherington, *Norman Lindsay: The Embattled Olympian* (Melbourne: Oxford University Press, 1973), pp 62–63.

30 McMullin, *Will Dyson* (2006), p 33.

31 ibid, p 34.

32 McMullin, *Will Dyson* (1984), p 36.

33 Lionel Lindsay, a knight of the realm and a close friend of Prime Minister Menzies, who lived on the upper North Shore of Sydney, wrote of Dyson's 'leftist politics' that his 'hatred of capitalism, and trust in the panaceas of Douglas Credit and Welfare Statism became ingrained': Lionel Lindsay, *Comedy of Life*, p 236.

34 McMullin, *Will Dyson* (1984), p 46 and following.

35 Norman Lindsay, *My Mask*, p 193.

36 Daryl Lindsay, *The Leafy Tree: My Family* (Melbourne: FW Cheshire, 1965), p 70.

37 For Norman Lindsay's account of the rift between him and Will and Ruby Dyson, see Norman Lindsay, *My Mask*, p 206. Dyson/Lindsay family gatherings must have been challenging.

38 June Helmer, *George Bell, the Art of Influence* (Richmond, Vic: Greenhouse, 1985), p 26.

39 ibid, p 28; Bernard Smith, *Australian Painting*, pp 163–65.

40 James MacDonald, writing in *Art in Australia*, Eleventh number, 1921, pages unnumbered.

41 ibid.

42 ibid, Sixth number, 1919, pages unnumbered.

43 Karen Johnson and National Library of Australia, *In Search of Beauty: Hilda Rix Nicholas' Sketchbook Art*, Portfolio Series (Canberra: National Library of Australia, 2012), pp 11–15. Hilda Rix Nicholas, *The Art of Hilda Rix Nicholas* (Sydney: A Hordern, 1919).

4 SYDNEY FOLLOWS MELBOURNE

1 Julian Ashton, *Now Came Still Evening On* (Sydney: Angus & Robertson, 1941), p 28.

2 ibid, p 79.

3 ibid, p 62.

4 William Moore, *The Story of Australian Art: From the Earliest Known Art of the Continent to the Art of To-Day*, vol 1, p 94. Moore added that 'a bright oil painting by Streeton' opened the eyes of South Australia's great landscape painter, Hans Heysen, 'to the fact that our Australia

sunshine was radically different from that of the European pictures': pp 94–95.

5 Ashton, *Now Came Still Evening On*, pp 88–89.

6 The president of the gallery, Chief Justice Sir Alfred Stephen, resigned his position in protest at Ashton's appointment.

7 Ashton, *Now Came Still Evening On*, pp 100–03. See also James MacDonald, *Australian Painting Desiderata [with a Portrait]* (Melbourne: Lothian Publishing, 1958), p 40; Bernard Smith, *Australian Painting, 1788–1970*, 2nd edn (Melbourne: Oxford University Press, 1971), p 117; Christopher Wray, *Arthur Streeton: Painter of Light* (Milton, Qld: Jacaranda, 1993), p 69.

8 Amy Lambert, *Thirty Years of an Artist's Life: The Career of GW Lambert, ARA* (Sydney: Australian Artist Editions, 1938), pp 15–17.

9 Ashton, *Now Came Still Evening On*, p 112.

10 Lambert, *Thirty Years of an Artist's Life*, p 25. Lambert, like Coates, married a woman who wrote his biography.

11 ibid, pp 23–24.

12 ibid, p 26.

13 ibid, p 29.

14 ibid, pp 29–31.

15 ibid, p 35.

16 Ashton, *Now Came Still Evening On*, p 112.

17 'Thea Proctor (1879–1966)', *Australian Dictionary of Biography*, vol 11, p 301. Barry Humphries, Andrew Sayers and Sarah Engledow, *The World of Thea Proctor* (St Leonards, NSW: Craftsman House in association with the National Portrait Gallery, Canberra, 2005), pp 23–24.

18 H Septimus Power and Max J Middleton, *The Art of H Septimus Power* (Adelaide: Rigby, 1974), pp 2–3.

19 'Fred Leist (1873–1945)', *Australian Dictionary of Biography*, vol 10, pp 70–71.

20 'Charles Bryant (1883–1937)', *Australian Dictionary of Biography*, vol 7, pp 469–70.

21 'Harold Parker (1873–1962)', *Australian Dictionary of Biography*, vol 11, pp 137–38.

22 'Benjamin Minns (1863–1937)', *Australian Dictionary of Biography*, vol 10, p 525.

23 'Girolamo Nerli (1860–1926)', *Australian Dictionary of Biography*, vol 10, pp 679–80.

24 Mary Eagle, John Jones, and ICI Australia, *A Story of Australian Painting* (Sydney: Macmillan, 1994), pp 118–19.

25 'Jessie Trail (1881–1967)', *Australian Dictionary of Biography*, vol 12, p 252.

26 Penelope Little and Bessie Davidson, *A Studio in Montparnasse: Bessie Davidson: An Australian Artist in Paris* (Melbourne: Craftsman House, 2003).

27 Stella Bowen, *Drawn from Life: Reminiscences* (London: Collins, 1940); Drusilla Modjeska, *Stravinsky's Lunch* (Sydney: Picador, 1999).

28 'William Hardy Wilson (1881–1955)', *Australian Dictionary of Biography*, vol 12, pp 531–33.

29 Modjeska, *Stravinsky's Lunch*.

30 Deborah Edwards, Rosemary Peel, and Denise Mimmocchi, *Margaret Preston* (Melbourne: Thames & Hudson, 2016).

5 LIFE IN LONDON

1 Arthur Streeton, Ann Galbally, and Anne Gray, *Letters from Smike: The Letters of Arthur Streeton, 1890–1943* (Melbourne: Oxford University Press, 1989), p 73.

2 ibid, p 74.

3 ibid. 'Dingbat' was a versatile term, used to describe those who were eccentric, different, or objects of scorn or derision.

4 ibid, p 75.

5 John Rothenstein and Charles Edward Conder, *The Life and Death of Conder [with Plates, Including Portraits]* (London: JM Dent & Sons, 1938), p 90.

6 Dimensions are 12.7 × 35.4 cm. Streeton, Galbally, and Gray, *Letters from Smike*, p 75.

7 Catalogue of the 'Exhibition of Australian Art in London: Grafton Galleries, Grafton Street, London W, 2nd April to 7th May 1898', held by National Library of Australia.

8 ibid.

9 Bernard Smith, *Documents on Art and Taste in Australia: The Colonial Period, 1770–1914* (Melbourne: Oxford University Press, 1975), pp 211–14.

10 ibid, p 215.

11 ibid, pp 215–16.

12 ibid, p 216.

13 ibid.

14 ibid, p 218.

15 ibid, p 219.

16 ibid, pp 218–19.

17 Streeton, Galbally, and Gray, *Letters from Smike*, p 77.

18 ibid, p 78.

19 HR Croll, *Tom Roberts: Father of Australian Landscape Painting* (Melbourne: Robertson & Mullens, 1935), p 57.

20 Streeton, Galbally, and Gray, *Letters from Smike*, p 93.

21 N Murdoch, *Portrait in Youth of Sir John Longstaff* (Sydney: Angus & Robertson, 1948), p 210.

22 Rothenstein and Conder, *The Life and Death of Conder*, pp 18–19.

23 Streeton, Galbally, and Gray, *Letters from Smike*, p 94.

24 Ann Galbally, *Charles Conder: The Last Bohemian* (Carlton South: Miegunyah Press, 2002), p 261.

25 Rothenstein and Conder, *The Life and Death of Conder*, p 191.

26 ibid, pp 190–91.

27 Barry Humphries, Andrew Sayers and Sarah Engledow, *The World of Thea Proctor* (St Leonards, NSW: Craftsman House in association with the National Portrait Gallery, Canberra, 2005), p 2.

28 Streeton, Galbally, and Gray, *Letters from Smike*, p 94.

29 ibid.

30 ibid.

31 See Tom Cross, *Artists and Bohemians: 100 Years with the Chelsea Arts Club* (London: Quiller, 1992).

32 ibid.

33 Amy Lambert, *Thirty Years of an Artist's Life: The Career of GW Lambert, ARA* (Sydney: Australian Artist Editions, 1938), pp 139–40.

34 Arthur Streeton et al, *Smike to Bulldog: Letters from Sir Arthur Streeton to Tom Roberts* (Sydney: Ure Smith, 1946), p 94.

35 Cross, *Artists and Bohemians*, p 37.

36 Croll, *Tom Roberts*, pp 78–83. What Sir Charles Cust said was true enough, but of little interest to Roberts, who was on a good little earner at one guinea a head. Roberts had to include as many as possible, even if it meant tolerating tiresome behaviour, like Cust's.

37 ibid, pp 78–79.

38 In 1957, Queen Elizabeth II returned the painting to Australia on permanent loan. It now hangs in the foyer to the Main Committee Room of the Australian Parliament.

39 Humphrey McQueen, *Tom Roberts* (Sydney: Macmillan, 1996), pp 485–87.

40 ibid, p 502.

41 ibid, p 503.

42 Croll, *Tom Roberts*, p 95. There were 146 flats in the block: McQueen, *Tom Roberts*, p 495.

43 McQueen, *Tom Roberts*, p 506.

44 Croll, *Tom Roberts*, pp 88, 95; McQueen, *Tom Roberts*, p 502.

45 Croll, *Tom Roberts*, pp 94–95.

46 McQueen, *Tom Roberts*, pp 506–09.

47 ibid, pp 29, 520.

48 Quoted in Helen Topliss and Tom Roberts, *Tom Roberts, 1856–1931: A Catalogue Raisonnee*, 2 vols (Melbourne: Oxford University Press, 1985), vol 1, p 25.

49 McQueen, *Tom Roberts*, p 527.

50 ibid, p 540.

51 Lambert, *Thirty Years of an Artist's Life*, p 26.

52 ibid, p 39.

53 ibid, p 38.

54 ibid, p 40.

55 ibid.

56 Barry Humphries, who met Thea Proctor in 1966, recounted how she told stories about 'her great love, George Lambert': Humphries, Sayers and Engledow, *The World of Thea Proctor*, p 2. Andrew Motion quotes one of George's closest companions (without identifying him or her), who thought they were lovers: 'You just had to see the way they were'. He also quotes Amy's niece, Dulcie, emphatically denying that they were lovers: 'It was my impression (but I might be wrong) that she was incapable of feeling any kind of passion or sexual feeling – for anybody': Andrew Motion, *The Lamberts: George, Constant & Kit*, 1st US edn (New York: Farrar, Straus and Giroux, 1987), p 44.

57 Motion, *The Lamberts*, p 44.

58 All Australia beats All England! McQueen, *Tom Roberts*, p 527.

59 Lambert, *Thirty Years of an Artist's Life*, p 46.

60 Dora Meeson Coates, *George Coates: His Art and His Life* (London: JM Dent, 1937), p 24.

61 ibid, pp 20–21.

62 Both were born in 1869.

63 Coates, *George Coates*, pp 22–24.

64 ibid, pp 27–28.

65 ibid, pp 29–30.

66 ibid, p 32.

67 ibid, pp 33–34.

68 ibid, p 35.

69 ibid.

70 ibid, p 36.

71 Rothenstein and Conder, *The Life and Death of Conder*, p 226.

72 Coates, *George Coates*, p 37.

73 ibid, pp 37–39.

74 ibid, pp 39–40.

75 Myra Scott, *How Australia Led the Way: Dora Meeson Coates and British Suffrage*, (Canberra: Office of the Status of Women, 2003). Dora Meeson's banner was used in the design of the Australian 2003 commemorative dollar coin, minted to celebrate the centenary of women's suffrage in Australia.

76 Coates, *George Coates*, p 43. Feminist issues abound. Readers wanting to read more about those affecting the Australian women artists in Edwardian London could start with: Angela Woollacott, *To Try Her Fortune in London: Australian Women, Colonialism, and Modernity* (Oxford: Oxford University Press, 2001) and Jillian Dwyer, 'The "Work" of Art: The National Gallery of Victoria Travelling

Scholarship 1887–1932', MA thesis, Monash University, 1997.

77 Coates, *George Coates*, p 44.

78 ibid, p 45.

79 ibid, p 67.

80 Daryl Lindsay, *The Leafy Tree: My Family* (Melbourne: FW Cheshire, 1965), p 119.

81 Coates, *George Coates*, p 62.

82 ibid, p 68.

83 Ross McMullin, *Will Dyson: Cartoonist, Etcher and Australia's Finest War Artist* (Sydney: Angus & Robertson, 1984), p 59.

84 Norman Lindsay, *My Mask: For What Little I Know of the Man Behind It, An Autobiography* (Sydney: Angus & Robertson, 1970), p 213.

85 McMullin, *Will Dyson* (1984), p 60.

86 Joanna Mendelssohn, *Lionel Lindsay: An Artist and His Family* (London: Chatto & Windus, 1988), p 124.

87 ibid.

88 Rose Lindsay, *Model Wife: My Life with Norman Lindsay* (Sydney: Ure Smith, 1967), p 121.

89 Norman Lindsay, *My Mask*, p 206. Rose Lindsay, *Model Wife*, pp 121–22.

90 The story of the bust-up of the Lindsay family is told in detail in Joanna Mendelssohn, *Letters & Liars: Norman Lindsay and the Lindsay Family* (Pymble, NSW: Angus & Robertson, 1996). Daryl's comment is found on p 54.

91 A phrase that Norman Lindsay used in his homage to Julian Ashton that forms the introduction to Julian Ashton, *Now Came Still Evening On* (Sydney: Angus & Robertson, 1941), p ix.

92 McMullin, *Will Dyson* (1984), p 63.

93 John Phillip Pigot and Hilda Rix Nicholas, *Hilda Rix Nicholas: Her Life and Art* (Carlton South, Vic: Miegunyah Press, 2000), pp 11–22. Hilda Rix Nicholas, *The Art of Hilda Rix Nicholas* (Sydney: A Hordern, 1919).

94 Pigot and Rix Nicholas, *Hilda Rix Nicholas*, p 23. See also Jeanette Hoorn, 'Letters from Tangiers: The Creative Partnership between Elsie and Hilda Rix in Morocco', in Robert Kelly and Veronica Dixon (eds), *Impact of the Modern: Vernacular Modernities in Australia 1870s–1960s* (Sydney: Sydney University Press, 2008).

95 Pigot and Rix Nicholas, *Hilda Rix Nicholas*, pp 23–26.

96 Karen Johnson and National Library of Australia, *In Search of Beauty: Hilda Rix Nicholas' Sketchbook Art*, Portfolio Series (Canberra: National Library of Australia, 2012), p 16.

97 *Art in Australia*, Sixth number, 1919, pages unnumbered.

98 Jeanette Hoorn and Hilda Rix Nicholas, *Hilda Rix Nicholas and Elsie Rix's Moroccan Idyll: Art and Orientalism* (Carlton, Vic: Miegunyah Press, 2012), pp 31–33. See also 'Rupert Bunny (1864–1947)', *Australian Dictionary of Biography*, vol 7, pp 479–80. For Bunny's career and fame in Paris, see Rupert Bunny et al, *Rupert Bunny: Artist in Paris* (Sydney: Art Gallery of New South Wales, 2009), pp 19 and following, and, especially, pp 102–03.

99 *Art in Australia*, Fifth number, 1918, pages unnumbered.

100 'Charles Bryant (1883–1937)', *Australian Dictionary of Biography*, vol 7, pp 469–70. AJ Daplyn called the Chelsea Arts Club the Australian artists' headquarters: AJ Daplyn, 'Australian Artists at the Academy and Salons', *Sydney Morning Herald*, 16 August 1913. Daplyn was a landscape painter. He was the first art instructor at the Royal Art School, Sydney, from 1885 to 1892, where Syd Long and Charles Conder were among his students: Alan McCulloch, *Encyclopedia of Australian Art* (New York: Frederick A Praeger, 1968), p 157.

101 Arthur Ransome, *Bohemia in London* (London: Chapman & Hall, 1907), pp 44–45, 78–81.

102 Bunny et al, *Rupert Bunny*, pp 162–63.

6 WAR

1 Dora Meeson Coates, *George Coates: His Art and His Life* (London: JM Dent, 1937), p 87.

2 Arthur Streeton, Ann Galbally, and Anne Gray, *Letters from Smike: The Letters of Arthur Streeton, 1890–1943* (Melbourne: Oxford University Press, 1989), pp 134–35.

3 HR Croll, *Tom Roberts: Father of Australian Landscape Painting* (Melbourne: Robertson & Mullens, 1935), pp 103–05.

4 ibid, p 105–10.

5 Winston Churchill, *The World Crisis, 1911–1918*, 4 vols (London, Odhams Press, 1938), vol 1, p 191.

6 Coates, *George Coates*, pp 89–90.

7 H Septimus Power and Max J Middleton, *The Art of H Septimus Power* (Adelaide: Rigby, 1974), p 4.

8 June Helmer, *George Bell, the Art of Influence* (Richmond, Vic: Greenhouse, 1985), p 42.

9 The expression 'total war' signifies warfare involving the civilian population. In a total war, civilians become legitimate targets of military violence, the entire economy may be mobilised to fight the war, and civilians are expected, and may be conscripted, to play a part in prosecuting the war. Total war was uncommon until the twentieth century.

10 Amy Lambert, *Thirty Years of an Artist's Life: The Career of GW Lambert, ARA* (Sydney: Australian Artist Editions, 1938), p 69.

11 Ross McMullin, *Will Dyson: Cartoonist, Etcher and Australia's Finest War Artist* (Sydney: Angus & Robertson, 1984), pp 107–13. Will Dyson, *Kultur Cartoons / Will Dyson*, (London: Stanley Paul, 1915).

12 John Hetherington, *Norman Lindsay: The Embattled Olympian* (Melbourne: Oxford University Press, 1973) p 95 and following.

13 Daryl Lindsay, *The Leafy Tree: My Family* (Melbourne: FW Cheshire, 1965), p 59.

14 Quoted in Hetherington, *Norman Lindsay*, p 132. Norman Lindsay saw his work on the posters as doing his duty – handing his 'services over to patriotic propaganda whenever it was required of me': Norman Lindsay, *My Mask: For What Little I Know of the Man Behind It, An Autobiography* (Sydney: Angus & Robertson, 1970), p 234. For the most part, war posters are beyond the scope of this book. Kirsty Grant et al, *Follow the Flag: Australian Artists and War, 1914–1945* (Melbourne: National Gallery of Victoria, 2015) has some fine examples.

15 Michael McKernan, *The Australian People and the Great War* (Sydney and London: Collins, 1984), p 29.

16 CEW Bean, *The Official History of Australia in the War of 1914–1918*, 12 vols (Sydney: Angus & Robertson, 1920–42), vol XI (1940), chapters IX and XI. The conscription debate in Australia followed a different path than in Britain. In Australia, sectarianism intruded on the debate, with Roman Catholic Archbishop Mannix accusing Prime Minister Hughes of wanting to conscript Australian men to fight on the Western Front to free up British troops to suppress the revolt in Ireland: see Patrick O'Farrell, *The Irish in Australia: 1788 to the Present*, 3rd edn (Sydney: UNSW Press, 2000); Patrick O'Farrell, *The Catholic Church in Australia: A Short History: 1788–1967* (London: Geoffrey Chapman, 1969). These differences make it difficult to read too much into the different outcomes of the conscription debates.

[17] Will Dyson, *'Conscript 'Em!' Cartoons by Will Dyson* (London: The Herald, 1915).

[18] McKernan, *The Australian People and the Great War*, p 29. The suffragettes were especially active in handing out white feathers. Some branches of the suffragette movement were pacifist, but Mrs Emmeline Pankhurst was 'one of the most virulent exponents of the measures demanded by the war extremists, Lloyd George, Carson and Northcliffe': E Sylvia Pankhurst, *The Life of Emmeline Pankhurst: The Suffragette Struggle for Women's Citizenship* (London: Werner Laurie, 1935), p 153. She supported 'conscription of men and women alike for national service, both military and industrial'.

[19] He wrote to the *Herald* denying that he was a pacifist: McMullin, *Will Dyson* (2006), p 150.

[20] McMullin's admiration for Dyson is evident from the titles of the two biographies: *Will Dyson: Cartoonist, Etcher and Australia's Finest War Artist*; and *Will Dyson: Australia's Radical Genius*.

[21] Compare McMullin's *Will Dyson* (1984), p 126, with *Will Dyson* (2006), p 155.

[22] If Dyson's justification for not volunteering was that he made a stronger contribution to the war effort by drawing cartoons than he would by serving in the trenches, the issues on that score were a little more complicated than they first seemed. Dyson's cartoons mocking the Germans supported the government line, but his conscription cartoons opposed it. Maybe Dyson was right on conscription and the government was wrong, but the question remained: who was to be the judge of when his cartoons contributed to the war effort, and when they ran counter to it?

[23] Lambert, *Thirty Years of an Artist's Life*, p 67.

[24] ibid, pp 69–74.

[25] American Hospital of Paris, 'Annual Report 1915' <(http://www.ourstory.info/library/2-ww1/AmHosp15/ahp1915.html1915> accessed January 2016.

[26] David Thomas and John Henshaw, *Rupert Bunny: 1864–1947*, Australian Art Library (Melbourne: Lansdowne Press, 1970), p 70.

[27] Barry Gregory, *A History of the Artists Rifles 1859–1947* (Barnsley, UK: Pen & Sword Military, 2006).

[28] Tom Cross, *Artists and Bohemians: 100 Years with the Chelsea Arts Club* (London: Quiller, 1992), p 46.

[29] Coates, *George Coates*, p 91.

[30] ibid, pp 91–94.

[31] McQueen, *Tom Roberts*, p 577.

[32] Christopher Wray, *Arthur Streeton: Painter of Light* (Milton, Qld: Jacaranda, 1993), p 129.

[33] Sir William MacPherson and TJ Mitchell, *Medical Services: General History*, 4 vols (London: HMSO, 1921), vol I, chapters IV and V.

[34] Sir Bruce Bruce-Porter, 'The History of Our Hospital' in Muir (ed), *Gazette of the 3rd London General Hospital*.

[35] The Royal Victoria Patriotic Building still stands in John Archer Way, Wandsworth <www.rvpb.com> accessed 23 October 2016.

[36] 'The War', *British Medical Journal*, 10 October 1914, p 644.

[37] Ward Muir, *The Happy Hospital* (London: Simpkin, Marshall, Hamilton, Kent & Co, 1918), p 518.

[38] Myra Scott, *How Australia Led the Way: Dora Meeson Coates and British Suffrage* (Canberra: Office of the Status of Women, 2003), p 251.

[39] ibid.

[40] Bruce-Porter, 'The History of Our Hospital'.

[41] The classes were: Class A – Fit for service at home or abroad; Class B – Temporarily unfit for service abroad; Class C – Fit for service at home

only; Class D – Unfit for service at home or abroad: Andrew Rawson, *British Army Handbook, 1914–1918* (Stroud, UK: Sutton, 2006), p 30.

[42] Coates, *George Coates*, p 98.

[43] Bruce-Porter, 'The History of Our Hospital'.

[44] CRW Nevinson, *Paint and Prejudice* (New York: Harcourt, 1938), p 105.

[45] Coates, *George Coates*, p 106.

[46] McQueen, *Tom Roberts*, p 581.

[47] Coates, *George Coates*, p 95.

7 GALLIPOLI

[1] Dudley McCarthy, *Gallipoli to the Somme: The Story of CEW Bean* (Sydney: John Ferguson, 1983), p 79. Peter Rees, *Bearing Witness: The Remarkable Life of Charles Bean, Australia's Greatest War Correspondent* (Crows Nest, NSW: Allen & Unwin, 2015), p 84. Bean's account reads as though General Bridges and Colonel White had the gift of prophecy. They may have. They were two of Australia's finest soldiers: see CEW Bean, *Two Men I Knew: William Bridges and Brudenell White, Founders of the AIF* (Sydney: Angus & Robertson, 1957), pp 1–2, 96.

[2] McCarthy, *Gallipoli to the Somme*, chapter 5, p 98 and following.

[3] For an overview, see ML Sanders and Philip M Taylor, *British Propaganda During the First World War, 1914–18* (London: Macmillan, 1982). The obsession with secrecy persisted until after Lloyd George became Prime Minister in December 1916.

[4] *Defence of the Realm Act 1914*, section 1.

[5] CEW Bean and HS Gullett, *The Official History of Australia in the War of 1914–1918*, vol XII (Sydney: Angus & Robertson, 1923), p v.

[6] Churchill's account of his exploits as a newspaperman covering the war in South Africa is given in Winston Churchill, *My Early Life: A Roving Commission*, Keystone Library edn (London: T Butterworth, 1930).

[7] CEW Bean, *The Official History of Australia in the War of 1914–1918*, 12 vols (Sydney: Angus & Robertson, 1921–42), vol III (1929), p 446.

[8] ibid, p 446.

[9] Colonel Charles à Court Repington, the military correspondent for *The Times*, claimed that the regulations were used 'as a cloak to cover all political, naval and military mistakes'. One cover-up, of which he famously complained, was a shortage of artillery shells. He was eventually prosecuted for breaching the regulations: ML Sanders and Philip M Taylor, *British Propaganda During the First World War, 1914–18* (London: Macmillan, 1982), pp 24–28.

[10] Bean and Gullett, *Official History*, vol XII, pp v–vi.

[11] ibid, p vi.

[12] For a painting made with an iodine brush, see CEW Bean (ed), *The Anzac Book*, 3rd edn (Sydney: UNSW Press, 2010), p 45.

[13] 'Ellis Silas (1885–1972)', *Australian Dictionary of Biography*, vol 11, pp 605–06.

[14] 'Neurasthenia' was the name of a nervous condition thought to be associated with overwork or prolonged mental strain. It was one of a number of terms used to describe the psychiatric effect of warfare. 'Shell shock' was another. 'Post-traumatic stress disorder' is a term used in similar contexts today.

[15] Silas Ellis, Service record, NAA: B2455. See also Ellis Silas and John Laffin, *An Eyewitness Account of Gallipoli*, 2nd edn (Kenthurst, NSW: Rosenberg Publishing, 2010), pp 6–9.

[16] ibid.

[17] ibid, p 3.

18 ibid.
19 'Ellis Silas', *Australian Dictionary of Biography*, vol 11, p 606.
20 Benson GC, Service record, NAA: B2455.
21 Benson Sketchbook, AWM: ART03605.
22 Hore LFS Major, Service record, NAA: B2455.
23 Diary of Major LFS Hore, Mitchell Library: PXE 702 and PXE 703.
24 Bazley AW, Service record, NAA: B2455; Crozier FR, Service record, NAA: B2455; Barker DV, Service record, NAA: B2455; Hewett WO 518, Service record, NAA: B2455; White CL, Service record, NAA: B2455; Ted Colles enlisted as Fredrick Collis – Collis F, Service record, NAA: B2455. See also 'Artists Who Served with the AIF' in this book.
25 Bean (ed), *The Anzac Book*, p 12.
26 Eltham WK, Service record, NAA: B2455; Roach Gilbert Thomas Meredith, Service record, NAA: B2455; Price Benjamin Henry Eyles, Service record, NAA: B2455.
27 Bean (ed), *The Anzac Book*, p 7.
28 CEW Bean's diary, entry for 21 January 1916, p 46, AWM38 3DRL 606/36/1.
29 For a detailed account of amateur publications by diggers of the Great War, see David Kent, *From Trench and Troopship: The Experience of the Australian Imperial Force, 1914–1919* (Alexandria, NSW: Hale & Iremonger, 1999).

8 THE 3RD LONDON GENERAL HOSPITAL
1 Dora Meeson Coates, *George Coates: His Art and His Life* (London: JM Dent, 1937), p 96.
2 Ward Muir, *Observations of an Orderly: Some Glimpses of Life and Work in an English War Hospital* (London: Simpkin, Marshall, Hamilton, Kent & Co, 1917). Ward Muir, *The Happy Hospital* (London: Simpkin, Marshall, Hamilton, Kent & Co, 1918). Ward Muir and W Noel Irving, *Happy – Though Wounded! The Book of the 3rd London General Hospital* (London: Country Life, 1917).
3 Ward Muir (ed), *Gazette of the 3rd London General Hospital* (London: 3rd London General Hospital, 1915–18).
4 The description of the hut comes from Muir, *Observations of an Orderly*, p 33 and following.
5 The description of the daily routine of the orderlies comes from notes by Noel Irving, quoted in Coates, *George Coates*, p 98 and following.
6 ibid, p 100.
7 The description of the process by which wounded men were evacuated from France comes from Richard C Travers, *Diggers in France: Australian Soldiers on the Western Front* (Sydney: ABC Books, 2008), p 96 and following.
8 The description of the arrival of trains at Wandsworth comes from Muir, *Observations of an Orderly*, p 204 and following.
9 The description of the procedure when the wounded arrived comes from ibid, p 93 and following.
10 Coates, *George Coates*, pp 99–100.
11 ibid, p 90.
12 ibid, p 100. Muir, *The Happy Hospital*, chapter III, p 35 and following.
13 Walker OB, Service record, NAA: B2455.
14 Muir (ed), *Gazette of the 3rd London General Hospital*. 'Square dinkum' was the forerunner of 'fair dinkum'. The terms may have shared a common origin in the phrase 'square and fair dinkum'. 'Dinkum oil' meant a rumour that was believable, and 'dinkum' by itself signified the truth. The menu of the Australian Glory Café at 1 Abbas Street, Heliopolis, in Cairo, boasted a 'Bill of Fare' of 'Square Dinkum Tucker'.

15 Sir William MacPherson and TJ Mitchell, *Medical Services: General History*, 4 vols (London: HMSO, 1921), vol 1, p 377, table III. Until I wrote this book, I was unaware that so many men wounded at Gallipoli were sent to London for treatment and recovery. It quickly became apparent that Trooper Walker was following a well-trodden path. My own grandfather was wounded at Gallipoli – shot in the leg on 29 August 1915. He was taken on board SS *Devanha* (a P&O cruiser turned hospital ship) and on 12 September 1915 was admitted to the 3rd London General Hospital, Wandsworth. He was a patient at Wandsworth until early 1916: Travers Reginald John Albert, Service record, NAA: B2455. Thanks to a clean bill of health from the 3rd London General Hospital, my grandfather lived well into his eighties. So, thank you, 3rd London General Hospital. I owe you one.
16 Coates, *George Coates*, p 107. Croll suggested that the presence of the Australian artists at Wandsworth 'was probably the reason why the War Authorities made so much use of it for AIF men': HR Croll, *Tom Roberts: Father of Australian Landscape Painting* (Melbourne: Robertson & Mullens, 1935), p 113.
17 Muir, *The Happy Hospital*, p 111.
18 Humphrey McQueen, *Tom Roberts* (Sydney: Macmillan, 1996), pp 583–84; 607–08. Croll, *Tom Roberts*, p 115.
19 Croll, *Tom Roberts*, p 111.
20 Anne Gray, 'Tom Roberts: La Vita Con Brio' in Anne Gray (ed), *Tom Roberts* (Canberra: National Gallery of Australia, 2015), p 23.
21 Croll, *Tom Roberts*, pp 112–13.
22 Noel Irving remembered that George Coates had fallen victim to this fate – 'I'm afraid George caught a tartar': Coates, *George Coates*, p 100.
23 ibid, p 102.
24 Croll, *Tom Roberts*, p 112.
25 Coates, *George Coates*, pp 103–04.
26 Muir, *Observations of an Orderly*, pp 80, 166.
27 Coates, *George Coates*, pp 105–07.
28 ibid, p 106.
29 ibid, p 107.
30 ibid.
31 ibid, pp 111–12.
32 Muir (ed), *Gazette of the 3rd London General Hospital*.
33 Coates, *George Coates*, p 104.
34 Muir (ed), *Gazette of the 3rd London General Hospital*. Extracts from the *Gazette* have recently been published in Simon McNeill-Ritchie, *Great Ward Poetry* (Bradford on Avon, Wiltshire: Hamilton Laird Publishing, 2014).
35 CRW Nevinson, *Paint and Prejudice* (New York: Harcourt, Brace and Co, 1938), pp 106–07.
36 Muir and Irving, *Happy – Though Wounded!*
37 Lorimer Vernon, Service record, NAA: B2455.
38 Muir (ed), *Gazette of the 3rd London General Hospital*.
39 Coates, *George Coates*, p 109.

9 THE WESTERN FRONT, 1916
1 William Riddell Birdwood, *Khaki and Gown: An Autobiography* (London: Ward Lock, 1942), p 302.
2 General Sir John Monash and FM Cutlack, *War Letters of General Monash* (Sydney: Angus & Robertson, 1935), pp 117–18.
3 J Maxwell, *Hell's Bells and Mademoiselles* (Sydney: Angus & Robertson, 1939), p 26. In a period of twelve months, Joe Maxwell won the Victoria Cross, the Distinguished Conduct Medal, and the Military Cross – twice!

4 The 3rd Division did not arrive in France until December 1916.

5 Nicholas George Matson, Service record, NAA B2455.

6 CEW Bean, *The Official History of Australia in the War of 1914–1918*, 12 vols (Sydney: Angus & Robertson,1921–42), vol III (1929), pp 697–98.

7 The Australians had only recently arrived on the Western Front when Captain Nicholas captured the gun. At that stage, British officers were treating them with disdain – see, for example, the incident described in Richard Travers, *Diggers in France: Australian Soldiers on the Western Front* (Sydney: ABC Books, 2008), p 82 and following. One manifestation of the British attitude was a reluctance to recommend Australian soldiers for the highest decorations. Later in the war, the Australian officers took control of the award of decorations to Australian soldiers. In this, as in so many other areas, it took time for the Australians to assert themselves.

8 Karen Johnson and National Library of Australia, *In Search of Beauty: Hilda Rix Nicholas' Sketchbook Art*, Portfolio Series (Canberra: National Library of Australia, 2012), p 20.

9 Nicholas Bryon Fitzgerald, Service record, NAA B2455.

10 Nicholas Athol Miller, Service record, NAA B2455.

11 Hilda Rix Nicholas, *The Art of Hilda Rix Nicholas* (Sydney: A Hordern, 1919), pages unnumbered.

12 Bean, *Official History*, vol III, p 932.

13 Catherine Speck, 'Meditations on Loss: Hilda Rix Nicholas's War', *Artlink*, vol 35, no 1, 2015, pp 40–43.

14 Quoted in Catherine Speck, *Beyond the Battlefield: Women Artists of the Two World Wars* (London: Reaktion Books, 2014), p 54.

15 Nicholas Bryon Fitzgerald, Service record. There were six boys in the Nicholas family. Five enlisted. Two were killed. Pray for them, and for their parents.

16 Jeanette Hoorn and Hilda Rix Nicholas, *Hilda Rix Nicholas and Elsie Rix's Moroccan Idyll: Art and Orientalism* (Carlton, Vic: Miegunyah Press, 2012), p 196.

17 Maria Tippett, *Art at the Service of War: Canada, Art and the Great War* (Toronto and London: University of Toronto Press, 1984), p 23.

18 ML Sanders and Philip M Taylor, *British Propaganda During the First World War, 1914–18* (London: Macmillan, 1982), pp 38–39. See also Cate Haste, *Keep the Home Fires Burning: Propaganda in the First World War* (London: Allen Lane, 1977).

19 Sanders and Taylor, *British Propaganda*, pp 38–43. See their account of the demarcation disputes that broke out between Wellington House, the Foreign Office and the War Office as to which organisation was best placed to run British propaganda.

20 ibid, pp 119–20. Tippett, *Art at the Service of War*, p 23.

21 *Military Service Act 1916*, sections 1 and 2.

22 IFW Beckett and Keith Simpson, *A Nation in Arms: A Social Study of the British Army in the First World War* (Barnsley, UK: Pen & Sword Military, 2014), p 13. The authors do not give details of the grounds on which exemptions were sought.

23 Sanders and Taylor, *British Propaganda*, pp 122–23.

24 David Boyd Haycock, *A Crisis of Brilliance: Five Young British Artists and the Great War* (London: Old Street, 2009), p 270. For an impressive catalogue of Muirhead Bone's wartime work, see the War Office (Great Britain), Sir Muirhead Bone, and CE Montague, *The Western Front: Drawings by Muirhead Bone ... With Text by CE Montague, Etc* (London: Country Life, 1917).

25 'Foreword', in Will Dyson, *Kultur Cartoons Will Dyson* (London: Stanley Paul, 1915).

26 Will Dyson, *Will Dyson's War Cartoons* (London: Hodder & Staughton, 1916). Lord Desborough was a useful and versatile acquaintance. He was a champion fencer, who also swam the Niagara rapids (twice); climbed the Matterhorn (three times); rowed across the English Channel; rowed for Oxford in the boat race (twice, winning both times, albeit once in a dead heat); and was amateur punting champion of the Upper Thames.

27 Dyson was thirty-six in 1916.

28 The Australian Constitution did not create or recognise Australian citizenship. Australian citizenship was first recognised with the enactment of the *Australian Citizenship Act 1948*. Until then, all Australians were British subjects.

29 Peter Edward Bastian, *Andrew Fisher: An Underestimated Man* (Sydney: UNSW Press, 2009), p 315 and following.

30 Publication and purchase of cartoons by Will Dyson, AWM93 18/7/5 Part 1.

31 ibid.

32 Dudley McCarthy, *Gallipoli to the Somme: The Story of CEW Bean* (Sydney: John Ferguson, 1983), p 262.

33 Letter from Collins to Dyson, 1 September 1916, AWM93 18/7/5 Part 1.

34 Letter from Birdwood to Collins, 27 September 1916, AWM93 18/7/5 Part 1.

35 Letter from War Office to the Official Secretary to the High Commissioner, 24 October 1916, AWM93 18/7/5 Part 1.

36 Publication and purchase of cartoons by Will Dyson; letter from Dyson to Collins, 9 October 1916: AWM93 18/7/5 Part 1. The Canadian war art scheme was more generous than the Australian. This was not the first time it was used as a stalking horse to squeeze a better deal for the Australian artists. For an account of the Canadian scheme, see Tippett, *Art at the Service of War*.

37 Tippett, *Art at the Service of War*, p 17 and following.

38 ibid, pp 23–26. Tippett accused General Charteris, the chief of British Military Intelligence, of being the roadblock, writing that 'His preference ... was that the British should have the job : ibid, p 24.

39 'Sir Robert Anderson (1865–1940)', *Australian Dictionary of Biography*, vol 7, p 62.

40 Lieutenant W Dyson – Appointment as official artist, AWM16 4351/2/13. Bean confirms the suspicion that Colonel Anderson may have been a thrusting figure. He describes him as 'by nature impatient, and ... aggressive when thwarted': Bean, *Official History*, vol III, p 175.

41 ibid.

42 Dyson W, Service record, NAA B2455; letter from Colonel Anderson to Headquarters, I Anzac Corps, 5 December 1916: Publication and purchase of cartoons by Will Dyson: AWM93 18/7/5 Part 1.

43 Letter from Colonel Anderson to Headquarters, I Anzac Corps, 5 December 1916; letter from Headquarters, I Anzac Corps, to Colonel Anderson, 10 December 1916: Publication and purchase of cartoons by Will Dyson, AWM93 18/7/5 Part 1.

44 Lt W Dyson – Appointment as official artist, AWM16 4351/2/13.

45 Minute paper, 3 June 1918, AWM93 18/7/5.

46 Dyson W, Service record.

47 CEW Bean diary, AWM38 3DRL 606/68/1.

48 EJ Rule, *Jacka's Mob*, 2nd edn (Sydney: Angus & Robertson, 1933), p 61. Captain EJ Rule MC MM was a member of the 14th Infantry Battalion, AIF. The title of his book commemorated Albert Jacka VC, but Rule, too, was a man of surpassing bravery.

49 Bean diary.

50 CEW Bean, *Gallipoli Mission* (Canberra: Australian War Memorial, 1948), p 111.

51 For a sympathetic review of Dyson's drawings, see J Wieland, 'Winter Witness: Will Dyson's *Australia at War* and Other War Drawings' in Anna Rutherford and James Murray Wieland, *War: Australia's Creative Response* (St Leonards, NSW: Allen & Unwin, 1997), p 100 and following.

52 Lindsay Daryl Ernest, Service record, NAA B2455.

53 Lindsay Reginald Graham, Service record, NAA B2455.

54 Daryl Lindsay, *The Leafy Tree: My Family* (Melbourne: FW Cheshire, 1965), pp 109–10.

55 CEW Bean, 'Will Dyson, Artist and Soldier', *Sydney Morning Herald*, 25 January 1938.

56 Daryl Lindsay, *The Leafy Tree*, p 111.

57 Bean, 'Will Dyson'.

58 Ross McMullin, *Will Dyson: Cartoonist, Etcher and Australia's Finest War Artist* (Sydney: Angus & Robertson, 1984), pp 52, 137.

10 THE WESTERN FRONT, 1917

1 Maria Tippett, *Art at the Service of War: Canada, Art and the Great War* (Toronto and London: University of Toronto Press, 1984), p 20.

2 Dudley McCarthy, *Gallipoli to the Somme: The Story of CEW Bean* (Sydney: John Ferguson, 1983), p 79.

3 Peter Rees, *Bearing Witness: The Remarkable Life of Charles Bean, Australia's Greatest War Correspondent* (Crows Nest, NSW: Allen & Unwin, 2015), p 309.

4 CEW Bean, *Gallipoli Mission* (Canberra: Australian War Memorial, 1948), p 6.

5 For an early thesis describing the Australian War Memorial's pictorial collection, see Jennifer Turnbull, 'Australian Artists in the Great War: The Origin and Nature of the Australian War Memorial's Pictorial Collection Representing the First World War – With Special Reference to George Lambert and Will Dyson', BA(Hons) thesis, University of Melbourne, 1969.

6 Bean, *Gallipoli Mission*, pp 6–7.

7 See, for example, the agreement with James Quinn, AWM93 18/7/13.

8 The solicitor as hero – something you don't see every day!

9 All but the sleepiest law students would know that the last clause as drafted was an agreement to agree, and unenforceable for uncertainty.

10 Compare Michael Scheib, 'Painting Anzac: A History of Australia's Official War Art Scheme of the First World War', PhD thesis, University of Sydney, 2015.

11 See the treatment of him in William Moore, *The Story of Australian Art: From the Earliest Known Art of the Continent to the Art of To-Day*, vol 1, pp xix, 25, 30, 35, 192, 216. Moore was a generous commentator – it was significant if he did not rate an artist highly. Similarly, Bernard Smith mentions Leist twice, but only in his capacity as a friend of George Bell, not as an artist in his own right: Bernard Smith, *Australian Painting, 1788–1970*, 2nd edn (Melbourne: Oxford University Press, 1971), pp 164, 233.

12 'Fred Leist (1873–1945)', *Australian Dictionary of Biography*, vol 10, p 70.

13 B Smith, *Australian Painting*, p 164.

14 'Fred Leist', *Australian Dictionary of Biography*.

15 Letter from Smart to Leist, 3 July 1917; list of items required by FS Leist: AWM93 18/7/8 Part 1.

16 Leist Frederick William, Service record, NAA B2455.

17 Power Harold Septimus, Service record, NAA B2455. See also H Septimus Power and Max J Middleton, *The Art of H Septimus Power* (Adelaide: Rigby, 1974), pp 2–5.

18 List of items required by HS Power, AWM93 18/7/8 Part 1.

19 CEW Bean diary, entries for 3 and 4 September 1917, AWM38 3DRL 606/88/1.

20 This account comes from Bean's diary, entry for 23 September 1917, supplemented by an entry made on 3 December 1931, AWM38 3DRL 606/88/1.

21 ibid.

22 Arthur Mason, 'Mr Fred Leist at the Front Painting the War', *Sydney Morning Herald*, 25 June 1918.

23 List of pictures by Lieutenant Leist, AWM93 18/7/8 Part 1.

24 Nowadays, carrier pigeons have their own Victoria Cross – the Dickin Medal, inaugurated in 1943. Two Australian pigeons have won it, both during the Hitler War <www.awm.gov.au/encyclopedia/dickin/> accessed 2 December 2015. The Dickin Medal is open to all animals. It is too much to hope that there would be a Victoria Cross for every species. Joyfully, the Victoria Cross Trust has taken the trouble to object to anybody being so wicked as to call the Dickin Medal 'the animals' VC'. On 4 September 2014, it announced on Twitter that 'there is NO such thing as an Animal VC'.

25 Australian Imperial Force (1914–21), *From the Australian Front* (London and Melbourne: Cassell and Company, 1917).

26 ibid, introduction.

27 AFC was the Air Force Cross.

28 The photographers and their work are beyond the scope of this book. Some references of interest include Jane Carmichael, *First World War Photographers* (London: Routledge, 1989); Frank Hurley, *Hurley at War: The Photography and Diaries of Frank Hurley in Two World Wars* (Broadway, NSW: Fairfax Library in association with Daniel O'Keefe, 1986); Frank Hurley, Robert Dixon, and Christopher Lee, *The Diaries of Frank Hurley, 1912–1941* (London and New York: Anthem Press, 2011).

29 Bragg BWP, Service record, NAA B2455; Crozier FR, Service record, NAA B2455; Davis JP, Service record, NAA B2455; Howie LH, Service record, NAA B2455; Lorimer Vernon, Service record, NAA B2455; Perks Stanley Frederick Sinclair, Service record, B2455; Picking Alfred Samuel Horace, Service record, NAA B2455; Shaw Stuart, Service record, NAA B2455. I was not able to find service records for CH Gould, P Huthnance, WL King, Allen M Lewi or Alf Saville.

30 Ian McCulloch, *Encyclopedia of Australian Art* (New York: Frederick A Praeger, 1968), p 257. Hartt CL, Service record, NAA B2455.

31 CEW Bean, *The Official History of Australia in the War of 1914–1918*, 12 vols (Sydney: Angus & Robertson, 1921–42) vol I (1921), p 7.

32 ibid, p 46.

33 Penleigh Boyd, *Salvage* (Canberra: Australian War Memorial Facsimile Editions, 1983 [1918]), preface.

34 McCulloch, *Encyclopedia of Australian Art*, p 92. Boyd TP, Service record, NAA B2455.

35 Bean, *Official History*, vol I, p 42. Andrew Rawson, *British Army Handbook, 1914–1918* (Stroud, UK: Sutton, 2006), p 6.

36 Bean diary, entry for 4 December 1916, AWM38 3DRL 606/67/1. Bean had pulled strings to secure a posting for Crozier as a runner on General Gellibrand's staff, where Gellibrand was happy for Crozier to take time out to paint: McCarthy, *Gallipoli to the Somme*, p 261.

37 Christopher Wray, *Arthur Streeton: Painter of Light* (Milton, Qld: Jacaranda, 1993), p 131.

38 Letter from Streeton to Fisher, 10 July 1917; letter from Smart to Streeton, 20 July 1917: AWM93 18/7/12.

39 Letter from Streeton to Fisher, 21 September 1917; letter from Smart to Streeton, 27 September 1917; letter from Streeton to Smart, 4 October 1917: AWM93 18/7/12.

40 Letter from Smart to Streeton, 11 October 1917, AWM93 18/7/12.

41 Streeton was laying it on thick. Private soldiers in the British army were paid 1s per day, but could choose to draw less than a shilling.

42 Letter from Streeton to Smart, 12 October 1917, AWM93 18/7/12.

43 Daplyn was a landscape painter. He was the first art instructor at the Royal Art School in Sydney, from 1885 to 1892, where Syd Long and Charles Conder were among his students: McCulloch, *Encyclopedia of Australian Art*, p 157.

44 Attachment to a letter from Streeton to Smart, 12 October 1917, AWM93 18/7/12.

45 Letter from Streeton to Baldwin Spencer, 28 April 1918, quoted in Wray, *Arthur Streeton*, pp 133–34.

46 Letter from Smart to Bean, 2 November 1917, AWM38 3DRL 6673/286.

47 'Baldwin Spencer (1860–1929)', *Australian Dictionary of Biography*, vol 12, pp 33–36. The Felton Bequest was a major funding mechanism for the gallery.

48 Arthur Streeton, Ann Galbally, and Anne Gray, *Letters from Smike: The Letters of Arthur Streeton, 1890–1943* (Melbourne: Oxford University Press, 1989), p 142.

49 ibid, p 143.

50 ibid.

51 Arthur Streeton, 'Australian Artists and War', *Argus*, 17 December 1917, p 4.

52 Ross McMullin, *Will Dyson: Cartoonist, Etcher and Australia's Finest War Artist* (Sydney: Angus & Robertson, 1984), pp 159–60. Dyson was in England from 13 November 1917 until 13 April 1918: Dyson W, Service record, NAA B2455.

53 Arthur Streeton, 'Artists and War', *Argus*, 11 May 1918.

54 A long list of Australian artists served in the ranks. See 'Artists Who Served with the AIF' in this book.

55 Letter from Smart to Bean, 28 December 1917, AWM38 3DRL 6673/286. Percy Spence was an Australian artist who worked in London between 1915 and 1926. He was a versatile artist, best known for his portraits: 'Percy Spence (1868–1933)', *Australian Dictionary of Biography*, vol 12, pp 29–30.

11 THE MIDDLE EAST

1 Letter from Smart to Bean, date unknown, AWM93 3DRL 6673/197.

2 Amy Lambert, *Thirty Years of an Artist's Life: The Career of GW Lambert, ARA* (Sydney: Australian Artist Editions, 1938), pp 71–72.

3 ibid, pp 73–74.

4 ibid, p 75.

5 ibid, pp 76–77.

6 CEW Bean and Australian War Memorial, *Anzac to Amiens: A Shorter History of the Australian Fighting Services in the First World War* (Canberra: Australian War Memorial, 1946), p 75.

7 CEW Bean, *The Official History of Australia in the War of 1914–1918*, 12 vols (Sydney: Angus & Robertson,1921–42) vol I (1921), p 130 note. See also R Hugh Knyvett, *'Over There' with the Australians* (London: Hodder & Stoughton, 1918), p 91 and following.

8 Bean, *Official History*, vol I, p 130 note.

9 Lambert, *Thirty Years of an Artist's Life*, pp 103–04.

10 Bean, *Official History*, vol I, p 130.

11 I was fortunate to know a veteran of the 'Wazza'. AM Cowper told the stories of the Wazza with a soldier's eye for detail. He was not nearly so forthcoming about the Western Front. Asked why he never took holidays in France, he answered: 'I've been to France. Didn't like it'. Cowper AM, Service record, NAA B2455.

12 Over the five years of the war, 416,809 men enlisted in the AIF: Bean, *Official History*, vol XI (1940), p 874.

13 Lambert, *Thirty Years of an Artist's Life*, p 78.

14 ibid. See also AB Paterson, 'Buffalo Shooting in Australia', *The Sydney Mail*, 7 January 1899.

15 Quoted in Anne Gray, George W Lambert, and National Gallery of Australia, *George W Lambert Retrospective: Heroes & Icons* (Canberra: National Gallery of Australia, 2007), p 137. *Across the Black Soil Plains*, now proudly displayed in the Art Gallery of New South Wales, was Lambert's first great painting.

16 Lambert, *Thirty Years of an Artist's Life*, pp 77–79.

17 ibid, p 83.

18 ibid, p 80.

19 Bean, *Official History*, vol VII (1923), p 649.

20 William Moore, *The Story of Australian Art: From the Earliest Known Art of the Continent to the Art of To-Day*, 2 vols (Sydney: Angus & Robertson, 1934), vol 1, p 151.

21 Bean, *Official History*, vol VII, p 649. See also Janet Maxwell Champion, *Lady of Kantara: A Biography of Dame Alice Chisholm, 1856–1954* (Turramurra, NSW: JM Champion, 1997).

22 Bean, *Official History*, vol VII, p 649. As if Allenby's disapproval would have stopped her! See also Jennifer Horsfield, *Rainbow: The Story of Rania Macphillamy* (Canberra: Ginninderra Press, 2007).

23 Jane Tolerton, 'Ettie Annie Rout, 1877–1936', in the *Dictionary of New Zealand Biography and Te Ara – The Encyclopedia of New Zealand*.

24 Lambert, *Thirty Years of an Artist's Life*, pp 82–83.

25 ibid, p 84.

26 ibid. The dimensions were 'six by four', that is, 6 × 4 inches.

27 HR Croll, *Tom Roberts: Father of Australian Landscape Painting* (Melbourne: Robertson & Mullens, 1935), p 26.

28 Ion L Idriess, *The Desert Column* (Sydney: Angus & Robertson, 1935), p 325.

29 Lambert, *Thirty Years of an Artist's Life*, p 85.

30 Bernard Smith, *Place, Taste and Tradition: A Study of Australian Art since 1788*, 2nd edn (Melbourne: Oxford University Press, 1979), p 242.

31 James S MacDonald and George W Lambert, *The Art and Life of George W Lambert* (Melbourne: Alexander McCubbin, Publisher, 1920), pp 24–27.

32 Publication and purchase of cartoons by Will Dyson; letter from Dyson to Collins, 9 October 1916: AWM93 18/7/5 Part 1.

12 FACE WOUNDS

1 AG Butler, *The Australian Army Medical Services in the War of 1914–1918*, 2nd edn, 3 vols (Melbourne: Australian War Memorial, 1938), vol III, p 329.

2 Major HD Gillies, *Plastic Surgery of the Face Based on Selected Cases of War Injuries of the Face Including Burns* (London: Oxford University Press and Hodder & Staughton, 1920), p 3 and following.

3 ibid, pp ix–x.

4 ibid, pp vii (Arbuthnot Lane), x (Gillies).

5 Butler, *The Australian Army Medical Services*, vol III, p 328.

6 Henry Tonks, Lynda Morris, and Norwich School of Art Gallery, *Henry Tonks and the 'Art of Pure Drawing'* (Norwich, UK: Norwich School of Art Gallery, 1985).

7 Gillies, *Plastic Surgery of the Face*, p x.

8 Butler, *The Australian Army Medical Services*, vol III, pp 328–29.

9 Not the same Colonel Anderson who attempted to help Dyson escape the clutches of the City of London local tribunal.

10 'Sir Neville Reginald Howse (1863–1930)', *Australian Dictionary of Biography*, vol 9, pp 384–86.

11 Daryl Lindsay, *The Leafy Tree: My Family* (Melbourne: FW Cheshire, 1965), pp 113–14.

12 ibid, p 114. 'Rhino' means 'nose' – as in 'rhinoceros'. Rhinoplasty is plastic surgery of the nose.

13 ibid, p 117.

14 Butler, *The Australian Army Medical Services*, vol III, p 320 and following. Gillies also used some of Lindsay's diagrams in his text, in addition to those by Tonks: Daryl Lindsay, *The Leafy Tree*, p 117. Gillies, *Plastic Surgery of the Face*.

15 Daryl Lindsay, *The Leafy Tree*, p 118. Tonks certainly made an impression. Helen Lessore, a student at the Slade School of Fine Art, described him as having 'large ears, hooded eyes, a nose dropping vertically from the bridge like an eagle's beak and a quivering camel-like mouth': Tonks, Morris, and Norwich School of Art Gallery, *Henry Tonks*, p 8. It was Tonks who had encouraged Dora Meeson to send one of her landscapes to the New English Art Club, adding that: 'We don't want anything of your husband's'.

16 Daryl Lindsay, *The Leafy Tree*, pp 119–21.

17 Ward Muir (ed), *Gazette of the 3rd London General Hospital*, December 1916 issue, p 67.

18 Ward Muir, *The Happy Hospital* (London: Simpkin, Marshall, Hamilton, Kent & Co, 1918), pp 143–44.

19 ibid, pp 146–47. See also Suzannah Biernoff, 'The Rhetoric of Disfigurement in First World War Britain', *Social History of Medicine*, vol 24, no 3, 2011, pp 666 –85.

20 Muir, *The Happy Hospital*, pp 147–48.

21 Francis Derwent Wood, 'Masks for Facial Wounds', *The Lancet*, 1917, p 949.

22 ibid, pp 949–51.

23 Muir (ed), *Gazette*, vol I, 1916, pp 205–06.

24 ibid.

25 Muir, *The Happy Hospital*, p 155.

13 AWAY FROM THE FRONT

1 The first issue of *Art in Australia* was published in 1916 by Sydney Ure Smith in Sydney.

2 John Phillip Pigot and Hilda Rix Nicholas, *Hilda Rix Nicholas: Her Life and Art* (Carlton South, Vic: Miegunyah Press, 2000), figures 1, 3 and 4–7.

3 Quoted in Catherine Speck, 'The Australian War Museum, Women Artists and the National Memory of the First World War', 'When the Soldiers Return': Conference Proceedings, Brisbane, 28–30 November 2007 (University of Queensland, 2009), pp 89 note 28, and 280.

4 *A Mother of France* <www.awm.gov.au/collection/ART03281/> accessed 21 December 2015.

5 Ray Howell, *Signaller at the Front* (Perth: Hesperian Press, 2001), p 55.

6 WH Downing et al, *WH Downing's Digger Dialects* (Melbourne: Oxford University Press in association with Australian War Memorial, 1990), p 210.

7 Come to think of it, these days, it is probably necessary to point out that it is possible to make socks by the process of knitting, and to describe what knitting is. Enough! My mother – a lifelong knitter, who lived not far from Grace Cossington Smith on the North Shore – will be turning in her grave.

8 Drusilla Modjeska, *Stravinsky's Lunch* (Sydney: Picador, 1999), p 226 and following.

9 ibid, p 205 and following.

14 THE WESTERN FRONT, 1918

1 Letter from Smart to Streeton, 29 January 1918, AWM93 18/7/12.

2 AWM93 18/7/2.

3 The camouflage of the British naval ships was called a 'dazzle' pattern. It was the brainchild of a British artist, Norman Wilkinson. See MRD Foot and Imperial War Museum (Great Britain), *Art and War: Twentieth Century Warfare as Depicted by War Artists* (London: Headline, 1990), p 21.

4 Cable from Fisher to Prime Minister's Department, 18 January 1918, AWM93 18/7/13.

5 Cable from Prime Minister's Department to Fisher, 28 March 1918, AWM93 18/7/13.

6 Ross McMullin, *Will Dyson: Australia's Radical Genius* (Carlton North, Vic: Scribe Publications, 2006), p 190. Dyson was in England from 13 November 1917 until 13 April 1918: Dyson W, Service record, NAA B2455.

7 Hurley's work was controversial because many of his photographs were either posed or composites of more than one original. For discussion of the exhibition and the controversy, see M Jolly, 'Australian First World War Photography: Frank Hurley and Charles Bean', *History of Photography*, no 23, Summer 1999; M Jolly, 'Composite Propaganda Photographs During the First World War', *History of Photography*, no 27, Summer 2003, pp 154–64.

8 WH Downing, *To the Last Ridge* (Sydney: Duffy & Snellgrove, 1998), p 120.

9 William Riddell Birdwood, *Khaki and Gown: An Autobiography* (London: Ward Lock, 1942), pp 322–33.

10 AWM93 18/7/13.

11 AWM93 18/7/9.

12 Quoted in Geoffrey Serle and Monash University, *John Monash: A Biography* (Melbourne: Melbourne University Press in association with Monash University, 1982), p 379.

13 Peter Rees, *Bearing Witness: The Remarkable Life of Charles Bean, Australia's Greatest War Correspondent* (Crows Nest, NSW: Allen & Unwin, 2015), p 132 and following.

14 ibid, p 357 and following.

15 Prue Joske, *Debonair Jack: A Biography of Sir John Longstaff 1861–1941* (Hawthorn, Vic: Claremont, 1994), pp 120 21.

16 Letters from Smart to Streeton, 22 January 1918; Streeton to Smart, 25 January 1918; Smart to Streeton, 29 January 1918; Smart to Streeton, 15 February 1918; Streeton to Smart, 20 February 1918; Smart to Streeton, 21 February 1918; Smart to Streeton, 12 April 1918; Streeton to Smart, 16 April 1918; and Smart to Streeton, 18 April 1918: AWM93 18/7/12.

17 Arthur Streeton, Ann Galbally, and Anne Gray, *Letters from Smike: The Letters of Arthur Streeton, 1890–1943* (Melbourne: Oxford University Press, 1989), p 149.

18 ibid, p 146. No good asking me. I have no idea how sleeping with boots on would stop a German bomb.

19 ibid, p 148.

20 ibid, p 149. Yes, green and gold – the whole cliché.

21 He was following the approach set out in the catalogue for the *9 by 5 Impression Exhibition*: HR Croll, *Tom Roberts: Father of Australian Landscape Painting* (Melbourne: Robertson & Mullens, 1935), p 26. See also Bernard Smith, *Documents on Art and Taste in Australia: The Colonial Period, 1770–1914* (Melbourne: Oxford University Press, 1975), p 207.

22 John Monash, *The Australian Victories in France in 1918*, 2nd rev edn (Melbourne: Lothian Book Publishing, 1923), p 143.

23 Streeton, Galbally, and Gray, *Letters from Smike*, p 148.

24 ibid, p 149.

25 CEW Bean diary, entry for 4 December 1916, AWM38 3DRL 606/67/1.

26 Notice for AIF Orders, 15 March 1918; letter from Treloar to Bean, 12 April 1918: AWM16 435/2/15.

27 Report of a committee appointed to select seven artists required for work in the Australian War Records Section, 10 April 1918, AWM16 435/2/15.

28 Letter from Treloar to Bean, 12 April 1918, AWM16 435/2/15.

29 Crozier FR, Service record, NAA B2455. See also letter from Gullett to Dodds, 17 August 1918, AWM16 435/2/15.

30 Benson GC, Service record, NAA B2455.

31 McCubbin LF, Service record, NAA B2455.

32 Scott, JF, Service record, NAA B2455.

33 Longstaff William Frederick, Service record, NAA B2455.

34 Letter from Treloar to Bean, 12 April 1918; letter from Treloar to Australian Corps, 21 June 1918, AWM16 435/2/15.

35 Letter from Bean to Treloar, 28 August 1918; letter from Treloar to Australian Corps Headquarters, 10 October 1918; AIF Orders by General Dodds, 23 September 1918 (date unclear) AWM16 435/2/15.

36 CEW Bean, *Anzac to Amiens*, 4th edn (Canberra: Australian War Memorial, 1961), p 242.

37 Bean diary, entry for 12 July 1918, AWM 3DRL 606/116/1

38 Cables from Fisher to Prime Minister's Department, 24 and 28 June 1918; letter from Pearce to Prime Minister's Department, 27 August 1918: AWM93 8/2/23.

39 Cable from Fisher to Prime Minister's Department, 31 August 1918, AWM93 8/2/23.

40 Cable from Bean to the Department of Defence, Melbourne, 14 September 1918, AWM16 4351/2/10. Bean, working his contacts as ever, went so far as to persuade Prime Minister Hughes to support the idea: Cable from Hughes to Watt, 21 October 1918, NAA A2 1920/1044. However, Hughes' cable arrived in Australia after the decision to approve funding for the composition paintings.

41 Amy Lambert, *Thirty Years of an Artist's Life: The Career of GW Lambert, ARA* (Sydney: Australian Artist Editions, 1938), pp 88–90.

42 AWM93 18/7/7 Part 1.

43 Cable from Fisher to Prime Minister's Department, 31 August 1918, AWM93 8/2/23.

44 Letter from Gullett to Trumble, 6 May 1919, AWM16 435/2/15.

15 PEACE, MEMORY AND COMMEMORATION

1 Catherine Speck, *Painting Ghosts: Australian Women Artists in Wartime* (St Leonards, NSW: Craftsman House, 2004), pp 87–89.

2 ibid. 'Vida Lahey (1882–1968)', *Australian Dictionary of Biography*, vol 9, pp 643–44.

3 Humphrey McQueen, *The Black Swan of Trespass: The Emergence of Modernist Painting in Australia to 1944* (Sydney: Alternative Publishing, 1979), p 98.

4 Alan McCulloch, *Encyclopedia of Australian Art* (New York: Frederick A Praeger, 1968), p 335. The generosity of Lord Woolavington's gift renders tacky the claim in Wikipedia that he paid £50,000 for his peerage. <en.wikipedia.org/wiki/James_Buchanan,_1st_Baron_Woolavington> accessed 14 January 2016.

5 Catalogue notes for *Menin Gate at Midnight*, AWM ART09807.

6 Among them, *Immortal Shrine*, AWM ART14196.

7 Arthur Streeton, Ann Galbally, and Anne Gray, *Letters from Smike: The Letters of Arthur Streeton, 1890–1943* (Melbourne: Oxford University Press, 1989), p 154.

8 Speck, *Painting Ghosts*, p 92 and following.

9 'Jessie Traill (1881–1967)', *Australian Dictionary of Biography*, vol 12, p 252.

10 'Margaret Preston (1875–1963)', *Australian Dictionary of Biography*, vol 11, pp 283–85.

11 Penelope Little and Bessie Davidson, *A Studio in Montparnasse: Bessie Davidson: An Australian Artist in Paris* (Melbourne: Craftsman House, 2003), p 69 and following.

12 Speck, *Painting Ghosts*, p 96. The Australian War Memorial holds one of Traill's watercolours: ART03552. It is an undistinguished sketch of a Rising Sun badge, cut into the chalk hills on the Wiltshire Downs. In 1886, Roberts made a fine series of paintings of A Battery of the NSW Field Artillery. During the Great War, he made a sketch of his son in uniform and portraits of his nephew, Gilbert Burchill, and of Colonel TS Woodburn, but little else. See Helen Topliss and Tom Roberts, *Tom Roberts, 1856–1931: A Catalogue Raisonnee*, 2 vols (Melbourne: Oxford University Press, 1985).

13 John Phillip Pigot and Hilda Rix Nicholas, *Hilda Rix Nicholas: Her Life and Art* (Carlton South, Vic: Miegunyah Press, 2000), p 35.

14 For a short history of the collection of war photographs, see CEW Bean and HS Gullett, *The Official History of Australia in the War of 1914–1918*, vol XII (1923), preface. The Australian War Memorial in Canberra did not open until November 1941: CEW Bean and Australian War Memorial, *Anzac to Amiens: A Shorter History of the Australian Fighting Services in the First World War* (Canberra: Australian War Memorial, 1946).

15 Cable from Watt to Fisher, 31 October 1918, NAA A2 1920/1044.

16 These were Streeton's words: Streeton, Galbally, and Gray, *Letters from Smike*, p 148.

17 Quoted in Dudley McCarthy, *Gallipoli to the Somme: The Story of CEW Bean* (Sydney: John Ferguson, 1983), p 362.

18 ibid, p 381. See also Peter Rees, *Bearing Witness: The Remarkable Life of Charles Bean, Australia's Greatest War Correspondent* (Crows Nest, NSW: Allen & Unwin, 2015), p 394. For the major general's salary, see Bean, *Official History*, vol XI (1940), p 207.

19 Bean, *Gallipoli Mission*, pp 4, 12.

20 ibid, pp 1–13.

21 ibid, p 14.

22 ibid, pp 14–15.

23 ibid, pp 15–16.

24 Amy Lambert, *Thirty Years of an Artist's Life: The Career of GW Lambert, ARA* (Sydney: Australian Artist Editions, 1938), p 108.

25 Bean, *Gallipoli Mission*, p 108.

26 Lambert, *Thirty Years of an Artist's Life*, p 103.

27 *Gallipoli* (film), director Peter Weir, Associated R&R Films, 1981.

28 Lambert, *Thirty Years of an Artist's Life*, pp 103–04.

29 Bean, *Gallipoli Mission*, p 109.

30 ibid, pp 109–10.

31 ibid, p 110.

32 Lambert, *Thirty Years of an Artist's Life*, p 112.

33 Spruce William Henry, Service record, NAA B2455.

34 Lambert, *Thirty Years of an Artist's Life*, pp 12, 104.

35 ibid, p 107.

36 ibid, pp 112–13.

37 ibid, pp 24, 121.

38 Ivers Thomas Henry, Service record, NAA B2455.

39 Lambert, *Thirty Years of an Artist's Life*, pp 128–29.

40 R Hugh Knyvett, *'Over There' with the Australians* (London: Hodder & Stoughton, 1918), p 117.

41 Turnour Donald Winterton, Service record, NAA B2455.

42 Letter from Bean to Leist, 22 August 1920, AWM38 3DRL 6673/304.

43 Richard White, of Hunters Hill, NSW, identified the gun. He has done a terrific job of restoring and maintaining the trophy gun of the same variety that now stands outside the Hunters Hill Council Chambers.

44 David Nash, *German Artillery, 1914–1918* (London: Almark Publishing, 1970), pp 17, 26, 27, and appendix 1, pp 44–45.

45 Bean, *Official History*, vol IV, p 814 including note 70.

46 Examples include *Australian Squadron in Blanche Bay, New Britain*, AWM ART07546; *Wireless Station, Bita Pika, Rabaul*, AWM ART03639 (the wireless station was the principal objective of the AN&MEF expedition); and *Waterfront at Rabaul*, AWM ART03634.

47 AWM93 18/7/6. See also Anne Gray, A Henry Fullwood, and Australian War Memorial, *A Henry Fullwood: War Paintings*, Australian War Memorial Artists Series (Canberra: Australian War Memorial, 1983), pp 29–30.

48 Even that most partisan of biographers, Ross McMullin, saw problems with the oils, but he found a way to praise them all the same: 'To mention that Dyson was not a seasoned practitioner in oil, and that in some of his figures he may have veered too closely towards caricature, is not at all to suggest that these slices of digger humour were sub-standard': Ross McMullin, *Will Dyson: Australia's Radical Genius* (Carlton North, Vic: Scribe Publications, 2006), pp 271–72.

49 Streeton, Galbally, and Gray, *Letters from Smike*, pp 49, 50, 148.

50 Robert Hughes, *The Art of Australia*, rev edn (Ringwood, Vic: Penguin Books, 1970), p 51.

51 Catalogue notes for *The Somme Valley Near Corbie*, AWM ART03497.

52 Bean, *Official History*, vol VI (1923), p 941 and following.

53 Streeton, Galbally, and Gray, *Letters from Smike*, p 150.

54 Catalogue notes for *Amiens, the Key of the West*, AWM ART12436.

55 Streeton, Galbally, and Gray, *Letters from Smike*, p 150.

56 AWM ART02991; AWM ART02993; AWM ART02997; AWM ART02998; AWM ART02999; AWM ART94169; AWM ART02990.

57 AWM ART03349; AWM ART03340; AWM ART03341; AWM ART03351; AWM ART03346; AWM ART03352.

58 AWM ART00098; AWM ART00107; AWM ART00100; AWM ART00101; AWM ART03589.

59 George Bell's biographer, June Helmer, described Bell's portraits as 'undistinguished as paintings … simply dull, factual records of soldiers who have attained high rank over the years': June Helmer, *George Bell, the Art of Influence* (Richmond, Vic: Greenhouse, 1985), p 44. Bell's composition painting, *Dawn at Hamel, 4 July 1918*, is also disappointing: AWM ART032590.

60 *Art in Australia*, Eleventh number, 1921, pages unnumbered.

61 Prue Joske, *Debonair Jack: A Biography of Sir John Longstaff 1861–1941* (Hawthorn, Vic: Claremont, 1994), pp 126–30.

62 AB Paterson, *Clancy of the Overflow* (1889).

63 Dora Meeson Coates, *George Coates: His Art and His Life* (London: JM Dent, 1937), p 118.

64 ibid.

65 AWM ART00199; AWM ART00197; AWM ART03644; AWM ART00202.

66 Coates, *George Coates*, p 121.

67 The organisation of the Royal Army Medical Corps (RAMC) is described in Andrew Rawson, *British Army Handbook, 1914–1918* (Stroud, UK: Sutton, 2006), pp 133–49. The elderly artists enlisted in the RAMC when they went to work as orderlies at the 3rd London General Hospital.

68 AG Butler, *The Australian Army Medical Services in the War of 1914–1918*, 2nd edn, 3 vols (Melbourne and Canberra: Australian War Memorial, 1938), vol II, p 356. See also Sir William MacPherson and TJ Mitchell, *Medical Services: General History*, 4 vols (London: HMSO, 1921), vol II, chapter II, especially p 42 and following.

69 Quoted in Peter Rees, *The Other Anzacs: Nurses at War, 1914–18* (Crows Nest, NSW: Allen & Unwin, 2008), 190–91.

70 Coates, *George Coates*, p 119.

71 ibid, p 123.

72 ibid, pp 149–50.

73 ibid, p 151.

74 ibid, p 152.

75 ibid, pp 64, 158–59.

76 ibid, p 170.

77 ibid, pp 179–80.

78 ibid, pp 91, 183. Sorry. It is the lawyer coming out in me.

79 CEW Bean, *Two Men I Knew: William Bridges and Brudenell White, Founders of the AIF* (Sydney: Angus & Robertson, 1957), introduction.

80 In 1921, George Benson and Frank Crozier painted a Pyramid picture of their own. It was a pastiche of Egyptian standards – pyramids, Arabs, orange-vendors and a Light-Horseman with a jaded expression on his face and a fag in his lips: *Training in the Desert, Mena*, AWM ART03607.

81 Ivers worked with Lambert from September 1919 until February 1920: Ivers Thomas Henry, Service record.

82 Lambert, *Thirty Years of an Artist's Life*, p 135.

83 ibid, pp 135–37.

84 *Art in Australia*, Twelfth number, 1921, p 9.

85 CEW Bean, *Gallipoli Mission* (Canberra: Australian War Memorial, 1948), p 110.

86 Ivers was 5 feet 7½ inches tall.

87 Daryl Lindsay, *The Leafy Tree: My Family* (Melbourne: FW Cheshire, 1965), p 123.

88 HR Croll, *Tom Roberts: Father of Australian Landscape Painting* (Melbourne: Robertson & Mullens, 1935), p 117.

89 Christopher Wray, *Arthur Streeton: Painter of Light* (Milton, Qld: Jacaranda, 1993), p 144.

90 Bell arrived back in Melbourne on 12 February 1920: Helmer, *George Bell, the Art of Influence*, p 46.

91 Joske, *Debonair Jack*, p 127.

92 Lambert, *Thirty Years of an Artist's Life*, pp 135–36.

93 ibid, p 141.

94 ibid, pp 143–44.

95 ibid, p 145.

96 ibid, p 144.

[97] ibid, p 150.

[98] The Australian War Memorial has the *Romani* painting: AWM ART09556.

[99] Bean, *Gallipoli Mission*, pp 109–10.

[100] The charge of the Light Horse at the Nek was made without horses – the Light Horse fought as infantrymen at Gallipoli. The use of crack cavalry troops in that way only added to the futility of the action at the Nek. Lambert, who idolised the Light Horse, did not resist the temptation to call both paintings 'charges'.

[101] Lambert, *Thirty Years of an Artist's Life*, pp 13, 102.

[102] ibid, p 105.

[103] Jimmy Olsen was Superman's sidekick. A cub reporter on the *Daily Planet* newspaper, Olsen was the quintessential nerd. Olsen and Bean even looked alike, sharing boyish looks and red hair. Sadly, however, the idea that Lambert based his portrait of Bean on Jimmy Olsen is only a dream. Olsen did not make his debut until April 1940.

[104] Bean, *Gallipoli Mission*, p 128.

EPILOGUE

[1] Prue Joske, *Debonair Jack: A Biography of Sir John Longstaff 1861–1941* (Hawthorn, Vic: Claremont, 1994), p 122.

[2] Ross McMullin, *Will Dyson: Australia's Radical Genius* (Carlton North, Vic: Scribe Publications, 2006), pp 231–42. Ruby was a victim of the Spanish influenza epidemic. She was thirty-two when she died. She left a daughter, Betty, aged eight, and a grieving husband. See William Dyson, *Poems: In Memory of a Wife, 1919* [byC WD [ie William Dyson] (London: Cecil, Palmer, 1920).

[3] The Balfour Declaration, 1926. For the text of the Declaration, see Arthur Berriedale Keith, *Speeches and Documents on the British Dominions 1918–1931* (London: Oxford University Press, 1948 [1932]), p 161.

[4] HR Croll, *Tom Roberts: Father of Australian Landscape Painting* (Melbourne: Robertson & Mullens), 1935, p 128.

[5] ibid, pp 126–27.

[6] Dora Meeson Coates, *George Coates: His Art and His Life* (London: JM Dent, 1937), pp 148–49.

[7] Arthur Streeton, Ann Galbally, and Anne Gray, *Letters from Smike: The Letters of Arthur Streeton, 1890–1943* (Melbourne: Oxford University Press, 1989), p 158.

[8] Hilda Rix Nicholas, quoted in *Art in Australia*, vol 1, no 1 (new series), no 12 (old series), 1921, p 69.

LIST OF IMAGES

The author thanks the galleries and/or copyright owners for granting permission to reproduce works in this publication. Every effort has been made to contact the copyright owners. Any omissions will be corrected in future editions, provided the author has been notified in writing.

The following abbreviations are used to describe the images and in the Notes:

AGB – Art Gallery of Ballarat
AGNSW – Art Gallery of New South Wales
AGWA – Art Gallery of Western Australia
AWM – Australian War Memorial
BVRG – Bega Valley Regional Gallery
CAGHM Castlemaine Art Gallery and Historical Museum
NAA – National Archives of Australia
NGA – National Gallery of Australia
NGV – National Gallery of Victoria
NLA – National Library of Australia
NPG – National Portrait Gallery
PHAC – Parliament House Art Collection
QGMA – Queensland Gallery of Modern Art
SLNSW – State Library of New South Wales
SHSM – Stratford Historical Society and Museum
V&A – Victoria and Albert Museum, London

COVER
Nicholas, Hilda Rix
A man 1921
oil on canvas framed: 104.6 × 98 cm; unframed: 92 × 75 cm
Australian War Memorial (ART19613)
By courtesy of Bronwyn Wright

TITLE PAGE
Coates, George
Australian official war artists 1916–1918 1920
oil on canvas overall: 124.2 × 104.5 cm
Australian War Memorial (ART15334)

PRINCIPAL ARTISTS
Tom Roberts (England; Australia, b 1856, d 1931)
Self Portrait 1924
oil on canvas, 61.2 × 51 cm
Art Gallery of New South Wales
Gift of the artist at the request of the Trustees 1924
Photo: AGNSW
958

Tom Roberts (England; Australia, b 1856, d 1931)
Smike Streeton age 24 1891
oil on canvas, 45.7 × 35.7 cm
Art Gallery of New South Wales
Purchased 1924
Photo: AGNSW
7442

George Coates (Australia; England, b 1869, d 1930)
Will Dyson (Sketch portrait)
oil on canvas, 76.1 × 59.3 cm
Art Gallery of New South Wales
Purchased 1921
Photo: AGNSW
941

George James Coates
Head of a Lady
Victoria and Albert Museum
P.32 – 1932

Hilda Rix Nicholas
Mrs George Matson Nicholas, Self Portrait of the Artist
c 1917
pastel on paper, 55.5 × 38 cm
Bega Valley Regional Gallery
By courtesy of Bronwyn Wright

Self Portrait with Gladioli 1922
by George Lambert (1873–1930)
oil on canvas
Collection: National Portrait Gallery, Canberra
Gift of John Schaeffer AO 2003
Donated through the Australian Government Cultural Gifts Program
2003.93

Grace Cossington Smith
Study of a head: self-portrait 1916
oil on canvas
26 × 21 cm
National Gallery of Australia, Canberra
Purchased 2010
2010.383
By courtesy of Ann Mills

1 BEING AUSTRALIAN

2 PAINTING AUSTRALIA
Ramon Casas
Tom Roberts 1883
oil on canvas on wood panel
32.7 × 24.5 cm
National Gallery of Victoria, Melbourne
Marie Therese McVeigh Bequest, 2005 (2005.584)

Tom Roberts (1856–1931)
Opening of the First Parliament of the Commonwealth of Australia by HRH The Duke of Cornwall and York (Later King George V) May 9, 1901 (1903)
On permanent loan to the Parliament of Australia from the British Royal Collection
Image courtesy of the Parliament House Art Collection, Canberra, ACT, and the Royal Collection Trust
© Her Majesty Queen Elizabeth II 2016

3 FROM HEIDELBERG TO LONDON – OR PARIS
Ruby Lindsay
Courtesy of the State Library of New South Wales

4 SYDNEY FOLLOWS MELBOURNE

5 LIFE IN LONDON
Walter Di Qual
*London showing 3rd London General Hospital, Wandsworth,
& Chelsea Arts Club* 2016

George W Lambert (Russia; Australia, b 1873, d 1930)
Miss Thea Proctor (1903)
oil on canvas, 90 × 69.8 cm
Art Gallery of New South Wales
Purchased under the terms of the Florence Turner Baker Bequest 1961
Photo: AGNSW
OA 12.1961

George Lambert
The sonnet c 1907
oil on canvas
113.3 × 177.4 cm
National Gallery of Australia, Canberra
Bequest of John B Pye in 1963
63.18

Dora Meeson (1869–1955)
The Women's Suffrage Banner: Trust the women … (1908)
Reproduced by permission of Lt Col Simon Hearder on behalf of the
heirs in copyright. Parliament House Art Collection, Canberra, ACT

Will Dyson
Labour wants a 'Place in the Sun'!
Cartoons, 1913

Hilda Rix Nicholas
La Robe Chinoise (The Chinese Dress) c 1913
oil on canvas
State Art Collection, Art Gallery of Western Australia
Purchased through the Sir Claude Hotchin Art Foundation,
Art Gallery of Western Australia Foundation, 1994
© Hilda Rix Nicholas c 1913
By courtesy of Bronwyn Wright

6 WAR
Dora Meeson
Leaving for the Front c 1918
oil on canvas
162.0 × 122.6 cm
Art Gallery of Ballarat
Purchased with funds from the Lawrence Clark Bequest, 1921

Will Dyson
The Goose Step, or the March of Civilisation
Kultur Cartoons, 1915

Norman Lindsay
Australia answers the War God's Call
© Barbara Mobbs
By courtesy of Barbara Mobbs and the Norman Lindsay Estate

Will Dyson
The Man Behind Conscription
Conscript 'Em!, 1915

Bunny, Rupert
Waiting to be X-rayed 1915
oil on canvas overall: 50.1 × 65.2 cm; Framed 59.0 × 74.3 × 8.4 cm
Australian War Memorial (ART50255)

Victoria Patriotic Asylum, Wandsworth AWM P11232.023

7 GALLIPOLI
Silas, Ellis
The landing 1916
pen and black ink on card overall: 19.8 × 24.4 cm (irreg)
Australian War Memorial (ART90807)

Silas, Ellis
In the trenches, Quinn's Post 1916
pen and black ink on card overall: 17.6 × 24.8 cm
Australian War Memorial (ART90798)

Colles, Ted
Something to remember us by! 1915
pen and ink and brush, watercolour and pencil on paper 29.0 × 20.2 cm
Australian War Memorial (ART00048)

Barker, David Crothers
At the landing and here ever since 1915
pen and brown ink, pencil and coloured pencil on paper 21.1 × 16.7 cm
Australian War Memorial (ART00025.002)

White, Cyril Leyshon
Kitch 1915
pen and ink, pencil and watercolour on paper 23.7 × 18 cm
Australian War Memorial (ART00013.002)

Hewett, Otho
Finis 1915
pen and ink on laid paper 32.5 × 20.3 cm
Australian War Memorial (ART00059)

Eltham, William Keith
North flank, Suvla from Anzac 1915
pencil, pen and ink on paper 20.4 × 32.4 cm
Australian War Memorial (ART00043)

Eltham, William Keith
South Flank – Gaba Tepe from Anzac 1915
pencil, pen and ink on paper 20.2 × 32.2 cm
Australian War Memorial (ART00056)

8 THE 3RD LONDON GENERAL HOSPITAL
Fullwood, A Henry
Balloon view of the 3rd London General Hospital, Wandsworth 1915
pencil, pen and ink and wash heightened with chinese white on paper
on board sheet: 36.7 × 53.8 cm; image: 36.7 × 53.8 cm
Australian War Memorial (ART19782)

Hut at Wandsworth AWM C01996

Hut at Wandsworth AWM H15252

Visiting day at Wandsworth AWM P11232.024
Lambert, George
Arthur Streeton 1917
oil on canvas overall: 76.4 × 63.5 cm
Australian War Memorial (ART19841)

Coates, George
*The arrival of the first Australian wounded from Gallipoli at the Third
London General Hospital, Wandsworth* 1915
watercolour with gouache and pencil on squared paper on cardboard
44 × 37 cm
Australian War Memorial (ART50234)

The Receiving Ward at Wandsworth
The Gazette of the 3rd London General Hospital, Wandsworth

Lieutenant Hugo Throssell VC recovering at Wandsworth AWM
P00516.003

Streeton, Arthur
Concert by Miss Hullah 1916
watercolour on paper sheet: 33.6 × 26.8 cm; image: 31.2 × 25.8 cm
Australian War Memorial (ART50161)

The art exhibition in the recreation room at Wandsworth
AWM P03451.006

George Coates
A Hero from Mons, nd
pencil
30.7 × 24.6 cm
Castlemaine Art Gallery and Historical Museum collection
Gift of the artist, 1926

Coates, George
Portrait of a soldier 1916
watercolour on board overall: 35.4 × 25 cm
Australian War Memorial (ART50016)

Cover of the *Gazette of the 3rd London General Hospital, Wandsworth*

9 THE WESTERN FRONT, 1916
Walter Di Qual
The Western Front 2016

George Nicholas and Hilda Rix at Buckingham Palace
Stratford Historical Society and Museum
By courtesy of Bronwyn Wright

Nicholas, Hilda Rix
Major George Matson Nicholas 1916
charcoal and pastel over pencil on paper sheet: 56 × 38 cm
Australian War Memorial (ART96807)
By courtesy of Bronwyn Wright

Hilda Rix Nicholas
These gave the world away 1917
oil on canvas
127 × 97 cm
National Gallery of Australia, Canberra
Ruth Robertson Bequest Fund in memory of Edwin Clive and
Leila Jeanne Robertson 2013
© Bronwyn Wright
2013.232
By courtesy of Bronwyn Wright

Dyson, Will
Coming out on the Somme 1916
charcoal, pencil, brush and wash on paper sheet: 58 × 47.4 cm;
image: 56 × 47.2 cm
Australian War Memorial (ART02276)

Dyson, Will
Entrance to Mouquet Farm dugouts 1917
charcoal and pencil on paper sheet: 42 × 57.5 cm (irreg);
image: 40.2 × 57.5 cm
Australian War Memorial (ART02219)

Dyson, Will
Signaller, 2nd Main Line Gun Battalion 1917
charcoal and pencil on paper sheet: 36.9 × 48.2 cm; image: 36.9 × 48.2 cm
Australian War Memorial (ART02323)

10 THE WESTERN FRONT, 1917
Power, H Septimus
War 1917
charcoal, watercolour, pencil, white gouache on paper mounted on
cardboard sheet: 46.8 × 60.7 cm (irreg); image: 46.8 × 60.7 cm
Australian War Memorial (ART03328)

Power, H Septimus
In the horse lines 1917
oil on hardboard unframed: 40.4 × 50.6 cm
Australian War Memorial (ART03305)

Leist, Fred
Gibraltar, Pozières 1917
watercolour over charcoal on paper sheet: 40 × 57.6 cm (irreg);
image: 37 × 46 cm
Australian War Memorial (ART02881)

Motorcycle despatch rider with pigeon basket AWM E00646

Fred Leist (Australia, b 1873, d 1945)
The pigeon loft 1917
oil on canvas, 63.4 × 76.2 cm
Art Gallery of New South Wales
Purchased 1934
Photo: AGNSW
843

Gould, Charles Henry
*Extract from Intelligence Report:- 'Yesterday two of our pigeons failed
to return'* 1917
pencil, pen and ink on paper sight: 17.4 × 24.4 cm
Australian War Memorial (ART02555)

Cecil Hartt
Don't you know what to do when you pass an officer?
Humorosities, 1917

Penleigh Boyd
Digger
Salvage, 1918

Norman Lindsay
The Slackers on the Beach
© Barbara Mobbs
By courtesy of Barbara Mobbs and the Norman Lindsay Estate

11 THE MIDDLE EAST
Lambert, George
Major Andrew Barton (Banjo) Paterson 1918
pencil on paper sheet: 30.4 × 19 cm (irreg); image: 18.6 × 16.5 cm
Australian War Memorial (ART02780)

Lambert, George
The Wassah, Cairo 1918
oil, pencil on wood panel overall: 22.2 × 30.6 cm
Australian War Memorial (ART02755)

Walter Di Qual
The Sinai Peninsula 2016

Lambert, George
Moascar, from Major 'Banjo' Paterson's tent 1918
oil on wood panel framed: 29.6 × 37.2 × 5.7 cm
Australian War Memorial (ART02774)

Lambert, George
Mrs Chisholm of Kantara 1918
pencil on paper sheet: 35.5 × 24.7 cm (irreg); image: 26.3 × 13.4 cm
Australian War Memorial (ART02756)

Lambert, George
Romani, Mount Royston in background 1918
oil, pencil on wood panel overall: 22.2 × 30.6 cm
Australian War Memorial (ART02704)

Lambert, George
Wadi bed between El Arish and Magdhaba 1918
oil on maple wood panel framed: 27.6 × 32.8 cm; unframed:
19 × 24 cm
Australian War Memorial (ART02679)

12 FACE WOUNDS
Cecil Hartt
We find the shrapnel helmets very useful
Humorosities, 1917

Daryl Lindsay
Diagram 3 Rhinoplasty after Low Nasal Loss
AWM *Official Medical History* vol III

Daryl Lindsay
Diagram 9 Fracture of the Mandible
AWM *Official Medical History* vol III

Daryl Lindsay
Diagram 10 *Fracture of the Mandible*
AWM *Official Medical History* vol III

Derwent Wood at Wandsworth AWM H07537

Derwent Wood at Wandsworth AWM H07538

13 AWAY FROM THE FRONT
Rae, Iso
Rue de la Gare (Station Street) 1918
pastel, gouache, pen and black ink, pencil on grey card overall:
63.1 × 48 cm
Australian War Memorial (ART19597)

Iso Rae
Étaples, 1915 1915
coloured chalks and charcoal
image 46.4 × 38 cm
sheet 55.2 × 46.1 cm
National Gallery of Australia, Canberra
Purchased 1980
80.3701

Nicholas, Hilda Rix
A mother of France 1914
oil on canvas overall: 72.6 × 60.2 cm
Australian War Memorial (ART03281)
By courtesy of Bronwyn Wright

Thea Proctor
Stunting c 1918
lithograph, printed in black ink, from one stone printed image
40.4 × 35.8 cm sheet 54.5 × 50.2 cm
National Gallery of Australia, Canberra
Rudy Komon Fund 1982
© Art Gallery of New South Wales
82.1
By courtesy of the Art Gallery of New South Wales

Grace Cossington Smith (Australia, b 1892, d 1984)
The sock knitter (1915)
oil on canvas, 61.8 × 51.2 × 1.7 cm
Art Gallery of New South Wales
Purchased 1960
Photo: AGNSW
© Estate of Grace Cossington Smith
OA 18.1960
By courtesy of Ann Mills

Grace Cossington Smith (Australia, b 1892, d 1984)
Reinforcements: troops marching (c 1917)
oil on paper on hardboard, 23.7 × 21.5 cm
Art Gallery of New South Wales
Purchased 1967
Photo: AGNSW
© Estate of Grace Cossington Smith
OA5. 1967
By courtesy of Ann Mills

Grace Cossington Smith (Australia, b 1892, d 1984)
The refugees (c 1918)
pencil on paper, 29 × 35.6 cm
Art Gallery of New South Wales
Thea Proctor Memorial Fund 1972
Photo: AGNSW
© Estate of Grace Cossington Smith
12.1972
By courtesy of Ann Mills

14 THE WESTERN FRONT, 1918
Bryant, Charles
Australian troops disembarking at Boulogne 1917
oil on canvas on board 48.8 × 64.3 cm × 6.1 cm
Australian War Memorial (ART00189)

Quinn, James Peter
General Sir William Birdwood 1918
oil on canvas framed: 93.2 × 80.5 × 9.8 cm; unframed: 76.4 × 63.6 cm
Australian War Memorial (ART03339)

Quinn, James Peter
Lieutenant General Sir John Monash 1918
oil on canvas framed: 100 × 87.2 × 7 cm
Australian War Memorial (ART03350)

Longstaff, John
Lieutenant General Sir John Monash 1919
oil on canvas framed: 136.5 × 108.3 × 10.5 cm; unframed: 120 × 92 cm
Australian War Memorial (ART02986)

Streeton, Arthur
Staff clerks at work, headquarters, St Gratien 1918
watercolour heightened with white, with pencil on paper image:
37.4 × 55.4 cm
Australian War Memorial (ART03502)

Streeton, Arthur
St Gratien: General Birdwood bidding farewell to headquarters staff 1918
watercolour with pencil on paper sheet: 37.2 × 55.4 cm; image:
37.2 × 55.4 cm
Australian War Memorial (ART03510)

Fullwood, A Henry
Villers-Bretonneux from Bussy 1918
watercolour with pencil on paper sheet: 39.2 × 56.6 cm (irreg); image:
34.4 × 53.6 cm
Australian War Memorial (ART50104)

Streeton, Arthur
Amiens Cathedral 1918
watercolour with pencil on paper sheet: 35.6 × 51 cm (irreg); image:
33.4 × 51 cm
Australian War Memorial (ART03491)

Streeton, Arthur
Souvenir, Amiens 1918
watercolour on paper sheet: 22 × 31.4 cm; image: 22 × 31.4 cm
Australian War Memorial (ART19783)

Fullwood, A Henry
Distant View of Amiens 1919
watercolour on paper sheet: 39.6 × 57.3 cm (irreg); image:
39.6 × 57.3 cm
Australian War Memorial (ART50007)

Fullwood, A Henry
Attack on Hamel-Vaire 1918
watercolour and gouache with charcoal on paper sheet: 39 × 56.8 cm;
image: 37.6 × 54.4 cm
Australian War Memorial (ART02493)

Streeton, Arthur
Chateau, Villers-Bretonneux 1918
pencil with yellow wash on paper sheet: 25.2 × 34.6 cm (irreg);
image: 25 × 34.6 cm
Australian War Memorial (ART12643)

Streeton, Arthur
Street in ruins, Villers-Bretonneux, France 1918
pencil and wash on buff paper sheet: 30.2 × 46 cm; image: 18 × 45.6 cm
Australian War Memorial (ART93003)

Streeton, Arthur
The Somme from above Corbie 1918
watercolour with pencil on paper sheet: 37.4 × 55.5 cm (irreg);
image: 24.6 × 55.5 cm
Australian War Memorial (ART12652)

Fullwood, A Henry
Valley of the Somme 1918
oil on canvas overall: 71.8 × 91.6 cm
Australian War Memorial (ART93176)

Fullwood, A Henry
Courtyard at Bertangles 1918
watercolour and gouache with pencil and charcoal on paper sheet:
38.6 × 56.2 cm (irreg); image: 35.6 × 54.8 cm
Australian War Memorial (ART02472)

Fullwood, A Henry
AIF aerodrome near Bertangles 1918
watercolour and gouache with pencil and charcoal on paper sheet:
40 × 57.2 cm
Australian War Memorial (ART02477)

Crozier, Frank
The beach at Anzac 1919
oil on canvas framed: 151.6 × 213 cm; unframed: 123.4 × 184.6 cm
Australian War Memorial (ART02161)

Crozier, Frank
Bombardment of Pozières, July 1916 1918
oil on canvas framed: 221.3 × 137 cm; unframed: 106.2 × 191.5 cm
Australian War Memorial (ART00240)

Scott, James F
Loft at Saint-Sylvestre-Cappel 1918
oil on canvas framed: 68.2 × 77.6 × 6.5 cm; unframed: 50.6 × 61 cm;
sight: 49.7 × 59.6 cm
Australian War Memorial (ART03383)

Longstaff, Will
Australians advancing from Villers-Bretonneux, August 8th 1918 1918
watercolour over pencil, heightened with white, with gouache on
paper sheet: 45.2 × 73 cm (irreg); image: 45.2 × 73 cm
Australian War Memorial (ART15522)

Longstaff, Will
Mont St Quentin 1918
watercolour over pencil on paper sheet: 41 × 67.4 cm;
image: 41 × 67.4 cm
Australian War Memorial (ART03001)

McCubbin, Louis
Looking towards the lines, Somme Valley 1918
watercolour on paper sheet: 36.6 × 37.8 cm; image: 36.6 × 37.8 cm
Australian War Memorial (ART03058)

Bell, George
German plane brought down near Ors, France November 1918
oil on wood panel 15.4 × 23.8 cm
Australian War Memorial (ART00125)

Bell, George
Le Cateau 1918
watercolour over pencil, heightened with white on paper 39.6 × 55.6 cm
Australian War Memorial (ART00111)

Streeton, Arthur
Péronne, looking towards Mont St Quentin 1918
watercolour with pencil on paper framed: 53.2 × 137.2 cm;
sheet 1: 18.5 × 54.5 cm; sheet 2: 18.8 × 55.2 cm
Australian War Memorial (ART03520)

Streeton, Arthur
Bellicourt: entrance to St Quentin Tunnel 1918
watercolour with pencil on paper sheet: 37.2 × 55.2 cm;
image: 37.2 × 55.2 cm
Australian War Memorial (ART03517)

15 PEACE, MEMORY AND COMMEMORATION
Lahey, Vida
Rejoicing and remembrance, Armistice Day, London, 1918 1924
charcoal, watercolour on paper sheet: 74.5 × 56 cm
Australian War Memorial (ART19592)
By courtesy of the Queensland Gallery of Modern Art

Longstaff, Will
Menin Gate at midnight 1927
oil on canvas overall: 137 × 270 cm; framed: 170 × 302 × 10 cm
Australian War Memorial (ART09807)

Streeton, Arthur
Australians burning effigy of Kaiser in square, Armistice Day 1918
watercolour heightened with white, with pencil on paper framed:
78.4 × 137.1 cm; unframed: 48.5 × 103 cm
Australian War Memorial (ART03523)

Evelyn Chapman (Australia, b 1888, d 1961)
(Ruined church, Villers-Bretonneux) 1918–1919
tempera on grey paper, 30.2 × 38.8 cm
Art Gallery of New South Wales
Gift of the artist's daughter Pamela Thalben-Bell 1976
Photo: AGNSW
© Estate of the artist
197.1976

Nicholas, Hilda Rix
A man 1921
oil on canvas framed: 104.6 × 98 cm; unframed: 92 × 75 cm
Australian War Memorial (ART19613)
By courtesy of Bronwyn Wright

Lambert, George
Anzac, from Gaba Tepe 1919
oil on wood panel framed: 23 × 31.5 cm; unframed: 13.7 × 22 cm
Australian War Memorial (ART02825)

Lambert, George
Lone Pine, looking towards the Nek, Walker's Ridge 1919
oil on wood panel overall: 13.8 × 21.8 cm
Australian War Memorial (ART02826)

Lambert, George
Study for dead trooper and detail of Turkish trench, Gallipoli 1919
oil on canvas overall: 35.7 × 45.8 cm
Australian War Memorial (ART02857)

Lambert, George
Balcony of troopers' ward, 14th Australian General Hospital, Abbassia 1919
oil and pencil on wood panel framed: 41.3 × 54.5 cm; unframed:
32 × 45.6 cm
Australian War Memorial (ART02815)

Lambert, George
The last tents at Moascar 1919
oil on canvas on wood panel overall: 30 × 50.8 cm
Australian War Memorial (ART02819)

Leist, Fred
Sinking of the Southland 1927
oil on canvas framed: 96.2 × 126.6 cm; unframed: 71.4 × 102.2 cm
Australian War Memorial (ART09829)

Leist, Fred
Australian infantry attack in Polygon Wood 1919
oil on canvas unframed: 122.5 × 245 cm; framed: 152.3 × 274 × 12.8 cm
Australian War Memorial (ART02927)

Grave of Lieutenant JEG Turnour AWM H15586

Power, H Septimus
Bringing up the ammunition, Flanders, Autumn 1917 1920
oil on canvas overall: 153 × 244.5 cm; framed: 183 × 274 × 14 cm
Australian War Memorial (ART03333)

Power, H Septimus
Bringing up the guns 1921
oil on canvas overall: 147.3 × 233.7 cm
Australian War Memorial (ART03334)

Bryant, Charles
Boulogne in wartime, January 1918 1923
oil on canvas framed: 85.5 × 116.4 cm; unframed: 73.7 × 104.7 cm;
sight: 72 × 102 cm
Australian War Memorial (ART03612)

Fullwood, A Henry
Attack on Péronne 1919
oil on canvas framed: 169 × 279.7 cm; unframed: 138.2 × 244.5 cm
Australian War Memorial (ART02503)

Dyson, Will
The amateur ('Who's cutting this hair, you or me?') 1920
oil on cardboard framed: 77.4 × 66.4 × 7.8 cm
Australian War Memorial (ART02434)

Streeton, Arthur
The Somme Valley near Corbie 1919
oil on canvas overall: 153 × 245.5 cm
Australian War Memorial (ART03497)

Streeton, Arthur
Bellicourt tunnel 1919
oil on canvas framed: 148.2 × 256 × 10.5 cm
Australian War Memorial (ART12437)

Streeton, Arthur
Amiens, the key of the west 1918
oil on canvas overall: 135.5 × 194.5 cm
Australian War Memorial (ART12436)

Arthur Streeton
Balloons on fire 1918
oil on canvas
63.4 × 76.2 cm
National Gallery of Victoria, Melbourne
Gilbee Bequest, 1918 (960-3)

Longstaff, John
General Sir Cyril Brudenell White 1921
oil on canvas framed: 93 × 80.5 × 10 cm; unframed: 76.8 × 64.2 cm
Australian War Memorial (ART02985)

Longstaff, Will
Australian 9.2 howitzer 1919
oil on canvas framed: 121.5 × 182.5 × 14.5 cm; unframed: 92 × 153 cm
Australian War Memorial (ART03004)

Scott, James F
4th Division Artillery and Infantry moving into battle 1919
oil on canvas framed: 166.8 × 217.5 × 15.5 cm
Australian War Memorial (ART03406)

Benson, George
The drover 1919–1920
oil on canvas framed: 127.5 × 153.5 × 11.5 cm;
unframed: 100.8 × 127.6 cm; sight: 97 × 123 cm
Australian War Memorial (ART00142)

Coates, George
Casualty clearing station 1920
oil on canvas framed: 141.8 × 212.4 × 10.5 cm
Australian War Memorial (ART00198)

Coates, George
First Australian wounded to arrive in England from Gallipoli 1921
oil on canvas 127.5 × 155cm
Australian War Memorial (ART0200)

Coates, George – Meeson, Dora
General William Bridges and his staff watching the manoeuvres of the 1st Australian Division in the desert in Egypt, March 1915 1922–26
oil on canvas overall: 116.9 × 160.3 cm
Australian War Memorial (ART09425)

Lambert, George
The Charge of the Australian Light Horse at Beersheba, 1917 1920
oil on canvas framed: 139.5 × 261.7 cm × 10 cm
Australian War Memorial (ART02811)

George W Lambert
A Sergeant of the Light Horse 1920
oil on canvas
77.0 × 62.0 cm
National Gallery of Victoria, Melbourne
Felton Bequest, 1921 (1182–3)

George W Lambert
The Official Artist 1921
oil on canvas
91.7 × 71.5 cm
National Gallery of Victoria, Melbourne
Felton Bequest, 1921 (1183–3)

Lambert, George
The charge of the 3rd Light Horse Brigade at the Nek, 7 August 1915 1924
oil on canvas framed: 179.5 × 333.2 × 10.5 cm
Australian War Memorial (ART07965)

Lambert, George
Anzac, the landing 1915 1920–22
oil on canvas framed: 235 × 405 × 15 cm;
unframed: 199.8 × 370.2 cm
Australian War Memorial (ART02873)

Lambert, George
Charles EW Bean 1924
oil on canvas 90.7 × 71.7 cm
Australian War Memorial (ART07545)

EPILOGUE
Will Dyson
Peace and Future Cannon Fodder
Daily Herald, 1919.

Adams, Brian, and William Dobell, *Portrait of an Artist: A Biography of William Dobell* (Milsons Point, NSW: Vintage, 1992).

American Hospital of Paris, 'Annual Report 1915' <http://www.ourstory.info/library/2-ww1/AmHosp15/ahp1915.html1915> accessed January 2016.

Ashton, Julian, *Now Came Still Evening On* (Sydney: Angus & Robertson, 1941).

Australian Imperial Force (1914–21), *From the Australian Front* (London and Melbourne: Cassell and Company, 1917).

Bastian, Peter Edward, *Andrew Fisher: An Underestimated Man* (Sydney: UNSW Press, 2009).

Bean, CEW, *Anzac to Amiens*, 4th edn (Canberra: Australian War Memorial, 1961).

—— *Gallipoli Mission* (Canberra: Australian War Memorial, 1948).

—— *Two Men I Knew: William Bridges and Brudenell White, Founders of the AIF* (Sydney: Angus & Robertson, 1957).

—— 'Will Dyson, Artist and Soldier', *Sydney Morning Herald*, 25 January 1938.

—— and Australian War Memorial, *Anzac to Amiens: A Shorter History of the Australian Fighting Services in the First World War* (Canberra: Australian War Memorial, 1946).

——, Henry Gullett, Arthur W Jose, SS Mackenzie, Ernest Scott, and FM Cutlack, *The Official History of Australia in the War of 1914–1918*, 12 vols (Sydney: Angus & Robertson, 1921–42).

—— (ed), *The Anzac Book*, 3rd edn (Sydney: UNSW Press, 2010).

Beckett, IFW, and Keith Simpson, *A Nation in Arms: A Social Study of the British Army in the First World War* (Barnsley, UK: Pen & Sword Military, 2014).

Biernoff, Suzannah, 'The Rhetoric of Disfigurement in First World War Britain', *Social History of Medicine*, vol 24, no 3, 2011, pp 666–85.

Birdwood, William Riddell, *Khaki and Gown: An Autobiography* (London: Ward Lock, 1942).

Bowen, *Stella, Drawn from Life: Reminiscences* (London: Collins, 1940).

Bunny, Rupert, Denise Mimmocchi, Deborah Edwards, David Thomas and Anne Gérard, *Rupert Bunny: Artist in Paris* (Sydney: Art Gallery of New South Wales, 2009).

Butler, AG, *The Australian Army Medical Services in the War of 1914–1918*, 2nd edn, 3 vols (Melbourne: Australian War Memorial, 1938).

Caban, Geoffrey, *A Fine Line: A History of Australian Commercial Art* (Sydney: Hale & Iremonger, 1983).

Carmichael, Jane, *First World War Photographers* (London: Routledge, 1989).

Champion, Janet Maxwell, *Lady of Kantara: A Biography of Dame Alice Chisholm, 1856–1954* (Turramurra, NSW: JM Champion, 1997).

Churchill, Winston, *My Early Life: A Roving Commission*, Keyston Library (London: T Butterworth, 1930).

—— *The World Crisis*, 1911–1918, 2 vols (London: Odhams Press, 1938).

Clark, Manning, *Select Documents in Australian History, 1851–1900* (Sydney: Angus & Robertson, 1977).

Coates, Dora Meeson, *George Coates: His Art and His Life* (London: JM Dent, 1937).

Croll, RH, *Tom Roberts: Father of Australian Landscape Painting* (Melbourne: Robertson & Mullens, 1935).

—— and Walter Murdoch, *I Recall: Collections and Recollections*, 1st cheaper edn (Melbourne: Robertson & Mullens, 1939).

Cross, Tom, *Artists and Bohemians: 100 Years with the Chelsea Arts Club* (London: Quiller, 1992).

Daplyn, AJ, 'Australian Artists at the Academy and Salons', *Sydney Morning Herald*, 16 August 1913.

Downing, WH, *To the Last Ridge* (Sydney: Duffy & Snellgrove, 1998).

——, JM Arthur, WS Ramson, and Australian War Memorial, *WH Downing's Digger Dialects* (Melbourne: Oxford University Press in association with Australian War Memorial, 1990).

Dwyer, Jillian, 'The "Work" of Art: The National Gallery of Victoria Travelling Scholarship 1887–1932', MA thesis, Monash University, 1997.

Dyson, Will, '*Conscript 'Em!' Cartoons by Will Dyson* (London: The Herald, 1915).

—— *Kultur Cartoons / Will Dyson* (London: Stanley Paul, 1915).

—— *Will Dyson's War Cartoons* (London: Hodder & Stoughton, 1916).

Dyson, William, *Poems: In Memory of a Wife, 1919 [by] WD [ie William Dyson]* (London: Cecil Palmer, 1920).

Eagle, Mary, John Jones, and ICI Australia, *A Story of Australian Painting* (Sydney: Macmillan, 1994).

Edwards, Deborah, Rosemary Peel, and Denise Mimmocchi, *Margaret Preston* (Melbourne: Thames & Hudson, 2016).

'Exhibition of Australian Art in London: Grafton Galleries, Grafton Street, London W, 2nd April to 7th May 1898' (catalogue), held by National Library of Australia.

Foot, MRD, and Imperial War Museum (Great Britain), *Art and War: Twentieth Century Warfare as Depicted by War Artists* (London: Headline, 1990).

Galbally, Ann, *Charles Conder: The Last Bohemian* (Carlton South: Miegunyah Press, 2002).

—— 'Shackled & Set Free: Art, Music and Theatre in Melbourne in the 1890s' in Thérèse Radic and Suzanne Robinson (eds), *Marshall-Hall's Melbourne: Music, Art and Controversy 1891–1915* (North Melbourne: Australian Scholarly Publishing, 2012).

Gallipoli (film), director Peter Weir, Associated R&R Films, 1981.

Garran, Robert, *Prosper the Commonwealth* (Sydney: Angus & Robertson, 1958).

Gillies, Major HD, *Plastic Surgery of the Face Based on Selected Cases of War Injuries of the Face Including Burns* (London: Oxford University Press and Hodder & Stoughton, 1920).

Grant, Kirsty, Susan Van Wyk, Alisa Bunbury, Kate Darian-Smith, Amanda Dunsmore, Ted Gott, Petra Kayser, Elena Taylor, and National Gallery of Victoria, *Follow the Flag: Australian Artists and War, 1914–1945* (Melbourne: National Gallery of Victoria, 2015).

Gray, Anne, 'Tom Roberts: La Vita Con Brio' in Anne Gray (ed), *Tom Roberts* (Canberra: National Gallery of Australia, 2015).

——, A Henry Fullwood, and Australian War Memorial, *A Henry Fullwood: War Paintings*, Australian War Memorial Artists Series (Canberra: Australian War Memorial, 1983).

——, George W Lambert, and National Gallery of Australia, *George W Lambert Retrospective: Heroes & Icons* (Canberra: National Gallery of Australia, 2007).

Gregory, Barry, *A History of the Artists Rifles 1859–1947* (Barnsley, UK: Pen & Sword Military, 2006).

Harington, Sir Charles, *Plumer of Messines* (London: John Murray, 1935).

Haste, Cate, *Keep the Home Fires Burning: Propaganda in the First World War* (London: Allen Lane, 1977).

Haycock, David Boyd, *A Crisis of Brilliance: Five Young British Artists and the Great War* (London: Old Street, 2009).

'Heidelberg School Review', *The Australian Critic*, 1 July 1891.

Helmer, June, *George Bell, the Art of Influence* (Richmond, Vic: Greenhouse, 1985).

Hetherington, John, *Norman Lindsay: The Embattled Olympian*

(Melbourne: Oxford University Press, 1973).

Hoorn, Jeanette, 'Letters from Tangiers: The Creative Partnership between Elsie and Hilda Rix in Morocco', in Robert Kelly and Veronica Dixon (eds), *Impact of the Modern: Vernacular Modernities in Australia 1870s–1960s* (Sydney: Sydney University Press, 2008).

—— and Hilda Rix Nicholas, *Hilda Rix Nicholas and Elsie Rix's Moroccan Idyll: Art and Orientalism* (Carlton, Vic: Miegunyah Press, 2012).

Horsfield, Jennifer, *Rainbow: The Story of Rania Macphillamy* (Canberra: Ginninderra Press, 2007).

Howell, Ray, *Signaller at the Front* (Perth: Hesperian Press, 2001).

Hughes, Robert, *The Art of Australia*, rev edn (Ringwood, Vic: Penguin Books, 1970).

Humphries, Barry, *Andrew Sayers and Sarah Engledow, The World of Thea Proctor* (St Leonards, NSW: Craftsman House in association with the National Portrait Gallery, Canberra, 2005).

Hurley, Frank, *Hurley at War: The Photography and Diaries of Frank Hurley in Two World Wars* (Broadway, NSW: Fairfax Library in association with Daniel O'Keefe, 1986).

——, Robert Dixon, and Christopher Lee, *The Diaries of Frank Hurley, 1912–1941* (London and New York: Anthem Press, 2011).

Idriess, Ion L, *The Desert Column* (Sydney: Angus & Robertson, 1935).

Irving, Helen, *The Centenary Companion to Australian Federation* (Cambridge and Melbourne: Cambridge University Press, 1999).

Johnson, Karen, and National Library of Australia, *In Search of Beauty: Hilda Rix Nicholas' Sketchbook Art*, Portfolio Series (Canberra: National Library of Australia, 2012).

Jolly, M, 'Australian First World War Photography: Frank Hurley and Charles Bean', *History of Photography*, no 23, Summer 1999, pp 141–48.

—— 'Composite Propaganda Photographs During the First World War', *History of Photography*, no 27, Summer 2003, pp 154–65.

Joske, Prue, *Debonair Jack: A Biography of Sir John Longstaff 1861–1941* (Hawthorn, Vic: Claremont, 1994).

Keith, Arthur Berriedale, *Speeches and Documents on the British Dominions 1918–1931* (London: Oxford University Press, 1948 [1932]).

Kent, David, *From Trench and Troopship: The Experience of the Australian Imperial Force, 1914–1919* (Alexandria, NSW: Hale & Iremonger, 1999).

Knyvett, R Hugh, *'Over There' with the Australians* (London: Hodder & Stoughton, 1918).

La Nauze, JA, *Alfred Deakin: A Biography*, 2 vols (Carlton, Vic: Melbourne University Press, 1965).

Lambert, Amy, *Thirty Years of an Artist's Life: The Career of GW Lambert, ARA* (Sydney: Australian Artist Editions, 1938).

Lindsay, Daryl, *The Leafy Tree: My Family* (Melbourne: FW Cheshire, 1965).

Lindsay, Lionel, *Comedy of Life: An Autobiography* (Sydney: Angus & Robertson, 1967).

Lindsay, Norman, *My Mask: For What Little I Know of the Man Behind It, An Autobiography* (Sydney: Angus & Robertson, 1970).

Lindsay, Rose, *Model Wife: My Life with Norman Lindsay* (Sydney: Ure Smith, 1967).

Little, Penelope, and Bessie Davidson, *A Studio in Montparnasse: Bessie Davidson: An Australian Artist in Paris* (Melbourne: Craftsman House, 2003).

McCarthy, Dudley, *Gallipoli to the Somme: The Story of CEW Bean* (Sydney: John Ferguson, 1983).

McCulloch, Alan, *Encyclopedia of Australian Art* (New York: Frederick A Praeger, 1968).

MacDonald, James, *Australian Painting Desiderata [with a Portrait]* (Melbourne: Lothian Publishing, 1958).

—— Frederick McCubbin, and Alexander McCubbin, *The Art of F McCubbin* (Brisbane: Boolarong Publications, 1986).

—— and George W Lambert, *The Art and Life of George W Lambert* (Melbourne: Alexander McCubbin, Publisher, 1920).

McKernan, Michael, *The Australian People and the Great War* (Sydney and London: Collins, 1984).

McMullin, Ross, *Will Dyson: Australia's Radical Genius* (Carlton North, Vic: Scribe Publications, 2006).

—— *Will Dyson: Cartoonist, Etcher and Australia's Finest War Artist* (Sydney: Angus & Robertson, 1984).

McNeill-Ritchie, Simon, *Great Ward Poetry* (Bradford on Avon, UK: Hamilton Laird Publishing, 2014).

MacPherson, Sir William, and TJ Mitchell, *Medical Services: General History*, 4 vols (London: HMSO, 1921).

McQueen, Humphrey, *The Black Swan of Trespass: The Emergence of Modernist Painting in Australia to 1944* (Sydney: Alternative Publishing, 1979).

—— *Tom Roberts* (Sydney: Macmillan, 1996).

Mason, Arthur, 'Mr Fred Leist at the Front Painting the War', *Sydney Morning Herald*, 25 June 1918.

Maxwell, J, *Hell's Bells and Mademoiselles* (Sydney: Angus & Robertson, 1939).

Mead, Stephen F, 'Bohemia & Brotherhood in Late Nineteenth Century Melbourne: Marshall-Hall's Involvement with the Cannibal and Ishmael Clubs' in Thérèse Radic and Suzanne Robinson (eds), *Marshall-Hall's Melbourne: Music, Art and Controversy 1891–1915* (North Melbourne: Australian Scholarly Publishing, 2012).

Melba, Nellie, and John Cargher, *Melodies and Memories* (West Melbourne: Nelson, 1980).

Mendelssohn, Joanna, *Letters & Liars: Norman Lindsay and the Lindsay Family* (Pymble, NSW: Angus & Robertson, 1996).

—— *Lionel Lindsay: An Artist and His Family* (London: Chatto & Windus, 1988).

Modjeska, Drusilla, *Stravinsky's Lunch* (Sydney: Picador, 1999).

Monash, General Sir John and FM Cutlack, *War Letters of General Monash* (Sydney: Angus & Robertson, 1935).

Monash, John, *The Australian Victories in France in 1918*, 2nd rev edn (Melbourne: Lothian Book Publishing, 1923).

Moore, William, *The Story of Australian Art: From the Earliest Known Art of the Continent to the Art of To-Day*, 2 vols (Sydney: Angus & Robertson, 1934).

Motion, Andrew, *The Lamberts: George, Constant & Kit*, 1st US edn (New York: Farrar, Straus and Giroux, 1987).

Muir, Ward, *The Happy Hospital* (London: Simpkin, Marshall, Hamilton, Kent & Co, 1918).

—— *Observations of an Orderly: Some Glimpses of Life and Work in an English War Hospital* (London: Simpkin, Marshall, Hamilton, Kent & Co, 1917).

—— and W Noel Irving, *Happy – Though Wounded! The Book of the 3rd London General Hospital* (London: Country Life, 1917).

—— (ed), *Gazette of the 3rd London General Hospital* (London: 3rd London General Hospital, 1915–18).

Murdoch, Nina, *Portrait in Youth of Sir John Longstaff (1861–1941)* (Sydney: Angus & Robertson, 1948).

Nash, David, *German Artillery, 1914–1918* (London: Almark Publishing, 1970).

Nevinson, CRW, *Paint and Prejudice* (New York: Harcourt, 1938)

O'Farrell, Patrick, *The Catholic Church in Australia: A Short History: 1788–1967* (London: Geoffrey Chapman, 1969).

—— *The Irish in Australia: 1788 to the Present*, 3rd edn (Sydney: UNSW Press, 2000).

Pankhurst, E Sylvia, *The Life of Emmeline Pankhurst: The Suffragette Struggle for Women's Citizenship* (London: Werner Laurie, 1935).

Paterson, AB, 'Buffalo Shooting in Australia', *The Sydney Mail*, 7 January 1899.

—— *Clancy of the Overflow* (1889).

Pigot, John Phillip, and Hilda Rix Nicholas, *Hilda Rix Nicholas: Her Life and Art* (Carlton South, Vic: Miegunyah Press, 2000).

Pike, Douglas, Bede Nairn, Geoffrey Serle, John Ritchie, and

Melbourne University Press, *Australian Dictionary of Biography Volumes*, 12 vols, 1788–1939 (Carlton, Vic: Melbourne University Press, 1996).

Pollard, Jack, *The Complete Illustrated History of Australian Cricket*, rev edn (Ringwood, Vic: Viking, 1995).

Power, H Septimus, and Max J Middleton, *The Art of H Septimus Power* (Adelaide: Rigby, 1974).

Ransome, Arthur, *Bohemia in London* (London: Chapman & Hall, 1907).

Rawson, Andrew, *British Army Handbook, 1914–1918* (Stroud, UK: Sutton, 2006).

Rees, Peter, *Bearing Witness: The Remarkable Life of Charles Bean, Australia's Greatest War Correspondent* (Crows Nest, NSW: Allen & Unwin, 2015).

—— *The Other Anzacs: Nurses at War, 1914–18* (Crows Nest, NSW: Allen & Unwin, 2008).

Rix Nicholas, Hilda, *The Art of Hilda Rix Nicholas* (Sydney: A Hordern, 1919).

Roberts, Tom, Ron Radford, Art Gallery of South Australia, and Art Exhibitions Australia, *Tom Roberts* (Adelaide and Sydney: Art Gallery of South Australia and Art Exhibitions Australia, 1996).

Rothenstein, John, and Charles Edward Conder, *The Life and Death of Conder [with Plates, Including Portraits]* (London: JM Dent & Sons, 1938).

Rule, EJ, *Jacka's Mob*, 2nd edn (Sydney: Angus & Robertson, 1933).

Rutherford, Anna, and James Murray Wieland, *War: Australia's Creative Response* (St Leonards, NSW: Allen & Unwin, 1997).

Sanders, ML, and Philip M Taylor, *British Propaganda During the First World War, 1914–18* (London: Macmillan, 1982).

Scheib, Michael, 'Painting Anzac: A History of Australia's Official War Art Scheme of the First World War', PhD thesis, University of Sydney, 2015.

Scott, Myra, *How Australia Led the Way: Dora Meeson Coates and British Suffrage*, (Canberra: Office of the Status of Women, 2003).

Serle, Geoffrey, and Monash University, *John Monash: A Biography* (Melbourne: Melbourne University Press in association with Monash University, 1982).

Silas, Ellis, and John Laffin, *An Eyewitness Account of Gallipoli*, 2nd edn (Kenthurst, NSW: Rosenberg Publishing, 2010).

Smith, Bernard, *Australian Painting, 1788–1970*, 2nd edn (Melbourne: Oxford University Press, 1971).

—— *Documents on Art and Taste in Australia: The Colonial Period, 1770–1914* (Melbourne: Oxford University Press, 1975).

—— *Place, Taste and Tradition: A Study of Australian Art since 1788*, 2nd edn (Melbourne: Oxford University Press, 1979).

Smith, Geoffrey, Arthur Streeton, and National Gallery of Victoria, *Arthur Streeton, 1867–1943* (Melbourne: National Gallery of Victoria, 1995).

Smith, James, *Argus*, Supplement, 11 September 1888.

Speck, Catherine, 'The Australian War Museum, Women Artists and the National Memory of the First World War', in 'When the Soldiers Return': Conference Proceedings, Brisbane, 28–30 November 2007 (University of Queensland, 2009), pp 277–90.

—— *Beyond the Battlefield: Women Artists of the Two World Wars* (London: Reaktion Books, 2014).

—— 'Meditations on Loss: Hilda Rix Nicholas's War', *Artlink*, vol 35, no 1, March 2015, pp 40–43.

—— *Painting Ghosts: Australian Women Artists in Wartime* (St Leonards, NSW: Craftsman House, 2004).

'Speech delivered by His Royal Highness the Duke of Cornwall and York at the Opening of the First Federal Parliament, 9th May 1901' (Australian Government Printer, 1901).

Streeton, Arthur, 'Artists and the War', *Argus*, 11 May 1918.

—— 'Australian Artists and War', *Argus*, 17 December 1917.

—— Ann Galbally, and Anne Gray, *Letters from Smike: The Letters of Arthur Streeton, 1890–1943* (Melbourne: Oxford University Press, 1989).

——, Tom Roberts, Robert Henderson Croll, and Charles Conder, *Smike to Bulldog: Letters from Sir Arthur Streeton to Tom Roberts* (Sydney: Ure Smith, 1946).

Thomas, David, and John Henshaw, *Rupert Bunny: 1864–1947*, Australian Art Library (Melbourne: Lansdowne Press, 1970).

Thoms, Albie, and Art Gallery of New South Wales, *Bohemians in the Bush: The Artists' Camps of Mosman* (Sydney: Art Gallery of New South Wales, 1991).

Tippett, Maria, *Art at the Service of War: Canada, Art and the Great War* (Toronto and London: University of Toronto Press, 1984).

Tolerton, Jane, 'Ettie Annie Rout, 1877–1936', in *Dictionary of New Zealand Biography and Te Ara – The Encyclopedia of New Zealand*, 2014.

Tonks, Henry, Lynda Morris, and Norwich School of Art Gallery, *Henry Tonks and the 'Art of Pure Drawing'* (Norwich, UK: Norwich School of Art Gallery, 1985).

Topliss, Helen, and Tom Roberts, *Tom Roberts, 1856–1931: A Catalogue Raisonnee*, 2 vols (Melbourne: Oxford University Press, 1985).

Travers, Richard C, *Diggers in France: Australian Soldiers on the Western Front* (Sydney: ABC Books, 2008).

Turnbull, Jennifer, 'Australian Artists in the Great War: The Origin and Nature of the Australian War Memorial's Pictorial Collection Representing the First World War – With Special Reference to George Lambert and Will Dyson', BA(Hons) thesis, University of Melbourne, 1969.

Twomey, Anne, *The Australia Acts 1986: Australia's Statutes of Independence* (Annandale, NSW: Federation Press, 2010).

Ure Smith, Sydney, Bertram Stevens, C Lloyd Jones, *Art in Australia* (1916–42).

'The War', *British Medical Journal*, 10 October 1914, pp 639–47.

War Office (Great Britain), Sir Muirhead Bone, and CE Montague, *The Western Front: Drawings by Muirhead Bone ... With Text by CE Montague*, Etc (London: Country Life, 1917).

Wills, Elizabeth, *The Royal Exhibition Building, Melbourne: A Guide* (Melbourne: Museum Victoria, 2004).

Wood, Francis Derwent, 'Masks for Facial Wounds, *The Lancet*, 23 June 1917, pp 949–51.

Woollacott, Angela, *To Try Her Fortune in London: Australian Women, Colonialism, and Modernity* (Oxford: Oxford University Press, 2001).

Wray, Christopher, *Arthur Streeton: Painter of Light* (Milton, Qld: Jacaranda, 1993).

INDEX

Page numbers in **bold** indicate images.
m indicates a map.

AUSTRALIAN ARMY

I Anzac Corps 106, 107, 108
1st Australian Division 97, 167
2nd Australian Division 97, 167
3rd Australian Division 110, 167
4th Australian Division 97, 167
5th Australian Division 72, 97, 167
13th Brigade 156
15th Brigade 156
16th Battalion 73
24th Battalion 99–100
53rd Battalion 188
59th Battalion 120
22nd Field Artillery Brigade 110
4th Light Horse Brigade 140
6th Light Horse Regiment 88
7th Light Horse Regiment 182
8th Light Horse Regiment 76

MILITARY HOSPITALS

1st General Hospital, Heliopolis 73
3rd London General Hospital 42m, 68–70, 80–94,
   125–127, 145, 165, 195–198
14th Australian General Hospital 183
17th Casualty Clearing Station 184

4th Division Artillery and Infantry Moving into Battle
   (Scott) 193, **194**
8 August 1918, battle of 161, 189
9 by 5 Impression Exhibition 14–17, 136, 161

A Hero from Mons (Coates) **92**
A Holiday at Mentone (Conder) 13
A Man (Rix Nicholas) front cover, **177**
A Mother of France 1914 (Rix Nicholas) **151**
A Sergeant of the Light Horse (Lambert) **202**, 203
A Summer Morning Tiff (Roberts) 13
Abbassia 183
Académie Colarossi 35
Académie de la Grande Chaumière 55
Académie Delécluse 35, 55
Académie Julian 26, 27, 30, 36, 58
Across the Black Soil Plains (Lambert) 34
Addison, Harwood 210
After the Day's Toil (Power) 36
AIF 65, 72, 73–75, 134, 149, 154, 157, 167, 169,
   173
AIF Aerodrome Near Bertangles (Fullwood) **164**
AIF Headquarters 106–107, 110, 144, 157
Albert 108, 167
Alexandra, Queen, see Queen Alexandra
Allegro con Brio: Bourke Street West (Roberts) 13
Allen, N 210
Allenby, Edmund 138
Allworth, LE 210
Amiens 156–157, 160, 191

Amiens Cathedral (Streeton) **160**
Amiens, the Key of the West (Streeton) **191**
An Essay on Australian Art and Literature.
   In recognition of Lambert's really excellent portrait of
   Mrs Paterson (Paterson) 134
Anderson, Jock 144
Anderson, Robert 106–107, 129
Anderson, W Wallace 210
Anglo-Australian relations 6–8, 15–17, 20–22,
   38–41, 71–73, 79, 105, 113–115, 133–134, 137,
   143, 169, 173, 207–209
Anzac (the battlefield), see Gallipoli
Anzac Beach 165, 180
Anzac Book, see *The Anzac Book*
Anzac uniform 181, 206
Anzac, from Gaba Tepe (Lambert) 180, **181**
Anzac, the Landing, 1915 (Lambert) 179, 180,
   200–201, 204, **205**, 206
April Girl (Roberts) 46
Arab Sheep Market (Rix Nicholas) 56
Armentières 72, 96
Armistice 157, 170, 174, 176–177, 188, 207
Arrival of Burke, Wills and King at the Deserted
   Camp at Cooper's Creek, Sunday Evening, 21st
   April 1861 (John Longstaff) 26, 41
Art Gallery of New South Wales 10, 32–34, 38,
   40, 193
Art Gallery of South Australia 36, 45
Art in Australia 56, 149
Art Society of New South Wales 32
Arthur Streeton (Lambert) **87**
Arthur Walker and his Brother Harold (Coates) 53
artist as historian 108–109, 111–112, 119–120,
   134, 141, 184, 195–206
artist as scientist 148
Artists Rifles 67
Ashmead-Bartlett, Ellis 71
Ashton, Julian 32–35, 38, 116
Ashton, William 58
At the Landing, and Here Ever Since (Barker) 76
Attack on Hamel-Vaire (Fullwood) 161, **162**
Attack on Péronne (Fullwood) **188**
Australia Answers the War God's Call (Norman
   Lindsay) **63**
Australia at War (Dyson) 155
Australia House 104, 128, 129, 154
Australian 9.2 Howitzer (Will Longstaff) **193**
Australian Corps 158, 160
Australian Imperial Force, see AIF
Australian Infantry Attack in Polygon Wood (Leist)
   168, 184, **186**
Australian nationhood 6–8, 20–22, 23–24, 79, 105,
   113–115, 169, 173, 207–209
Australian Natives' Association 7
Australian Naval and Military Expeditionary Force
   188
Australian Official Photographs and Pictures
   exhibition 155–156
Australian Official War Artists 1916–1918 (Coates)
   title page, 198

Australian Troops Disembarking at Boulogne (Bryant)
   154–155
Australian War Memorial 114, 151, 174–175, 177,
   179, 191, 192, 199
Australian War Museum, see Australian War
   Memorial
Australian War Records Section 114, 128, 165, 177,
   179, 184, 203
Australians Advancing from Villers-Bretonneux,
   August 8th 1918 (Will Longstaff) 167, 168
Australians Burning Effigy of Kaiser in Square,
   Armistice Day (Streeton) **176**

Bailed Up (Roberts) **18–19**
Bailey, ES 210
Bailey, G 210
Balcony of Troopers' Ward, 14th Australian General
   Hospital, Abbassia (Lambert) **183–184**
Baldwin, HF 123
Baldwin, Stanley 64
Balfour, John 179, 205
Ballman, J 210
Balloon View of the 3rd London General Hospital,
   Wandsworth (Fullwood) **81**
Balloons on Fire (Streeton) 191, **192**
Barker, David 76–77, 210
Barrau, Laureano 10–11
Barton, Edmund 20, 41
Batham, PA 210
Battle of 8 August 1918, see 8 August 1918, battle
   of
Battle of the Somme, see Somme, Battle of the
Bazley, AW 76–77, 179
Bean, Charles 71–73, 76–77, 79, 105, 108–112,
   114–115, 117–120, 125, 130–131, 132 - 134,
   158, 165–166, 168, 169, 173, 177–181, 184, 186,
   199–200, 203, 205–206
Beaverbrook, Lord 105, 113
Beersheba 133, 140–141, 169, 200–202
Bell, George 30, 47, 58, 59, 63, 116, 127, 131, 155,
   170, 192, 198, 203
Bellicourt 170–173, 189–190
Bellicourt, Entrance to St Quentin Tunnel (Streeton)
   170, **172**, 191
Bellicourt Tunnel (Streeton) 189, **190**, 191
Benson, George 75–76, 165–167, 194–195, 210
Bertangles 164
Big Picture (Roberts) 22, **23**, 24, 44–45
Bigge, Arthur 44
Bird, Bolton 8
Birdwood, William 75, 77, 95, 105, 106–107, 123,
   156, 157, 160, 178, 192
Birmingham, Bishop of 103
black and white artists 20, 28–30, 36, 59, 75, 103,
   104, 111, 116, 188
Blackett, PC 210
Blamey, Thomas 163
Blangy 191
Blashki, Myer 4, 26, 80, 91, 127
Bleach AC 210

Bloody Angle 73, 75
Bohemia in London (Ransome) 59
Bombardment of Pozières, July 1916 (Crozier) **166**, 167–168
Bone, Muirhead 102–103, 106–107
Booth, JLC 210
Bostock, C 210
Boulogne 154, 187
Boulogne in Wartime, January 1918 (Bryant) 187, **188**
Bowen, Stella 36
Boyd, Martin 125
Boyd, Merric 125, 210
Boyd, Penleigh 124–125, 210
Bragg, Bernie 123, 210
Breitmeyer, Mrs Louis 41
Bridges, William 71, 114, 200
Bringing up the Ammunition, Flanders, Autumn 1917 (Power) 187
Bringing up the Guns (Power) 168, **187**
British Journal of Nursing 69
Britton, FC 210
Broodseinde Ridge 100
Brooks, Ernest 77, 123
Brown, Frederick 43, 210
Browne, George 210
Bruce-Porter, Harry Edwin Bruce 68–70, 84, 89, 91–94, 147–148
Brudenell White, Cyril, see White, Cyril Brudenell
Bryant, Charles 36, 58, 154–155, 158, 168, 187–188
Buchanan, CWF 210
Buchanan, HS 179
Budworth, Charles 163
Bunny, Rupert 25, 56, 59, 67, 149
Burgess, Arthur 127, 168–169
Burne, Harry 210
Butler, JS 210
Butterworth, Isabel 36
Buvelot, Louis 10, 189

Cadell, JH 210
Cairo 133, 137, 183, 199
Cambridge Hospital, Aldershot 142
Campbell, CB 210
Cannibals, Prehistoric Order of 4, 5, 26–27, 29, 30, 51, 53, 80
Cape Helles 75
Carolus-Duran, Charles 11
carrier pigeons 120–123
Carrington, Lord 6
cartoonists 5, 20, 29–30, 54–55, 63–65, 111
Casas, Ramon 10–12
Caseldine, GW 210
Cash, A 210
Casualty Clearing Station (Coates) 195, **196**, 197–198
censorship 71–73, 77, 79, 100–102, 109, 113, 123, 173
Cézanne, Paul 9, 153
Chamberlain, Joseph 58
Chapman, Evelyn 176
Chapple, WC 210
Charles EW Bean (Lambert) 206
Chateau, Villers-Bretonneux (Red Chateau) (Streeton) 161, **162**
Chaulnes 191
Chauvel, Henry 192

Chelsea Arts Club 43–44, 46, 50, 53, 58, 67, 68, 70, 116, 129, 143
Chesterton, GK 103
Chisholm, Alice 136–138
Churchill, Winston 61, 72
Clancy of the Overflow (Paterson) 6, 134, 195
Clark, GHP 210
Clemenceau, Georges 'Tiger' 163, 208
Coates, Dora, see Meeson, Dora
Coates, George (married Dora Meeson) 3–5, 26, 27–28, 30, 43, 50–54, 58, 59, 60, 63, 67, 70, 80, 86, 89–90, 91–94, 112, 127–129, 149, 155, 195–200, 207–209
Coates, HF 210
Coleman, WR 210
Colles, Ted 76–77, 210
colonial inferiority complex 6–8, 17, 38–41, 79, 105, 113–115, 207–208
Colville, George C 210
Coming Out on the Somme (Dyson) 108, **109**
commercial artists, see black and white artists
Concert by Miss Hullah (Streeton) **92**
Conder, Charles 3, 9, 13–18, 27, 28, 35, 37, 38, 40, 42–43, 51–52, 59, 208
Conder, Stella Maris 42–43
Conscript 'Em! (Dyson) 64
conscription 64–65, 112
Constable, John 40
Constantinople 183
Corbie 157, 162, 164, 189
Cormon's *atelier* 25
Cornwall and York, Duchess of, see Princess of Wales
Cornwall and York, Duke of, see Prince of Wales
Corser, PW 210
Cossington Smith, Grace 5, 36, 152–153, 176
Cossington Smith, Mabel 153
Cossington Smith, Madge 153
Coulson, HO 210
Courtyard at Bertangles (Fullwood) **104**
Cox, Charles 191
Cremorne Pastoral (Streeton) 18
cricket 7, 60
Croll, Robert 1, 10–11
Cross, Stan 20
Cross, T 210
Crozier, Frank 76–77, 123–124, 125, 165–168, 173, 210
Crusading at Anzac, AD 1915 (Silas) 75
Curlew Camp 18
Currie, Arthur 163
Cust, Charles 44

Dagnan-Bouveret, Pascal 28
Dalley-Cooper, LC 210
Damascus 184, 201
Daplyn, Alfred 127
Dardanelles, see Gallipoli
Darley, Frederick 25
Darnley, Countess of 41
Darvall, HL 210
Dattilo-Rubbo, Antonio 153, 176
Davidson, Bessie 36, 177
Davis, John 124, 210
de Groot, Mr and Mrs Maurice 52
de la Bere, Stephen 80, 94
De Mestre, Roy 210
Defence of the Realm Act 1914 71

deference to the British, see Anglo-Australian relations
Degas, Edgar 9, 28
dentistry 90–91, 145
Desborough, Lord 103
Desolation (Rix Nicholas) 100
Dewson, 'Digger' 110
di Luca, Luigi 201
Diagram 3 Rhinoplasty after Low Nasal Loss (Daryl Lindsay) **144**
Diagram 9 Fracture of the Mandible (Daryl Lindsay) **144**
Diagram 10 Fracture of the Mandible (Daryl Lindsay) **144**
Dibbs, George 33
Dickenson, Eric H 210
Dickinson, Sidney 17–18
Digger (Boyd) **125**
Digger Dialects (Downing) 152
Digging in at Pope's Hill: The End of a Great Day (Silas) 75
Distant View of Amiens (Fullwood) **161**
Dobbs, Wilson 210
Dominions and Dominion status 207–208
'Don't you know what to do when you pass an officer?' (Hartt) **124**
Dowd, JH 80, 92, 94
Downing, WH 152
Drake-Brockman, EA 179
Dubois, B 210
Duchess of Cornwall and York, see Princess of Wales
Duke of Cornwall and York, see Prince of Wales
Dunstan, G 210
Durand, Haviland 210
Dyson, Ambrose 30
Dyson, Jean, see Lindsay, Jean
Dyson, Ruby, see Lindsay, Ruby
Dyson, Ted 4, 26, 55, 129
Dyson, Will (married Ruby Lindsay) 4–5, 26, 29–30, 54–55, 58, 59, 63–65, 95, 103–112, 115, 120, 124, 125–130, 141, 155, 158, 165, 188, 198, 207–208

Early Summer (Streeton) 39
Edward VII, King, see King Edward VII
Egypt 1, 75, 79, 114, 132, 135, 137, 178, 184, 199
Elder, Edith 53
Eldon, Countess of 41
Elmes, P 210
Eltham, William 77–78, 180
Entrance to Mouquet Farm Dugouts (Dyson) **111**
Errazuriz, Madame 42
Étaples 31, 56, 99, 150–151
Étaples, 1915 (Rae) **150**
Evergood, Miles, see Blashki, Myer
Extract from Intelligence Report: 'Yesterday two of our pigeons failed to return' (Gould) **122**, 123

face wounds 90–91, 142–148
Fagan, WB 80
Fantin-Latour, Henri 28
Farrow, W 210
Feint, A 210
Felton Bequest 128
Fenwick, GM 210
Ferdinand, Archduke 60
Fine Arts Society 203
Finis (Hewett) **77**

Finley, F 210
Fire's On! Lapstone Tunnel (Streeton) 19, 33, 191
First Australian Wounded to Arrive in England from Gallipoli (Coates) **197–198**
Fisher, Andrew 64, 103–112, 113, 115, 116, 125–130, 141, 154–155, 157–158, 168–170, 177
Floriana Hospital 88
Foley, _ (initial unknown) 210
Folingsby, George 12–13, 25
Foott, Cecil 195, 199
Ford, Emily 53
Foulet, LC 210
French Salon, see Salon
Frith, WP 14–15
From the Australian Front Xmas 1917 123–124
Fromelles 72, 97
Fullwood, Albert Henry 32–33, 35–36, 38, 43, 45, 58, 63, 70, 80, 86–87, 91, 127–128, 131, 155, 158–164, 170, 188
Fullwood, Clyda 36

Gaba Tepe 80
Galbraith, IH 115–116
Galilee 184
Gallipoli 71–79, 88–89, 95, 97, 99, 123, 125, 158, 165, 167, 173, 178–183, 184, 199
Gallipoli (Weir) 180
Gallipoli Mission 178–183, 205
Gallipoli Mission (Bean) 178–180, 206
Gallop, H 210
Garran, Robert 20
Garrard, GF 210
Gates, R 210
Gathering Mistletoe (Frederick McCubbin) 13
Gazette of the 3rd London General Hospital 80, 88, 92, 94, **94**, 145
Geach, Portia 27
Geer, HR 210
Gellibrand, John 163, 192
General Sir Cyril Brudenell White (John Longstaff) 191–192, **193**
General Sir William Birdwood (Quinn) **157**
General William Bridges and His Staff Watching the Manoeuvres of the 1st Australian Division in the Desert in Egypt, March 1915 (Pyramid picture) (Coates and Meeson) 198, **199**, 200
German New Guinea 188
German Plane Brought Down Near Ors, France (Bell) 170, **171**
Gérôme, Jean-Léon 11
Gibraltar, Pozières (Leist) 120, **121**
Gillbee Bequest 26, 41
Gillies, Harold 142–144
Gilmour, GL 119
Glasgow, William 163, 192
Glisy 191
Glossop, John 192
Godley, Alexander 163
Golden Fleece, see *The Golden Fleece*
Golden Summer, Eaglemont (Streeton) 33
Goodchild, J 210
Gootch, T 210
Gordon, LF 210
Gould, GH 123, 210
Goya, Francisco 1
Grafton Galleries 37, 128, 155–156
Grand Marché, Tangier (Rix Nicholas) 56
Grandmère (Rix Nicholas) 56

Grey Day on the Hawkesbury (Streeton) 19
Griffiths, Thomas 195
Gruner, Elliott 210
Gullett, Henry 119, 186

Haig, Douglas 96, 158, 163
Haig, Florence 52–53
Haking, Richard 72
Hale, CF 210
Hall, Bernard 27, 30, 75
Hallett, CM 210
Hamel 157, 161
Hamilton, Ian 77
Handfield, G 210
Happy Hospital (Muir) 147–148
Happy – Though Wounded! (Muir and Irving) 94
Hartt, Cecil 124, 210
Hawkes, JS 210
Hawkesbury River (Streeton) 39, 41
Hay, A 210
Hazebrouck 117
Head of a Lady (Coates) **4**
Heasely, CJ 210
Heath Robinson machines 94
Heidelberg School 3, 17–18, 20, 25, 45
Heliopolis 137
Henderson, AE 210
Henry, George 54
Herring, Edmund 191, 192
Hewett, Otho 76–77
Hewitt, WO 210
Heysen, Hans 36, 128
Hoare, FG 210
Hobbs, Joseph 157, 163
Hogarth, William 47
Holden, Edith 94
home front 149–153
Hop 20
Hopetoun, Lord 20–22, 45
Hore, Leslie Francis Standish 76
Horniman, Mr and Mrs Elmslie 51
Howe, HV 179
Howell, Arthur 152
Howie, LH 124, 210
Howse, Neville 144, 192
Hughes, Billy 64, 103–104, 155, 168–170
Hughes, Robert 189
Humorosities (Hartt) 124
Humphries, Mrs Barry 43
Hunter Rogers, G 179
Hurley, Frank 123, 156
Huthnance, P 124, 210
Hutton, Edward 19

Idriess, Ion 140
Imperial Institute 44
Impressionism, French 9–11, 13, 14, 19, 39, 41
impressionism more broadly, including the painting of impressions, see impressions
impressions 11, 13, 19, 161, 163–164, 169
In the Horse Lines (Power) 118, 119
In the Trenches, Quinn's Post (Silas) **75**
Ingres, Jean-Auguste-Dominique 1
Irving, Noel 80, 85–86, 94
Ismalia 134, 136
Ivers, Harry 184, 201–203, 210

Jack, Richard 105, 128
Jacka, Albert 195
Jacko (the Turks) 180
Jackson, Alfred 158
Jacobs, RC 210
Jess, Carl 158
John, Augustus 42–43, 50, 51, 128
Johnson, B 210
Johnson, JJ 210
Johnson's Jolly 182
Justelius, H 210

Kantara 136–138, 184
Kavanagh, Charles 163
Keane, HV 210
King Edward VII 21–22, 41, 44
King George V 99
King, WL 124, 210
Kirk, Paul 80
Kitch (Leyshon-White) **77**
Kitchener, Lord 61, 69
Kitchin-Kerr, CF 210
Klotz, Louis 163
Knox, Edward 25
Krupp 15 centimetre sFH13-L17 model heavy field howitzer 186
Kultur Cartoons (Dyson) 63, 103

la peinture anglaise (painting like the English) 28, 41, 43, 51, 58, 187
La Robe Chinoise (Rix Nicholas) 56, **57**
Labour Wants a 'Place in the Sun'! (Dyson) **55**
Lahey family 174
Lahey, Jack 174
Lahey, Noel 174
Lahey, Romeo 174
Lahey, Vida 174
Lambert, Amy 34–35, 46–50, 58, 183, 184, 201, 203–204
Lambert, Constant 46
Lambert, George 5, 33–35, 38, 43, 46–50, 54, 58, 59, 63, 66–67, 87–88, 112, 127–129, 132–141, 155, 169, 179–184, 200–208
Lambert, Maurice 35, 201
Lancet 147–148
landscapes and landscape painting 3, 10–20, 23, 32–33, 34, 38–41, 45–46, 116, 138–141, 149, 158–164, 189, 191
Lane, Arbuthnot 142
Lang, WE 210
Latimer, F 210
Laurens, Jean-Paul 28, 58
Lawson, Henry 25
Le Cateau 170
Le Cateau (Bell) **171**
Leane, Raymond 192
Leaving for the Front (Meeson) **62**, 149
Leicester Galleries 155
Leist, Fred 36, 58, 113, 116–123, 125, 126, 127–129, 155, 158, 165, 168, 184–187
Lejeune, Louis-François 1
Lewi, Allen 124, 210
Leyshon-White, Cyril 76–77
Lieutenant General Sir John Monash (John Longstaff) **158**
Lieutenant General Sir John Monash (Quinn) **157**
Light Horse 133, 138, 140–141, 155, 184, 202–203

Lind, Ruby, see Lindsay, Ruby
Lindsay, Daryl 55, 63, 109–111, 124, 128, 143–145, 165, 203, 210
Lindsay, Jack (son of Norman and Katie Lindsay) 29
Lindsay, Jean (formerly Jean Dyson) 28, 55
Lindsay, Katie (first wife of Norman Lindsay) 29–30, 54
Lindsay, Lionel (married Jean Lindsay) 4, 26, 27, 28, 54–55, 128, 193
Lindsay, Norman (married Katie Lindsay, then Rose Lindsay) 4, 20, 26, 28–30, 54–55, 63–64, 128–129, 149
Lindsay, Percy 4, 26
Lindsay, Reg 109–110, 207, 210
Lindsay, Rose (second wife of Norman Lindsay) 29–30, 54–55
Lindsay, Ruby (married Will Dyson) 29–30, 54–55, 58, 59, 106, 109–110, 207
Linlithgow, Marquis of, see Hopetoun, Lord
Lister Lister, William 32–33, 36, 38
Little, G 210
Lloyd George, David 42, 105, 208
Lloyd, N 210
Loft at Saint-Sylvestre-Cappel (Scott) 166, 168
London Showing 3rd London General Hospital, Wandsworth, & Chelsea Arts Club (Di Qual) 42m
Lone Pine 180, 182
Lone Pine, Looking Towards the Nek, Walker's Ridge (Lambert) 182
Longstaff, John 25–26, 34, 41–43, 53, 59, 63, 127, 129, 131, 149, 154–155 , 157–158, 165, 167, 170, 191, 193, 198, 203, 208
Longstaff, John junior 207
Longstaff, Ralph 193, 207
Longstaff, Reginald 207
Longstaff, Topsy 26
Longstaff, Will 167–168, 174–176, 193, 195, 210
Looking Towards the Lines, Somme Valley (Louis McCubbin) 168
Lorimer, Vernon 94, 124, 210
Lost (Frederick McCubbin) 13
Lotty and a Lady (Lambert) 47
Loureiro, V 210
Low 20
Lowther, C 210
Luxmore, RH 210

MacColl, Dugald 40, 43
MacDonald, James 3, 9–11, 13, 141, 165–166, 210
Mackay, Iven 191
Mackennal, Bertram 25, 36, 43, 126–128
Macqueen, KR 210
Maghdaba 139
Major Andrew Barton (Banjo) Paterson (Lambert) 134
Major George Matson Nicholas (Rix Nicholas) 99
Manet, Édouard 28
Marshall, VF 210
Marshall-Hall, George 27
Masks for Facial Disfigurement Department, see Tin Noses Shop
Masterman, Charles 102–103
Mattinson, L 210
Maxwell, Joe 96

May, Phil 20
McCubbin, Frederick 3, 13–14, 27, 31, 34, 37–38, 75, 165, 167
McCubbin, Louis 165, 167–168, 210
McKinley, Michael 210
McLean, Hugh 210
McMillan, William 8
McMullin, Ross 65
McNicoll, Walter 158, 191
McPherson, A 210
McPhillamy, Rania 137–138
Meek, HG 210
Meeson, Dora (married, finally, to George Coates) 4, 27–28, 43, 50–54, 58, 59, 60–62, 67–68, 70, 127, 149, 195–200, 203, 208
Melba, Nellie 7, 17
Meldrum, Max 4, 26
Menin Gate 119, 174–176
Menin Gate at Midnight (Will Longstaff) 174–175, 176
Men's League for Women's Suffrage 52
Mère et Fils (Quinn) 58
Messines 112
Middle East 132–141, 136m
Military Service Act 1916 102–107
Minns, Benjamin 36, 37
Mison, MS 210
Miss Jessica Strubelle (Coates) 51
Miss Thea Proctor (Lambert) 47, 48, 49
Mission, see Gallipoli Mission
Mitchell, Helen, see Melba, Nellie
Mme Hartl as La Tournabuoni (Roberts) 46
Moascar 134–137, 184
Moascar, from Major 'Banjo' Paterson's Tent (Lambert) 137
Molony, FH 210
Monash, John 96, 157–158, 160, 163, 191, 192
Monet, Claude 9, 25, 28
Mont St Quentin 157
Mont St Quentin (Will Longstaff) 167, 168
Montauban 108
Montgomery, Bernard 158, 163
Montgomery, W Mont 210
Moore, George 210
Moore, William 10–11
Moore-Jones, H 210
Moorhouse, Mollie 60
Morel, Jeanne (married Rupert Bunny) 56
Mosman's Bay (Roberts) 18
Moss, WK 210
Mouquet Farm 97, 111, 167
Mrs Chisholm of Kantara (Lambert) 137–138
Mrs George Matson Nicholas, Self Portrait of the Artist (Rix Nicholas) 4
Muir, Ward 80, 94, 145–148
Mulock, FC 80
Murray, ACS 210
Murray, Chris 210
Murray, Harry 192

Napoleon I on his Imperial Throne (Ingres) 1
National Art Gallery of New South Wales, see Art Gallery of New South Wales
National Collection of War Pictures 155
National Gallery Art School and National Gallery School, see National Gallery of Victoria Art School
National Gallery of Victoria 10, 19, 25, 27, 32, 38, 128, 203

National Gallery of Victoria Art School 10, 12–13, 25, 27, 29, 30, 31, 38, 75, 76
nationhood, see Australian nationhood
Negro Boy, Morocco (Rix Nicholas) 56
Nek, the, see The Nek
Nerli, Girolamo 36
neurasthenia 73, 75, 195
Nevinson, CRW 80, 128
New Art School Kensington (London) 31
New English Art Club 43–44, 53, 54
Newell, H 210
Newland, Henry 143–144
Nicholas, Bryon 99–100, 207
Nicholas, Frank 99–100, 207
Nicholas, George Matson 98–100, 120, 207
Nicholl, W 210
Nightingale, Florence 53, 94
Noonan, F 210
North Flank, Suvla from Anzac (Eltham) 78

O'Dwyer, Ida 195–196
Official Australian Medical History of the Great War: The Australian Army Medical Services in the War of 1914–1918 (Butler) 144
Official History: The Official History of Australia in the War of 1914–1918 (Bean et al) 72, 98, 119, 124, 136–137, 179, 187
official photographers 102, 123, 156
official war artists' scheme – Australia 95, 103–112, 113, 115–116, 125, 128–131, 149, 158, 164, 165, 168–170, 173, 177, 195, 201–202, 203
official war artists' scheme – Australian army 165–168, 173, 193–195
official war artists' scheme – Britain 95, 100–103, 105, 112, 113
official war artists' scheme – Canada 95, 105, 113, 128–129, 132–133, 149, 158, 177–178
OG1 and OG2 trenches 99
Ogilvie, Edward 19
Olsen, Jimmy 206
Olsson, Julius 58
On Our Selection (Rudd) 30
On the Road – Retreat and Escape December, 1812 (Vereshchagin) 1
Opening of the First Parliament of the Commonwealth of Australia by HRH The Duke of Cornwall and York (Later King George V) May 9, 1901, see Big Picture (Roberts)
Orlando, Vittorio 208
Orpen, William 43, 128

painting à la mode anglaise, see la peinture anglaise
painting à la mode française (painting like the French) 25, 28, 39, 40, 41, 43, 46, 51, 59
Palestine 114, 132–133, 155, 169, 183
Pals battalions 67
Pankhurst, Emmeline 53
Pankhurst, Sylvia 42
Paris Salon, see Salon
Parker, Harold 36
Parkes, Henry 6, 19, 33
Parkinson, Ray 4, 26, 29
Passchendaele 98
Passchendaele battle, see Third Ypres
Paterson, Andrew Barton 'Banjo' 6, 134–136, 195
Paterson, H 210
Paterson, Jack M 210
Paterson, Mrs 'Banjo' 134

Peace and Future Cannon Fodder (Dyson) **208**
Peachey, Adrian John 210
Pearce, George 104, 107, 113–115 , 141, 169–170
Peninsula, see Gallipoli
Percival, Cecil 210
Perks, S 124, 210
Péronne 157, 170–171, 176, 188,
Péronne, Looking Towards Mont St Quentin (Streeton) **172–173**
Phillips Fox, Emanuel 34
photographers, see official photographers
Picking, AH 124, 210
Pieneman, Jan Willem 1
pigeons, see carrier pigeons
Pissaro, Camille 9
plastic surgery 142–148
Plastic Surgery of the Face (Gillies) 142–143
plein air painting 1, 13, 19, 32, 201
Plumer, Herbert 8
Polygon Wood 119–120, 184–187
Port Said 137
Portrait of a Soldier (Coates) **93**
portrait painting, portraiture 4, 19, 25, 27, 58, 63, 116, 149, 157–158, 191–193, 206
post-traumatic stress disorder 69, 109
Power, Harold Septimus 36, 58, 59, 63, 113, 116–119, 126–129, 155, 158, 165, 168, 187
Pozières 97, 99, 125, 165–166, 173
Prehistoric Order of Cannibals, see Cannibals, Prehistoric Order of
Preston, Margaret 36, 177
Prince of Wales 21–24, 41, 44
Princess of Wales 21–23, 41, 44
Pro Humanitate (Rix Nicholas) 100
Proctor, Thea 33, 35, 43, 47–49, 150–151
propaganda 63–64, 100–102, 173
Putney Bridge, London (Roberts) 45
Puvis de Chavannes, Pierre 28

Queen Alexandra 41
Queen Mary's Hospital, Sidcup 143–145
Queen Victoria 21
Quinn, James 26, 28, 38, 43, 45, 58, 59, 63, 128–129, 155, 157–158, 170, 192, 198
Quinn's Post 75

Rabaul 188
Rae, Alison 36, 56
Rae, Iso 36, 56, 150
Rain, Steam and Speed–the Great Western Railway (Turner) 41
Ramsay, Hugh 27, 34–35
Ransome, Arthur 59
Rawlinson, Henry 163
Ready for the Concert (Coates) 92
Record, AG 210
Red Chateau 161–162
Red Cross 89
Reinforcements: Troops Marching (Cossington Smith) **152**, 153
Rejoicing and Remembrance, Armistice Day, London, 1918 (Lahey) 174, **175**
Rembrandt, Harmenszoon van Rijn 15, 119
Renoir, Pierre-Auguste 9, 28
Retour de la Chasse (Rix Nicholas) 56
Riggall, Louisa B 210
Rix, Elizabeth (mother of Hilda Rix Nicholas) 31, 55–56, 99, 207

Rix, Elsie (sister of Hilda Rix Nicholas) 31, 55–56, 99, 207
Rix, Henry (father of Hilda Rix Nicholas) 31
Rix, Hilda, see Rix Nicholas, Hilda
Rix Nicholas, Hilda 4–5, 31, 55–56, 59, 95, 98–101, 149, 177, 207–209
Roach, GTM 210
Robbins, EL 210
Roberts, Caleb 19, 44, 203
Roberts, Tom 1, 9–20, 27, 32, 35, 37–42, 44–46, 51–52, 56, 59, 60–61, 63, 68, 70, 80, 89–91, 127–128 , 145, 160–164, 177, 189, 203, 208–209
Robertson, James 191
Rodin, Auguste 25, 28
Roll Call (Silas) 75
Romani 138
Romani, Mount Royston in Background (Lambert) **138**
Rosenthal, Charles 163, 191
Rosetti, Dante Gabriel 42
Ross, Cyril 210
Rothenstein, Albert 43
Rothenstein, John 13, 42–43
Rothenstein, William 43
Rout, Ettie 137–138
Royal Academy 14, 16–17, 30, 45, 47, 51, 53, 58, 93, 116, 117, 178, 208
Royal Academy of Arts, see Royal Academy
Royal Army Medical Corps 70, 80, 125
Royal Victoria Patriotic Asylum 68, 69
Rubens, Peter Paul 47
Rudd, Steele 30
Rue de la Gare (Station Street) (Rae) **150**
Ruined Church, Villers-Bretonneux (Chapman) **176**
Rule, EJ 108–109
Russell, John Peter 10, 25, 35, 59
Russell-Coleman, Wm 210
Ruthven, William 'Rusty' 192
Ryan, PV 210

Salon 9–10, 14, 16–17, 30, 33, 35, 51, 56, 58, 116, 208
Salvage (Boyd) 124
Samuels, C 210
Saville, Alf 124, 210
Schmidt, Florence 43
Scott, EG 210
Scott, JF 167–168, 193–195, 210
See, the Conquering Hero Comes (Handel) 42
Self Portrait (Roberts) **3**
Self Portrait with Gladioli (Lambert) **5**
Senlis 108
Sennett, Henry 210
Shaw, Stuart 124, 210
Shearing the Rams (Roberts) 18
shell shock, see post-traumatic stress disorder
Shepheard's Hotel, Cairo 133
Sheppard, WH 210
shirkers, see slackers
shrapnel helmets, see steel helmets
Sickert, Walter 43, 73
Sidcup, see Queen Mary's Hospital, Sidcup
Signaller, 2nd Main Line Gun Battalion (Dyson) 111, **112**
Silas, Ellis 73–75, 210
Simpson, Brian 210
Sinai Peninsula **136m**, 137–141, 200
Sinclair-MacLagan, Ewen 163

Singer Sargent, John 43
Sinking of the 'Southland' (Leist) 184, **185**
Sisley, Alfred 28
Sister and her 'Boys' (Dowd) 92
slackers 64–66, 126–130
Slade School of Fine Art 27, 43, 53, 143–144
Small, Fred 210
Smart, Henry 77, 115–116, 125–131, 132, 154, 157, 158, 169–170, 195
Smike Streeton age 24 (Roberts) **3**
Smith, Bernard 19, 141
Smith, Ernest (father of Grace Cossington Smith) 153
Smith, HW 210
Smith, James 13–17
Smyth, Nevill 195
Snowdon, Arthur 25
socialism and socialists 54, 64, 112, 129, 169, 177–178
Something to Remember Us By! (Colles) **76**
Somme Valley 98, 108, 110, 111, 150, 156–157, 158–164 , 189–191
Somme, Battle of the 96–99, 100, 108
Sommers, Jack 210
South Flank, Gaba Tepe from Anzac (Eltham) **78**, 180
Souvenir, Amiens (Streeton) **161**
Sowden, William 7
Spence, Percy 131
Spencer, Baldwin 126–129, 203
Spruce, William 182
St Gratien 160
St Gratien: General Birdwood Bidding Farewell to Headquarters Staff (Streeton) **159**
St Ives 31, 58
St John's Wood Art School 35
St Martin in the Fields 174
St Quentin 98
Staff Clerks at Work, Headquarters, St Gratien (Streeton) **159**
steel helmets 142
Steer, Philip 43
Stevenson, RAM 39–41
Stevenson, Robert Louis 39
'Still Glides the Stream, and Shall For Ever Glide' (Streeton) 13, 33, 39
Storr, A 210
Stott, William 80,
Street in Ruins, Villers-Bretonneux, France (Streeton) 161, **162**
Streeton, Arthur 3, 9, 12–19, 27, 32–33, 35, 37–43, 49, 52, 54, 59, 60, 63, 68, 80, 87–88, 91, 113, 125–131, 154–155, 158–164, 165, 170, 172–173, 176, 188–191, 198, 203, 208–209
Streeton, Nora 60, 203
Streeton, Oliver 60, 203
Streeton's Sydney Sunshine Exhibition 19
Strubelle, Jessica 51
Study for Dead Trooper and Detail of Turkish Trench, Gallipoli (Lambert) **182**
Study of a Head: Self Portrait (Cossington Smith) **5**
Stunting (Proctor) **151**, 152
Sturgess, RW 210
Suez Canal 134, 138
suffrage movement 52–53, 55
Suvla 75
Swallows and Amazons (Ransome) 59
Sydney Harbour from Milson's Point (Roberts) 18

Taylor, W 210
Territorial Army 68, 84
The Amateur ('Who's cutting this hair, you or me?') (Dyson) **188**
The Anzac Book 76–79, 115, 124, 125, 142, 180–181
The Arabian Nights 45
The Arrival of the First Australian Wounded from Gallipoli at the Third London General Hospital, Wandsworth (Coates) **90**
The Attack of the 4th Brigade, AIF, at Bloody Angle (Silas) 75
The Bathers (Lambert) 47
The Battle of Borodino (Lejeune) 1
The Battle of Romani, 4 August 1916 (Lambert) 200, 205
The Beach at Anzac (Crozier) **165**, 167
The Blue Hat (Lambert) 47
The Charge of the 3rd Light Horse Brigade at the Nek, 7 August 1915 (Lambert) 180–182, **204**, 205, 206
The Charge of the Australian Light Horse at Beersheba, 1917 (Lambert) 133, 140–141, 169, 200, **201**, 202
The Children's Orchestra (Coates) 51
The Conversation (Bell) 47
The Drover (Benson) **194**, 195
The Duke of Wellington and Officers and Soldiers of the Allied Army at the End of the Battle of Waterloo (Pieneman) 1
The Fighting Temeraire Tugged to her Last Berth to be Broken Up (Turner) 41
The Golden Fleece (Roberts) 18, 39, 41
The Goose Step, or the March of Civilisation (Dyson) 63
The Home Front, see home front
The Landing (Silas) **74**
The Last Tents at Moascar (Lambert) 184, **185**
The Light that Failed (Coates) 92
The Man Behind Conscription (Dyson) 64, **65**
The Man from Snowy River (Paterson) 8
The Middle East, see Middle East
The Mother (Lambert) 47
The Nek (Gallipoli) 180–182, 205–206
The Official Artist (Lambert) **202**, 203
The Pigeon Loft (Leist) **122**, 123
The Purple Noon's Transparent Might (Streeton) 19
The Refugees (Cossington Smith) 153
The Sinai Peninsula (Di Qual) **136m**
The Slackers on the Beach (Norman Lindsay) 129
The Sleeper Awakened (Roberts) 45
The Sock Knitter (Cossington Smith) **152**, 153
The Somme from Above Corbie (Streeton) 162–164
The Somme Valley Near Corbie (Streeton) 189
The Sonnet (Lambert) **49**
The Sphinx (Gallipoli) 180
The Towpath, Putney (Roberts) 45
The Wassah, Cairo (Lambert) **135**
The Wazza, Cairo, see Wazza, Cairo

The Western Front (Di Qual) **97m**
The Western Front, see Western Front
The Women's Suffrage Banner: Trust the Women … (Meeson) 52
These Gave the World Away (Rix Nicholas) 100, **101**
Thiepval 167
Third of May, 1808 (Goya) 1
Third Ypres 96, 98, 117, 119
Throssell, Hugo 89, 91
Tin Noses Shop 147
Titian 40
Tom Roberts (Casas) 11, **12**
Tonks, Henry 43, 53–54, 143–145
Townsend, GK 210
Trafalgar Square 174
Traill, Jessie 36, 177
Travelling Scholarship, National Gallery of Victoria 25–27, 34, 58
Travelling Scholarship, New South Wales Society of Artists 34
Treaty of Versailles 208
Treloar, John 114–115, 165, 177, 198, 200, 203–204
Trevelan, R 210
Trinnick, JB 210
Tronville 191
Turnbridge, AL 210
Turner, JMW 15, 40–41, 42, 45
Turnour, John 120, 184, 186–187

Valley of the Somme (Fullwood) **163**, 164
van Dyck, Anthony 179
van Gogh, Vincent 25, 153
Vaughan Williams, Ralph 42
Velasquez, Diego 15, 179
Vereshchagin, Vasily 1
Victoria Gully (Gallipoli) 76
Victoria, Queen, see Queen Victoria
Villers Bretonneux 98, 156–157, 160–164, 189
Villers-Bretonneux from Bussy (Fullwood) 160

Waden, R 210
Wadi Bed between El Arish and Magdhaba (Lambert) 139, 140, 201–202
Waite, JC 22
Waiting to be X-rayed (Bunny) 66, 67
Wales, Prince of, see Prince of Wales
Wales, Princess of, see Princess of Wales
Walker, Arthur 53, 94
Walker, DC 210
Walker, Harold 53, 157, 192
Walker, Oswald 88–89
Waller, M Napier 210
Wandsworth and Wandsworth Hospital, see 3rd London General Hospital
War (Power) **118**, 119
War and Peace (Tolstoy) 1

war art, tradition of 1
war artists' schemes, see official war artists' scheme
war correspondent as historian 114, 177–180
War Office 67, 102, 105, 107, 116, 195
War Propaganda Bureau, see Wellington House
War Records Office – Canada 113–114
War Records Section – Australia, see Australian War Records Section
Ward, Thomas 39–40
Watts, George Frederic 40
Waugh, Ralph W 210
Wazza, Cairo 133–135
'We find the shrapnel helmets very useful' (Hartt) 142
Wellington House 100–102
Wells, HG 103
Wenban, R 210
Western Front **97m**, 112, 129, 140, 150, 156–157, 158, 186, 188, 195; 1916: 95–112; 1917: 113–131, 1918: 154–173
Wheeler, Chas 210
Whistler, James McNeill 28, 42
White CL 210
White, Cyril Brudenell 71, 114, 157, 191–192, 200
Wilde, Oscar 28
Wilkins, Hubert 123, 179
Will Dyson (Sketch Portrait) (Coates) **4**
Will Dyson's War Cartoons (Dyson) 103
Williams, FA 210
Williams, Henry 50–51
Williamson, Lillie (married Tom Roberts) 19, 44, 203
Williamson, Mrs JC 41
Wilson, Henry 163
Wilson, William Hardy 36
Wilson, Woodrow 208
Windsor, Duke of 58
Winter, HE 210
Wisdom, Evan 191
Wise, BR 54
Withers, Alfred 70, 80, 91
Withers, Walter 17, 38
Wolf, E 210
Women's Social and Political Union 52
Wood, Francis Derwent 43, 67, 70, 80, 91, 94, 128, 146–148
Woolavington, Lord 174
Woolcott, H 210
Wrecked Coast of Northumberland (Turner) 41
Wright, JC 210
Wynne Prize 34

York, Duchess of 58
Ypres 98, 110, 112, 117, 119